D1457450

Philosophy and the Novel

Philosophy and the Novel

Alan H. Goldman
College of William & Mary

OXFORD
UNIVERSITY PRESS

OXFORD
UNIVERSITY PRESS

Great Clarendon Street, Oxford, OX2 6DP,
United Kingdom

Oxford University Press is a department of the University of Oxford.
It furthers the University's objective of excellence in research, scholarship,
and education by publishing worldwide. Oxford is a registered trade mark of
Oxford University Press in the UK and in certain other countries

© Alan H. Goldman 2013

British Library Cataloguing in Publication Data

Data available

ISBN 978–0–19–967445–9

Printed in Great Britain by the
MPG Printgroup, UK

Links to third party websites are provided by Oxford in good faith and
for information only. Oxford disclaims any responsibility for the materials
contained in any third party website referenced in this work.

For Joan again, who shares my love of novels and all else.

Acknowledgments

Parts of Chapters 2 and 4 appeared in *The Journal of Aesthetics & Art Criticism*; parts of Chapters 6 and 7 appeared in *Philosophy and Literature*. I thank those journals for permission to include those sections, now revised and expanded. Briefer versions of Chapter 6 were read at colloquia at the University of Miami and University of Tel Aviv. I thank attendees at those sessions for their comments. Robert Stecker sent constructive criticism of one chapter, and Eva Dadlez and Derek Matravers provided very helpful comments on the entire manuscript. The chapter on interpretation benefitted from exchanges with Noël Carroll. Remaining errors would be entirely my responsibility, if there were any. I thank Peter Momtchiloff and Eleanor Collins for their encouragement and efficiency. I am grateful, as I have been for the past ten years, for the continued support of the William R. Kenan, Jr., Foundation.

Contents

PART I
Philosophy of Novels

1

Introduction
Philosophical content and literary value

I

Why should philosophers read novels? The first reason is the same reason why anyone should: for pleasure, as it is usually called, although not the sort of pleasure we get from nodding half asleep in front of the TV or in a warm bath. It is instead the satisfaction that John Rawls subsumed under what he called the Aristotelian Principle, although Aristotle never described it explicitly, the satisfaction derived from the full and vigorous exercise of our human faculties or capacities.[1] The physical equivalent is intense exertion in a competitive sport, but here we are speaking of the full and interactive exercise of our mental capacities: perceptual, imaginative, emotional, and cognitive. For a work of art to so engage these capacities simultaneously and interactively is the mark of aesthetic value, as I argued in an earlier book with that title.

Pleasure here lies in appreciating aesthetic value. Aesthetic value lies in the capacity of a work to engage us in this broad and full way, not simply in the more superficial pleasure derived immediately from its surface sensuous or formal qualities. I take it that literary value is simply the value of literary works of art as such, the aesthetic or artistic value of works of literature. It therefore demands the same broad analysis in terms of full engagement. To be so captured by a work of art or literature is to appreciate its aesthetic value, at the same time to lose oneself in the world of the work, to seem to enter for a time that alternative world.

---

[1] John Rawls, *A Theory of Justice* (Cambridge, MA: Harvard University Press, 1971), p. 426; Aristotle, *Nicomachean Ethics*, 1174a–1177a.

A narrower but perhaps currently dominant view of aesthetic and literary value derives from formalists, such as Clive Bell, who wrote at the birth of Modernism in art early in the 20th century.[2] For them, aesthetic experience and the value inherent in it involved an immediate perceptual grasp only of the sensuous "significant form" in aesthetic objects or artworks, although this appreciation of form was said to produce a unique emotional response. Literary formalists are concerned not only with the immediate perception of sensuous qualities of language and with structural relations within sentences, but also with more subtle, larger formal relations within narratives and elaborations of language and style in literary works. But their focus remains narrow.

For pure aesthetic formalists, even expressive qualities are not aesthetically relevant.[3] For them, aesthetic properties are only sensuous or structural. But being strident, soothing, serene, jarring, vibrant, or melancholy seem intuitively to be as genuine aesthetic properties as being unified, elegant, or disjointed. Indeed, the expressivist theory of aesthetic value earlier championed by Romantics such as Tolstoy, although equally narrow, has as much historical claim to validity as the formalist theory. And the broader theory that includes the exercise of cognition and imagination in the apprehension, or constitution, of aesthetic value has deeper and philosophically more impressive roots. For Kant, Dewey, and more recently Monroe Beardsley, appreciation of aesthetic value is not limited to the apprehension of aesthetic properties usually cited as such, but consists in the full and harmonious engagement of different mental capacities (although it is significant that perceiving the usually cited aesthetic properties typically requires responding affectively to what is imagined or thought).

A main argument for the broader view of aesthetic experience and literary value then focuses on the indissoluble link between grasp of form itself and the exercise of cognitive, imaginative, and emotional capacities. The apprehension of formal structure in a novel, for example, often depends on seeing how its characters and the moral relations between them develop in the course of its narrative, and this "seeing" requires thought and reflection as well as emotional or empathetic reactions. In regard to some of the novels we will analyze, the formal structure in *Pride and Prejudice* consists partly in the way the main characters move gradually

---

[2] See, for example, Clive Bell, *Art* (London: Chatto & Windus, 1914).
[3] See, for example, Peter Kivy, *Once Told Tales* (Oxford: Wiley-Blackwell, 2011), chs 3–4.

from an initial antagonism to a perfect blend, while in *The Sun Also Rises* the theme of moral malaise reinforces and is reinforced by the repetitive or cyclical structure of the narrative, and in *Nostromo* the theme of social chaos and moral disintegration goes hand in hand with the novel's somewhat chaotic formal structure, its rapid and nearly incomprehensible shifts in time and space. The elegance of *Pride and Prejudice*, the chilling power of *Nostromo*, a large part of their great literary value, depends on this perfect union of form and content, grasped through imagination, feeling, and thought operating together.

While apprehension of form depends on all these capacities, prominently including cognition, grasp of philosophical theses implicit in the novels in turn depends in part on appreciation of formal structure. In the novels we will consider how these theses relate to the nature of moral agency, its development, lack of development, or disintegration. We appreciate Elizabeth Bennet's and Homer Wells' states of moral maturity, what is involved in their mature moral agency, by seeing how they get there. And how they get there is brought home in the unfolding structure of the novels. While we might be able in retrospect to describe their end states independently, and describe their developments in nonliterary terms, access to these descriptions is greatly facilitated and reinforced by our implicit feeling for the developing structures of the narratives as we read.

All great works of art engage us on all these levels simultaneously, but they do so in different ways. Musical works, for example, engage us cognitively as well as perceptually in grasping their complex forms, revealed in part through our affective or emotional reactions as we imaginatively anticipate resolutions of tensions in the unfolding melodies and harmonic progressions. Novels cognitively challenge us on more levels while typically lacking the immediately perceived sensuous beauty of musical tones. But there is perceptual engagement with novels as well, both with the rhythms and textures of the language, and, more directly linked with cognition, in the grasp of the larger structural patterns, formal relations between characters, settings, and incidents in the works, captured in large-scale quasi-perceptual images. (Formalists do capture part of aesthetic value.) As in musical pieces, these patterns often involve building dramatic tension and its ultimate resolution, prompting emotional engagement along with perceptual and cognitive.

In novels there is the additional formal aspect of form or style matching content, again combining perception and cognition. Grasping this match can be a source of aesthetic pleasure even without much sympathy for the content or beauty in the form. Among the novels we will examine, *Nostromo* sacrifices formal coherence or linear narrativity to express the theme of fragmentation in the characters' psyches, while, under one acceptable interpretation, *The Sun Also Rises* is relentlessly repetitive in formally expressing the lack of development in its characters. The role of cognition in interpreting such works is linked also to its ascribing such broad themes that reveal coherence or unity across otherwise diverse elements in the works. Uncovering these themes, a major part of interpreting many novels, reveals their underlying content, what they are ultimately about, at the same time showing how separate strands of the narratives relate to each other in formal patterns captured in quasi-perceptual images.

As mentioned, in the novels addressed in this book, themes relate to developing moral relations among the characters, which elicit our emotional responses as we imaginatively identify with these characters and with the morally charged situations in which they find themselves. In identifying with fictional characters, we imagine being those characters in those situations, and we empathetically feel the emotions we ascribe to them.[4] Our interpretations guide what affective responses are appropriate—emotional responses are appropriate when they fit acceptable interpretations—but the interpretations develop out of the ways we affectively respond as well. And as we interpret, our imaginations fill out the fictional worlds of the works beyond what is explicitly stated in the texts. Thus perception, cognition, emotion, and imagination combine and blend in the appreciation of literary works, as they do in appreciating other forms of art, which is why we speak of novels as literary art. Proper appreciation is fully controlled by the texts while at the same time structuring the worlds of the texts. It is both receptive and at the same time active in its interpretive responses.

As indicated, such appreciation is a deep pleasure or end in itself, and the various aspects of it are inherent ingredients of aesthetic value. There is also an instrumental benefit of reading novels that can be considered an aspect of their aesthetic value, as it is an immediate consequence of appreciation in the sense defined. I speak again of the escape from our mostly

---

[4] These claims are of course empirical. I rely on psychological evidence provided by the authors mentioned in notes 6–8, on my own reading experience, on informal surveys of the extent to which my experience is shared, and on you, the reader's own experience with novels.

satisficing efforts in the real world into the more intentionally created and aesthetically pleasing alternative worlds of artworks. In light of the full engagement of our mental capacities in appreciating musical or visual art, it is not amiss to speak of occupying the worlds of symphonies or paintings, but it is far more common and intuitive to refer to the fictional worlds of novels, defined as the set of propositions imagined to be true in properly reading and interpreting the texts. We all know what it is to get lost or wrapped up in a good novel, forgetting to call it a night as we continue to turn the pages. The cares of the day will seem more distant, if remembered at all. Such value from being so engaged and having these alternative worlds to occupy might be pejoratively described as escapist, but it is not to be underestimated.

Returning to the intrinsic components of appreciation and its object, aesthetic value or literary value as a subclass, the first point I am emphasizing here is that cognitive engagement is an essential element in appreciation, typically united indissolubly with perception, emotion, and imagination. I noted the central cognitive–interpretive task of finding underlying unifying themes in the narratives of novels. Although defined by their content, they also play a formal or structural role in tying together otherwise diverse elements. Themes in serious novels often relate to fundamental human interests, especially in the social and ethical dimensions of interpersonal relations. Such is the stuff of dramatic conflict, which is the stuff of absorbing narratives.

I will focus in the second half of this book on the themes of moral development, moral motivation, obedience to moral rules, and moral disintegration. These are typical of many serious novels, and I have chosen canonical examples. Such themes, of course, do not simply serve a formal function. *Pride and Prejudice*, for example, is not just about moral development. In interpreting the unfolding of this motif throughout the novel, we infer implicit claims about the nature and causes of such development in the characters, and in us, in so far as the characters are sufficiently like us for us to identify with them. When such claims or theses are plausible, we engage with them more readily, and in inferring them in the course of interpretation, we naturally at the same time evaluate their plausibility. This is as much part of our cognitive engagement with novels as is our grasp of larger structural features emphasized in much professional literary criticism. And cognitive engagement is as much part of appreciating literary or aesthetic value as are perception, emotion, or imagination. That recurrent themes function to unify structure does not preclude our reflection on the substantive theses implicit in them, and the latter is more often a conscious cognitive focus than the former, emphasized by formalist critics.

I am not claiming that all novels, or even all good ones, contain profound themes or make interesting or controversial or enlightening claims about them. Just as musical works engage us cognitively without teaching us about our social or moral world, so do poems and many novels. Novels of an entire genre, the mystery genre, which I will examine in the fourth chapter (and claim many instances of which to have high aesthetic or literary value), challenge us to continuously interpret as we read, yet typically lack edifying theses about overarching themes. What I am claiming is that when we do infer naturally to such theses in the course of interpreting the sorts of novels that will occupy us in Part II, their evaluation is an integral part of our cognitive (and emotional) engagement with these works, which in turn is an integral part of their aesthetic or literary value, their value as literary art. Such reflective cognitive exercise, as much as perceptual, emotional, and imaginative engagement, is part of appreciation, and to appreciate a literary work is to grasp its literary value.

As noted, part of such cognitive exercise is the evaluation of thematic theses for truth or plausibility. When the themes are such as I have described above, and the theses are therefore philosophical, literary critics may not very often concern themselves with their analyses or truth. But that most recent literary criticism is mainly formalist and concerned with the details of language and expression does not imply that evaluation of implied theses beyond mere identification of themes is not a proper part of literary interpretation. What it does suggest is that philosophers might well have something to contribute to the interpretation of great literature. The test of literary value is engagement on all mental levels including cognitive, not the learning of moral lessons, but cognitive and emotional engagement can include reflective moral evaluation. Literature is better suited to engage us in that way than are the other arts, so that such reflection is a typical part of literary appreciation and value, a subclass of aesthetic value.

II

In evaluating philosophical or moral theses implicit in novels, we can learn important general philosophical truths. This appears to be an instrumental benefit of reading novels, but obviously an important one for philosophers and one concurrent with cognitive activity inherent in literary appreciation. There is no sharp line to be drawn between aspects of aesthetic experience intrinsic to aesthetic value and benefits from that experience that are of only instrumental value. In the case of literary value, the line, such as it is, falls between aspects of appreciating while reading and at the same time (or shortly thereafter) reflecting on what one has read, and more remote effects of such engagement with literature. What one learns by grasping and reflecting on themes and theses in novels falls perhaps in the border area. But it is a significant part of our cognitive engagement with many novels, and it can be considered intrinsic to the appreciation of those works, and so an aspect of their literary value.

Before expanding on how such learning occurs in the course of reading and interpreting novels, I turn briefly to other instrumental benefits often cited by philosophers of literature, but less immediately related to the exercise of our mental capacities in literary appreciation. I refer to the development of these capacities—again imaginative, emotional, and perceptual–cognitive—through their exercise. Just as exercising our muscles generally improves our physical abilities, so does exercising our minds develop our mental capacities.

Begin with imagination. Many philosophers of literature claim that in reading a novel we imagine that the story is being told to us as true, or, more significantly, if we identify with certain of the characters, we imagine being them or finding ourselves in their situations and personal relations. In my view readers do not so much imagine the content of fictional narratives, or imagine that someone is reporting the story to them as fact, as much as they suspend disbelief in that content. But in doing so they may well identify with the fictional characters, see themselves in those characters' shoes, and imagine reacting to their situations. Authors of novels imagine novel situations for us that we might not otherwise encounter. In real life we decide how to respond to various situations by envisioning an array of possible responses and probable outcomes or ensuing situations. Reading novels might provide us with imaginary templates that facilitate such real-life reflection, broadening our powers of imaginative reflection. So it can be plausibly claimed (although I have not seen any experimental confirmation of the claim).

Just as actors playing roles or reading novels on tapes or discs imagine themselves to be the characters they are playing in order to imitate their expressive behavior or voices, so in silently reading we at least sometimes imagine ourselves to be the characters we read about or to be in the situations they are in.[5] When we do so, and when the situations resemble real-life highly emotionally charged contexts, we naturally respond emotionally, either empathetically or sympathetically, just as we do to actors whom we know to be playing fictional characters. We either know how the characters would feel and through identification or empathy feel the same ways, or we respond sympathetically to the situations and thereby come to know how the characters would feel.[6] We vicariously experience the events in the novels as observers or participants and so respond emotionally, most readily with negative emotions in reaction to imagined danger, frustration, or loss. Imagination prompts emotion.

Just as when we think of something pleasant or frightening we can respond to this imaginary thought, and just as our empathetic and sympathetic reactions come to extend to distant people through verbal mediation, so can we respond to fictional characters or events. That they are fictional does not block emotional response any more than recognition of the fictional status of pornography blocks sexual response.[7] It is true that visual pornography involves real people, albeit acting. But readers of written pornography also react with sexual responses (or so I imagine). Such reactions are not purely physical, but involve contentful mental states as well, some empathetic.

Knowledge of fictionality might even encourage empathetic emotional response, as we drop our suspicion of real people's motives and any obligation to respond with helpful action.[8] A belief that something is fictional occupies an area of the brain isolated from that responsible for emotional responses, which helps to explain empathy with fictional characters.[9] Similarity between a character as described and a reader facilitates the process, but is not necessary, as we empathize also with fictional animals and science fiction aliens. And there are devices authors

[5] The analogy between readers and actors is drawn by Peter Kivy, *The Performance of Reading* (Oxford: Blackwell, 2006).

[6] See Susan Feagin, *Reading with Feeling* (Ithaca, NY: Cornell University Press, 1996), pp. 97–8.

[7] The point is made by Blakey Vermeule, *Why Do We Care about Literary Characters?* (Baltimore: Johns Hopkins University Press, 2010), p. 17.

[8] So argues Suzanne Keen, *Empathy and the Novel* (Oxford: Oxford University Press, 2007), pp. xiii, 4.

[9] Patrick Hogan, *Cognitive Science, Literature and the Arts* (London: Routledge, 2003), p. 185.

use to encourage identification with their characters, such as first-person narration, free indirect discourse (third-person narration but in the character's language or perspective), direct description of characters' mental states, and present tense. When saying the words in direct quotation to ourselves, for example, we play the role of the character speaking, and this makes it easier to identify with the character more generally.

Thus reading novels is claimed to increase both our powers of imagination and our ability to empathize with people less similar or more distant from ourselves, broadening our repertoire of responses to situations that might arise. Whether this increased empathetic capacity leads to more moral behavior is another question entirely. Despite empathy's being a main component in fully competent moral agency, and granting for the sake of argument that reading can broaden our tendency to empathize, it is far more doubtful and equally lacking in evidential support that novel readers become more altruistic.[10] First, better knowledge of the feelings and motives of those with whom we might interact can make us more wary of them or aid us in controlling or exploiting them, just as it can motivate us to help. Second, identifying and empathizing with evil fictional characters could reinforce immoral attitudes, if empathizing with good characters could encourage altruism. Third, while authors of novels report empathizing with the characters they create, there is no evidence that they tend to be more moral or altruistic than others.

A second major component of competent moral agency beyond the emotional ability to empathize is the cognitive–perceptual ability to grasp and weigh the morally relevant features of complex interpersonal contexts. Here Martha Nussbaum and those who follow her have claimed that reading novels is an invaluable tool in teaching or developing this moral capacity. I will discuss her position in Chapter 5 and more fully in Chapter 7, but I mention it here as a third morally related instrumental benefit of novel reading. Nussbaum cites the novels of Henry James as prime examples of heavily nuanced descriptions of morally complex interpersonal relations perfectly suited to develop readers' capacities to finely discriminate morally relevant features of such contexts that she takes to be typical in life.[11] Since we not only empathize with fictional characters, but vicariously experience the highly problematic situations

[10] Skeptical doubts are raised by Keen, *Empathy and the Novel*, pp. xiii, 4.
[11] Martha Nussbaum, *Love's Knowledge* (Oxford: Oxford University Press, 1990).

in which they find themselves, that we should thereby learn to respond in more finely tuned ways by learning to better characterize these types of situations in relevant moral terms is again not implausible.

I do not wish to deny that reading novels might develop our imaginative, emotional, and cognitive–perceptual discriminatory capacities, or that such development might (a bigger might) enable us to respond to real people and situations in more morally appropriate ways. If forced to draw a distinction that may be largely verbal, I would side with skeptics who deny that such instrumental benefits of reading novels are an essential part of their literary value. The reason is that, as separable consequences, they are significantly removed from the real measure of such value, the full engagement of these faculties while reading. By contrast, it is far more plausible to claim that the evaluation of thematic theses uncovered in the process of interpreting, and the learning that occurs in that process of evaluation, are part of the cognitive engagement that is part of the appreciation of the literary value of novels that contain such theses, such as those we will interpret in Part II. We must now confront the skeptical arguments against this claim, indeed against the idea that we can learn much of philosophical importance from novels.

III

The two most prominent skeptics on this topic are Peter Lamarque and Richard Posner. Both adhere to mainly formalist theories of aesthetic or literary value. Lamarque is not officially a formalist; he insists that great works of literature contain themes of central human interest: "love and conflict, honor and shame, self and other."[12] But he sees the function of these themes as mainly formal, as uniting various aspects of works under unifying concepts, providing organizing vision that binds together incidents and characters.[13] For him the literary value of themes has little to do with their reflecting any truth about the real world.[14] Literary value derives from the manner of expression, not the content:[15] That a theme is to be found in a novel is no reason to believe that it implies any

[12] Peter Lamarque, *The Philosophy of Literature* (Oxford: Blackwell, 2009), p. 273.
[13] Lamarque, *The Philosophy of Literature*, p. 150.
[14] Lamarque, *The Philosophy of Literature*, p. 237.
[15] Peter Lamarque, "Literature and Truth," in Gary Hagberg and Walter Jost, eds, *A Companion to the Philosophy of Literature* (Oxford: Blackwell, 2010), p. 376.

proposition true of the real world, as opposed to the fictional world of the novel. We do not typically encounter such grand themes in daily life, which is mostly occupied with trivial matters not to be duplicated in fine art.[16] Furthermore, the bare statement of such a theme is likely itself to sound utterly trivial.[17] Lamarque approvingly cites Jerome Stolnitz, who extracts as truth from *Pride and Prejudice* only that "stubborn pride and ignorant prejudice keep attractive people apart," rightly described as "pitifully meager."[18]

For Lamarque only the elaboration of such a theme throughout the novel is of literary interest. But since every literary work elaborates its themes in a unique way, since the personal relations in which these themes are embodied are unique, we cannot generalize from them to real-life situations.[19] If a primary aim of literature were to convey truths, literary works would need to present evidence and arguments, but they do not.[20] Nor do critics provide them. And even if we could extract nontrivial truths from literary works, they could not be essential to the works' literary value, since many fine works of literature serve no such function. The question for Lamarque is not whether we can learn from literature, but whether such learning is part of literary value.[21] According to him, when we do learn about the real world from fiction, we mainly learn about distant times and places, but such historical facts are not the sort of truths that will interest us here.

Posner echoes many of the same arguments.[22] He too warns against trying to extract practical lessons from literary works. We should not, for example, learn not to trust our children from reading *King Lear*, he tells us. Like Lamarque, he admits nevertheless that we can learn from literature, but he denies that doing so contributes to literary value. He is more insistent that such value lies in formal properties: in harmonizing disparate elements, relating characters, settings, and themes, and changing

[16] Peter Lamarque and Stein Haugom Olsen, *Truth, Fiction, and Literature* (Oxford: Clarendon, 1994), p. 455.

[17] Lamarque, "Literature and Truth," p. 376.

[18] Jerome Stolnitz, "On the Cognitive Triviality of Art," in Peter Lamarque and Stein Olsen, eds, *Aesthetics and the Philosophy of Art* (Oxford: Blackwell, 2003), pp. 338–9.

[19] Lamarque and Olsen, *Truth, Fiction, and Literature*, pp. 378, 395.

[20] Lamarque and Olsen, *Truth, Fiction, and Literature*, p. 368.

[21] Lamarque, "Literature and Truth," p. 367.

[22] Richard Posner, "Against Ethical Criticism," in Stephen George, ed., *Ethics, Literature, Theory* (Lanham, MD: Rowman & Littlefield, 2005).

pace and viewpoints. And although he admits that we can empathize with fictional characters, he points out that the effects of doing so can be for better or worse, a claim with which I have agreed.

Unlike Lamarque, however, who identifies what we learn from novels as mainly historical facts about distant times and places, what Posner grants we can learn is much of what I want to claim. He admits that we learn about people from vicariously experiencing the events in novels in which fictional characters are involved, "building models of human behavior" that are a "source of insight into human nature and social interactions."[23] Literature is a "path to a better understanding of the needs, problems, and point of view of human types that we are unlikely to encounter firsthand ... expanding our emotional as well as our intellectual horizons." It "helps us to fashion an identity for ourselves."[24] Who needs philosophical friends with enemies like this? Posner is mainly concerned again to deny that all this counts as part of the literary value of novels or poems. (Skeptics often use poems as examples, which I take to be totally different in this regard from novels in lacking extended narrations.) I have characterized the divide over this question as in large part a verbal matter, but since verbal matters matter to philosophy, I want to answer the specific points of both Lamarque and Posner.

The most general point of rebuttal is that the largely formalist theory of aesthetic or literary value that they assume is too narrow, just as outdated as the purely expressivist theories of the earlier Romantics. As noted above, the broader view of aesthetic experience and value that includes cognitive, imaginative, and emotional engagement with artworks, along with perceptual grasp of their formal structures, can claim a deeper and more exalted ancestry than the formalism that dates only from the birth of modernism in the post-Romantic age. I have argued that cognitive engagement is part of aesthetic appreciation, and that cognitive engagement includes the evaluation of implicit theses related to the broad themes in novels. Such theses, or specific slants on the themes, are, like the themes themselves, rarely explicitly stated and virtually never argued for in fictional narratives. But inferring to implicit themes and more specific theses or perspectives on them is part and parcel of interpreting novels. That the theses may not be explicitly intended by the authors of the

---

[23] Posner, "Against Ethical Criticism," pp. 70–1.
[24] Posner, "Against Ethical Criticism," pp. 72–3.

works in which we infer them is also irrelevant according to the theory of interpretation I will defend at length in the next chapter.

That we do not find interesting or important thematic theses or philosophical truths in all good novels does not imply that properly inferring their presence in some novels is not essential to appreciating the literary value of those works as a major part of our cognitive engagement with them. While I claim that all great art engages us cognitively on some level or in some way, not all need do so in the same way. Our cognitive engagement with a symphonic movement can consist in determining after reflection on multiple listenings detailed broad structure; with a painting it might consist in determining textual or historical references or in placing it in a proper historical narrative that will affect the way it is perceived. Musical works, abstract paintings, and most detective novels might not teach us much about psychological capacities and motivations, and might not impart many philosophical truths about moral agency, but many serious novels do, and reflecting on their psychological and philosophical theses is an essential part of appreciating what they have to offer readers, their literary value.

We might or might not learn something new from pondering such implicit theses: they might instead test by concrete example or pull together abstract claims into a more unified body of knowledge. If we know, for example, different theories of moral development, we might see how they can apply together to the ways the characters in *Pride and Prejudice* or *Huckleberry Finn* develop. We might see concretely the degree to which cognitive or emotional growth engenders moral development, as the development of these characters emphasizes and therefore implicitly claims the predominance of one or the other. Of course, bald statements of such theses implicit in the themes of novels are not themselves of literary value, although they may be of philosophical importance. To be of literary value, the theses must be embodied in or woven into narrative, characterization, and even setting, formal structure, and prose style of the novels. My descriptions of the novels to be interpreted in the chapters to follow provide ample examples.

That such thematic theses even when present are not argued for does not imply that we cannot learn by first conceiving and then reflecting on them as we read. We learn from testimony and from life experience more than we learn from being presented arguments, especially about the dynamics of interpersonal relationships and what is morally required in them. We can similarly learn from the vicarious experience of reading fiction. As to Lamarque's point that themes are uniquely developed in novels and Posner's similar warning against generalizing from such works as *King Lear*, uniqueness in complex objects is no obstacle to generalizing from the set of their properties that may be instantiated elsewhere as well. My house is unique—there is no duplicate—but that does not mean that I have not learned what it is like to live in a house by living in it. Each chess game is unique, but chess players learn to win future games by assiduously studying past ones. Similarly, each person and personal relationship is unique, but we properly generalize from the people we know, whether real people or fictional characters.

When Posner tells us not to generalize to our children from King Lear's, he should have instead advised us to generalize only to children sufficiently similar to Lear's (better your children than mine). Surely we should learn not to trust *them*, and we are fortunate to learn this from reading rather than life. When Jerome Stolnitz could find no more interesting thesis in *Pride and Prejudice* than the one he enunciates, this reflects only how cognitively shallow his reading of that novel is. Here I can only ask the reader to compare my reading in Chapter 5 and issue a promissory note for detailed and interesting theses about moral development and moral agency. Similarly, we can state the theme of *Nostromo* baldly and trivially as the effect of the social environment on individual ambitions and projects, but it is spelled out in such devastating detail in the novel's narratives that we learn much in reverse about what is necessary for personal integrity, a healthy psyche, and moral agency as an ingredient in both. This is certainly the kind of theme we can encounter throughout life, and if this were not generally true of the themes we find elaborated in great novels, why else would they be of perennial human interest, as Lamarque claims?

There remains the point that narrations and descriptions in novels are asserted not as true of the real world, but only as fictionally true, true in the make-believe worlds of the novels. Lamarque claims that they therefore provide no reasons to believe anything about the actual world. It seems that in order to know that what is asserted in fiction is also true of the real world, we would already have to know that it is true of the real world, in which case we would learn nothing. Other philosophers have responded to this worry by claiming that fictional narratives can extend our knowledge in the same way that any thought experiments can: by helping us to trace the implications of concepts we already possess, implications that we might not yet be aware of.[25] I would extend this claim to learning the consequences of acting on principles we might or might not previously accept. We have only to recognize that the situations in which the characters act on these principles are relevantly like those we might encounter, that we might act in similar ways in those circumstances, and that similar consequences would likely ensue.

I want to claim yet more: that we can learn from novels not only consequences of acting on various principles, and conceptual truths such as what is involved in fully developed moral agency, but philosophically important empirical facts such as how such agency develops or decays. To show how we can learn empirical facts from fictions, we need to think of the epistemological roles of foundations, coherence, and testimony. Playing the role of foundations here is the knowledge we bring to the novels we read, which is then extended through considerations of coherence and the testimony of the authors. We judge the similarity of relationships and events in novels to those we might encounter by seeing whether they cohere with what we already know and by judging the reliability of the authors—whether they are writing of what they know by first-hand experience, and whether they intend to write realistically. We judge the reliability of any testimony in the same way, by whether the testifier seems trustworthy, knowledgeable, and intending to tell the truth, and by whether the testimony coheres with our prior knowledge.

Such coherence and appreciation of an author's style can inform us as to whether the author aims at realism, although biographical knowledge of the author might be required to judge her first-hand experience of contexts such as those she portrays. When an author passes these tests, we can accept her explicit and implicit claims as we would other testimony. Likewise, when we judge the characters and narratives in a novel to be plausible and relevantly similar to people we might encounter and trains of events in which we might be involved, we can learn from our vicarious experience in reading much as we learn from real-life experience. Surely what is gained from such experience is not limited to conceptual knowledge.[26]

---

[25] Among the philosophers who compare fictional narratives to thought experiments are Noel Carroll, "The Wheel of Virtue: Art, Literature, and Moral Knowledge," *Journal of Aesthetics and Art Criticism*, 60 (2002): 3–26; Mitchell Green, "How and What We Can Learn from Fiction," in *A Companion to the Philosophy of Literature*.

[26] Compare Eileen John, "Reading Fiction and Conceptual Knowledge," *Journal of Aesthetics and Art Criticism*, 56 (1998): 331–48, p. 335.

IV

All the novels to be interpreted in this book elaborate themes relating to the moral dimensions of interpersonal relations, such themes as are common to many or most great novels. In each one, main characters must make crucial moral decisions that culminate long processes of development in their relations with others. In climactic contexts, Darcy must decide whether to propose to Elizabeth a second time, Huck Finn must decide whether to return his runaway slave friend Jim to his owner, Jake Barnes must decide whether to continue his relationship with Brett, Homer Wells must decide whether to return to the orphanage and accept a personal rule to provide abortions on demand, and Nostromo faces the decision whether to steal the silver. Each decision when made seems not to result from a dispassionate weighing of utilities and disutilities, costs and benefits, but to be necessitated by the prior development or lack of development in the character's character. The real self, or lack of unified self, then emerges in the decision. In each case the reader not only witnesses the decision, but vicariously experiences the full extended process of development that leads to it and the ensuing consequences. We share the character's search for individual identity, for integrated selves and relations with others that confirm our self-images, and we see the social pressures that bear on the outcomes.

In daily life the testing ground of our moral beliefs and principles lies in the consequences of our decisions and in our observations of the decisions of others. These observations can extend to actions of fictional characters. And here there is an additional advantage. We observe not only the decisions, but the entire processes leading up to them, in contrast to the very intermittent witnessing of other, real people. And in fiction we notice not only actions, but readily inferable or directly described mental states of the characters making the decisions.

Real people often try to hide their motives and decision-making processes; fictional characters do so far less often.[27] Of course sometimes (and often in mystery novels) we must judge characters indirectly, by how they are represented in the statements or mental states of other characters, who may be more or less reliable, and it is then crucial to keep track of

---

[27] Compare David Novitz, *Knowledge, Fiction, and Imagination* (Philadelphia: Temple University Press, 1987), p. 136.

the perspective through which we are observing. But this in itself is an important cognitive skill to be exercised in real life as well as in reading.[28] In general, we can see in fictional narratives patterns in character development and ways of living that are obscured in real life by interrupted vision and distracting noise.

The commonality of terms when we speak of a character's character is probably no accident. Every fictional character has a character that is a prime object of interest for readers. In reflecting on ourselves, we are naturally interested in the characters and lives of others. We read fiction in part because we are social animals who are interested in other people and in how they will react to our actions. Like Miss Marple, we assimilate new acquaintances to those we know, real or fictional. We gauge our own actions and seek to make sense of our experiences by comparing them to those of others, real or fictional. In seeking knowledge of how to live, we often look to role models, and these too can be provided by fiction as well as life.

In good fiction, as in real life, we should not expect perfect models explicitly teaching us moral lessons, but characters of mixed virtue who challenge our moral sense in grappling with problematic contexts and relations, characters in moral quandaries such as Huck Finn, Nostromo, and Homer Wells and Dr. Larch in *The Cider House Rules*. In contributing to the literary value of these novels, such characters are far better than perfect models of virtue or vice. Again it is the stimulation of our moral sensibilities in reflecting on the actions of fictional characters that contributes to the overall engagement of our mental faculties that is the mark of aesthetic experience and value. It is not the truth of moral theses advocated in novels that is aesthetically relevant, as current so-called aesthetic moralists claim, but their power to so engage us.

Nevertheless, the practical knowledge we acquire in observing fictional models can result in fine-tuning those principles we intuitively and often naively accept. If we want to know, for example, when we should obey or disobey the accepted ethical rules of our society, we cannot do much better than a careful reading and character analysis of *The Cider House Rules*, as I will show in Chapter 7. There we will find no simple meta-rule, such as "Always obey society's reasonable rules even when

---

[28] According to Lisa Zunshine, acquiring this skill, as well as the more general skill of reading others' minds, is a main reason for reading novels. Lisa Zunshine, *Why We Read Fiction* (Columbus: Ohio State University Press, 2006).

you know you can do better in the individual case," or "Never obey when you know you can do better." Instead, we are presented with situations in which a character must accept or reject a social rule, and once we see which decision should be made, sometimes to obey at the sacrifice of net benefits and sometimes to disobey, we can use these situations as settled cases to which to compare others that might arise.

Philosophers can give us abstract arguments complete with fine distinctions on this and similar topics,[29] but even if we can remember and keep their arguments and distinctions in mind (doubtful), we will be more strongly motivated by our revised views by having lived through, vicariously or otherwise, the consequences of acting on the inadequately nuanced earlier versions of moral guidelines. To be motivated to make the revisions, we must bring our values or moral intuitions to bear on those vicariously experienced consequences, but the same is true in evaluating philosophers' arguments. Once we know what it is like to live by certain principles, we can readily accept, reject, or modify those principles according to the values we bring to bear.

Fictional narratives show us what it is like to live in certain ways. In real life we learn to live with others by interacting with them, not by learning a set of rules or taking ethics courses. Because our experience in the real world is limited, extending it through the vicarious experience of reading can be an important source of practical knowledge. And this knowledge is the immediate byproduct of being cognitively and emotionally challenged by the fiction, hence one indication of its literary value.

The focus of chapters other than Chapter 7 will not be on such practical moral knowledge, but on related conceptual and factual theses concerning the nature of moral agency and moral motivation, and on how they develop and decline or fragment. Here we learn not only how to make finer moral discriminations, normative moral truths such as when we should obey rules and when we should not, but philosophically important general truths about the nature of morality, and especially about moral agency, about what is involved in becoming a fully mature and competent moral agent, and how such agency can disintegrate under social pressures. The nature of moral development will be inferred from an interpretation of *Pride and Prejudice*, and the nature of

---

[29] See Alan Goldman, *Practical Rules: When We Need Them and When We Don't* (Cambridge: Cambridge University Press, 2002).

moral motivation from *Huckleberry Finn*. Finally, we will see how moral agency can fail to fully develop or disintegrate under extreme pressure of violence, frustration, moral compromise, and temptation in *Nostromo*. I have chosen these books because of the salience of these themes in them, but also because they are among the most widely read in the canon, and a philosophical book of this sort will be of less interest to those who have not read any of the works discussed.

Before those analyses in Part II, I need to spell out the theories of value and interpretation suggested earlier here and draw out their implications. The theory of interpretation, showing how interpreting novels aims at appreciating their value, will be fully defined and defended in the next chapter. Interpretation, I claim, aims at explanation of a text as written that maximizes its literary value for the reader. I will use *The Sun Also Rises* to confirm one of the major implications of this view—the acceptability of mutually incompatible interpretations—in Chapter 3. If different explanations enhance different values in a text, then more than one may be equally acceptable. Incompatible interpretations of the lead characters in Hemingway's novel as morally developing and as stagnating instantiate this possibility. Chapter 4 will illustrate and confirm the theory of literary value described in this introduction by showing how it explains the great appeal of mystery fiction. I will show how such fiction, or the better works within the genre, engage us on all the levels indicated, demonstrating that the great appeal of these works can be explained in terms of their aesthetic value.

Indeed, all the novels to be discussed afford confirmation of the theory by engaging our perceptual, cognitive, imaginative and emotional capacities, their resultant high literary value being another excellent reason to turn our philosophical interpretive attention to them. In judging this book, I would recommend reading or rereading some of the novels discussed in Part II. See whether your interpretations bring out the themes and theses regarding moral agency that I attribute to them, whether your cognitive engagement with these theses is part of your appreciation of these novels. See too whether your emotional engagement with the characters involves reactions to their moral development or lack of it, and whether the parallels and contrasts in the moral relations among the characters partially determine the formal structures of these novels. In *The Sun Also Rises*, I think you will find the characters either sharing or contrasting in moral development or atrophy; in *The Cider*

House Rules, you will see a complete array of characters' attitudes toward rules; in *Pride and Prejudice*, a similar array of developments and stunted developments; and in *Nostromo*, a variety of ways moral personalities can disintegrate under extreme social pressure.

If cognitive grasp of these moral and psychological theses is so indissolubly linked with grasp of formal structures and with empathetic emotional reactions in imaginatively identifying with these characters and their complex and challenging moral situations, then all these are equally aspects of literary appreciation, of appreciating literary value. Interpretation aims to bring out and enhance such value, as I will argue in the next chapter. Thus philosophers should read novels not just for pleasure, but to add their interpretations, which should be of literary interest. In any case, they will find nontrivial philosophical theses in the great novels I address.

2

Interpreting novels

I

The task of an art or literary critic is to be an interpreter, not simply to evaluate on the one hand or to describe or pick out random properties of works on the other, but to select those properties that are value relevant and to guide the audience to appreciation and proper evaluation by showing how those properties are relevant, how they contribute to the values of the works.

On the surface, those critical activities that count as interpretations of literary or other artworks make up a very diverse class. Interpreting literature may consist in giving the meanings of phrases in context, explaining the place of an episode in a plot, analyzing psychological features of characters or their motives as inferred from their actions or stated thoughts, showing formal patterns implicit in plot or character developments, stating the broad theme or historical, moral, political, or religious significance of a work as a whole, or the broader explanatory scheme (Freudian, Marxist, Christian) into which it fits.

Interpretations of other artworks vary even more. An art critic or interpreter of a painting might point out how the shadows reveal diverse sources of light, what a certain interplay of colors expresses, how certain represented objects in the painting function symbolically, why certain spatial perspectives are distorted, the historical significance of the absence of traditional elements, or how the depicted relations among characters illustrate the climax of a biblical story. A music critic will explain the place of various passages in the overall structure of a work, will describe its expressive qualities, or describe the historical importance of the work or some of its techniques in a style or tradition. Performers who are said to be interpreting musical works may simply play certain passages with emphasis, or alter their dynamics or tempi slightly.

At the least, then, interpretations may state what parts or whole works mean, represent, or express, how parts relate to each other, or how works relate to others in a historical narrative. In light of the diversity of these interpretive activities, it might seem that we should heed Wittgenstein's warning and resist seeking a common core or essence. But there is a common function if not common phenomenology to these activities, a function shared with activities called interpretive outside art as well. They all seek to facilitate understanding, and in the case of art and literature, appreciation.

Interpreters who do not merely translate from foreign tongues facilitate understanding by providing explanations of various kinds. Thus, if we specify the kinds of understanding and explanation at which interpretations of the arts aim, and if the kinds of understanding sought and hence explanations provided are similar across arts, then we might derive a unified account of interpretation. The characteristic they share is functional, a common aim. As suggested, interpretive explanation aims at understanding and ultimately at appreciation. Interpretation aims ultimately to facilitate appreciation in all the arts, and this is the key to its proper characterization. Appreciating a work is grasping its values. Hence interpretation aims to show how the elements of a work contribute to its value as art. Art and literary criticism seeks ultimately and essentially to uncover and make comprehensible to us the values of the works examined. In leading to evaluations supported by reasons in the form of accurate descriptions, interpretations indicate the sources of value in art and literary works, helping audiences to fully appreciate the works.

In the introduction I suggested a theory of aesthetic and literary value (defended in an earlier book) according to which an artwork of any kind is aesthetically valuable to the extent that it engages all our mental faculties simultaneously: perceptual, imaginative, cognitive, and emotional. Thus interpretation aims to show how a work and its elements engage us on all these levels. In novels, we interpret characters, actions, and events by showing how they contribute to or express broader themes (cognitively unifying the work), how they add psychological depth or expressive atmosphere, how they challenge our moral assumptions, or create formal relations such as contrasts and parallels. In showing how such elements engage or fail to engage us in these ways, interpretation aims at evaluation supported by reasons or accurate descriptions, resulting in full appreciation of whatever values are inherent in the works.

II

Grasping what is common to interpretation across the several arts will correct some misconceptions and resolve some disputes regarding literary criticism specifically. In all art criticism, interpretation falls between description and evaluation. Evaluation depends on interpretation, which in turn depends on noninterpretive descriptions of works and their elements. This does not imply, however, an exclusive distinction between interpretation and description, and certainly not one that is drawn, as is common, in epistemic terms. Based on the fact that there is often more room for disagreement in interpretation than in noninterpretive descriptions of artworks, many philosophers claim that interpretation is invariably weaker epistemically than description, that an interpreter cannot know, or cannot knowingly know, that her interpretation is correct.[1] Descriptions, by contrast, can be known to be true.

But many of the activities described above as interpretive can produce true descriptions that can be known to be true. A reader of *Death of a Salesman*, *The Prime of Miss Jean Brodie*, and *The Sun Also Rises* can know that Willy Loman is self-deceptive, that Jean Brodie is manipulative, and that Jake Barnes has suffered a war injury that has left him impotent, and the reader can correctly describe them as such. These descriptions are interpretations, albeit obvious ones, of the dialogue in the plays and novel or of noninterpretive descriptions of these characters and their actions. If uniquely correct, interpretations such as these are a subclass of true descriptions, not a contrasting class (but not all interpretations, I will argue below, are uniquely correct).

How, then, do we distinguish interpretations from other sorts of descriptions of works? Part of the distinction lies in the difference between directly perceiving and inferring. Many elements of works that we can directly perceive can be described without being interpreted. Interpretations are most often inferred on the basis of such direct perceptual encounters. In addition, elements of works that can be described without being or needing to be interpreted are those about which all observers (without perceptual defects in regard to the type of work in question) can agree, despite possibly disagreeing in interpretations of

---

[1] See, for example, Robert J. Matthews, "Describing and Interpreting a Work of Art," *Journal of Aesthetics and Art Criticism*, 36 (1977): 5–14; Annette Barnes, *On Interpretation* (Oxford: Basil Blackwell, 1988), chs 2, 3.

the works. Noninterpretive descriptions of artworks and their parts elicit virtually universal agreement. Hence, even the direct perception of elements and their properties, if their description is a matter of dispute, counts as interpretation. Ascriptions of certain expressive properties, say sadness in musical phrases, can fall into either class depending on context.

A central claim here is that all artistic media present us with elements that can be described without being interpreted, and that such elements constrain acceptable interpretations of the works that contain them. This is perhaps most obvious in painting and music, where such directly perceivable parts include colored shapes or notes and their formal relations. As is well known, Arthur Danto has argued that visual artworks must be vehicles of interpretation in order to be artworks, since, in this age of the avant-garde, there may be physically indistinguishable objects that are not art.[2] In so far as interpretation is required for and often implicit in appreciation of artistic values, I agree with this claim. But I want to note here that it is compatible with the fact that colored shapes as well as clearly represented objects are parts of paintings and can be described without being interpreted. Such elements make up the data or evidence for acceptable interpretations, which cannot be incompatible with their agreed descriptions.

If, as I claim, a unified account of artistic interpretation is possible, then there must be counterparts in literature. Given the criterion of direct perception that elicits near universal agreement in its description, noninterpretive elements in literary art are not simply physical ink marks on paper. We do not perceive such marks and infer that they are there to represent words with meanings. Instead, we directly perceive words and sentences, and, if not defective in our understanding of the language used, we will agree on the standard meanings of these words. Having standard semantic content is part of what makes a mark or sound a word. Sometimes words are ambiguous, and when they remain so in context, then interpretation is required to specify the meanings that work best in the work. We must infer to those meanings that best explain the use of those words in those contexts. But if this were not the exception, then reading novels would be an impossibly long and arduous task.

---

[2] Arthur Danto, *The Transfiguration of the Commonplace* (Cambridge, MA: Harvard University Press, 1981), ch. 1.

Ordinarily we directly perceive words as words, and we agree as to their literal meanings, which ordinarily persist in a relatively stable manner over time. Texts are therefore to be defined in terms of standard lexical meanings at their times of production. Those proficient in the language used in various texts are those who are familiar with the language as used at those times. When we understand the relevant language, we can agree on what the text is (in a given published edition), despite disagreeing on its proper interpretation. We can also often agree, for example, on the events, settings, and character traits explicitly described in a novel, and on the ways they are literally described, despite disagreeing on the significance of those elements. Texts containing such descriptions constrain acceptable interpretations in much the way that colored shapes and notes constrain interpretations of paintings and musical works.

This distinction between noninterpretive descriptions and interpretations has been challenged. Richard Shusterman, for example, argues that what we take to be descriptive fictional facts in a work depends on our interpretation of it. His example (borrowed from Richard Wollheim) is that of Hamlet's declared love for his father, which, under a Freudian interpretation, becomes a rationalization rather than a fact.[3] But what is a fact in the text is Hamlet's declaration of love for his father and the words he uses to make that declaration, however it is interpreted. There remains here, as in other conceivable examples, a level of description, a use of words with agreed ordinary meanings, that is noncontroversial.

Shusterman also points out that what descriptions we choose to pick out for attention in a work depend on our interpretation of it. This I cheerfully accept. In like manner, scientific theory guides observation and experiment, which nevertheless can be distinguished from theory and, crucially, can serve as a constraint on acceptable theories. In like manner too, those painted shapes to which we attend on a canvas will be those we take to be relevant to the significance and aesthetic value of the painting. The shapes can nevertheless be described without being interpreted. Philosophers sometimes deny distinctions simply by pointing out that one of the terms exerts an influence on the other (as in value–fact, theory–observation). But such arguments are not sound. That interpretation influences noninterpretive description does not erase the distinction

---

[3] Richard Shusterman, "Interpretation, Intention, and Truth," *Journal of Aesthetics and Art Criticism*, 46 (1987–8): 399–411, p. 403.

between them. Interpretation can be distinguished on the other side from evaluation as well, although our interpretations will depend on which aesthetic values we take to be realizable in the perception and appreciation of the works in question.

The line between noninterpretive description and interpretation must sometimes be drawn finely, even though the distinction is real and crucial for understanding the constraints on acceptable interpretations. Some examples may help to indicate where the line lies. To point out that a musical passage leads back to the tonic key is to describe it noninterpretively, even though one requires minimal musical training in order to understand that description. But to claim that the passage is there simply to form a bridge back to the tonic is to interpret it, however obviously. Similarly, we can directly perceive without needing to interpret expressive qualities in music, say the sadness in a particular phrase. But we may need to interpret the phrase as an expression of sadness if it can be viewed and played otherwise and therefore serve a different function in the piece. Finally, to say that a character in a novel acted as he did for a particular reason may be a noninterpretive description, if the action and its motive are described in ordinary terms in the novel. But it is an interpretation if it is inferred as most coherent with the explicit descriptions, given the style and context of the work.

Thus the same sentence may describe or interpret, depending on whether it is inferred as an explanation for what is explicitly stated in the text, as opposed to its being a mere restatement. In novels, where to draw the line can be affected by the reliability and sincerity of the narrator. A description of a character's motives, for example, should be taken at face value only when, as is ordinarily the case, we judge the narrator to be reliable and sincere. If we take the narrator to be unreliable or ironic in the instance, as we find on several occasions and with different narrators in *Nostromo*, then we must interpret seeming descriptions as meaning or implying something else. There will remain a descriptive level, however, in that it will remain true that the narrator described the matter as he did.

It should be pointed out here that the logical relations between noninterpretive descriptions, interpretations, and evaluations do not imply any order in actually perceiving and describing works of art. We might first note explicitly the evaluative aesthetic properties of a work, which might suggest or even presuppose an implicit interpretation, and only later focus on those descriptive properties that prompt our evaluative and interpretive responses. We may use a critic's interpretation to direct or redirect our perception and appreciation of a work. The critic may well offer interpretations on different levels. She might interpret a character as acting a certain way for a certain reason, then interpret that motive as indicative of a longer-term character trait, and then interpret that trait as contrasting with other characters or explaining their reactions.

Having located interpretation on the map with description and evaluation, we can now make explicit the account of it that has been implicit in our examples and previous discussion. It follows from that discussion that interpretation is a certain kind of inference to the best explanation. In interpreting elements of artworks we explain why they are placed in those contexts, for example, to convey a certain meaning, suggest a certain theme, express a certain feeling, or lead into the development section. In interpreting whole works we explain their artistic points, what broad themes they express, how they fit into various traditions, what artistic values they serve. The explanatory account of interpretation requires that there be uninterpreted data to be explained. In interpreting literature we seek to explain why words occur where they do, why passages constructed from them are placed where they are, why characters and events are described as they are, and so on. All this presupposes standard semantic content as part of the data to be explained. Words are to be interpreted as ironic or symbolic when we can show that the work or passage is more interesting, coherent, or expressive if those words (with those standard meanings) are understood in those ways. (I address authorial intention at length below.)

III

The claim that interpretation is inference to the best explanation for artworks and their parts in itself leaves open the kind of explanation at which it aims. If we held that interpreters aim at causal explanations, then we might arrive at the view that they aim to uncover artists' intentions, since these will figure prominently as causes in the production of artworks. The central question for evaluation will then be whether the artist succeeded in fulfilling the artistic aims she intended, and for interpretation what those aims or intentions were. If interpretations of works are explanations of their elements, of how the elements contribute to the values of the works, then according to this account we would ask why the artist placed the elements there as she did: what were her intentions that caused her to place them there as she did?

There is certainly something to be said for interpreting a work as its creator intended it to be taken, if those intentions are discoverable in the work or outside it. One of the values to be derived from appreciating art is the ability to see the world of the work, and derivatively perhaps the real world as well, from another viewpoint, through the imaginative eyes or genius of an artist. In all works with representational content, there is at least one implicit point of view from which that content is represented. A point of view may itself be part of the representation, and, as such, it may not always be that of the artist or author. But for a complete view of the world of a work, it is always worth asking what the artist's own view of that world is, and this normally involves thinking about the artist's intentions. If an interpreter ignores the way an artist intends her work to be understood, then he sacrifices that opportunity to see through the artist's eyes.

Thus, the interpretation that captures an artist's or author's intention is not just one possible reading among others with initially equal claim. Instead, it is one that has a value not realizable in other interpretations, a value that must be overridden if other interpretations are to be acceptable.

Recognizing an artist's achievement or successfully intended solution to an artistic problem is part of the full appreciation or engagement with a work. My account is not exclusive of the intentionalist's valid point on appreciation, but is more inclusive than it. Recognizing Constable's brilliant success in his attempts to capture sunlight in painting affects the way we perceive and react to his works. We come to see as subtle and dazzling at the same time what might otherwise be seen as ordinary landscapes. Seeing the world of a novel through the author's eyes, with the optimism of a Jane Austen or pessimism of a Hemingway or Conrad, is certainly a valuable way to engage cognitively and emotionally with it. Doing so can expand our viewpoint and change the way we see our world and the characters in it, certainly part of the value of reading novels. Knowing Hemingway's place in the moral malaise of post-World War I Europe allows us to better appreciate the terse but sometimes lyrical prose style, the repetition and seemingly nondeveloping plot, and the cynicism of the characters in *The Sun Also Rises*.

But if interpretation aims to facilitate the full appreciation of values in a work, why must we limit those values to those specifically intended by the artist? If critics are to facilitate the appreciation of artistic value, shouldn't they aim to maximize that value for their audiences? Surely it is strange to limit the value derivable from a work in this way, when such a limit lowers the amount of value that might otherwise be derived. At least the burden of proof must lie with the theory that seeks to enforce such a limit. At the same time it must be emphasized that value-maximizing explanations must remain true to texts as written, to what is straightforwardly described within them. We cannot, for example, interpret *Macbeth* as lacking the porter's scene or *Moby Dick* as lacking some of the longer and more tedious descriptions of whales on the ground that those works would be even better without those passages.

The main question is whether we can properly ascribe values to works that were not specifically intended by their creators. Certainly artists can achieve less than they intend in their works. It seems equally plausible and only fair that they can achieve more than they intend. It is also plausible but perhaps less fair that they can achieve precisely what they intend when what they intend is not worth achieving, so that their success is no justification for positive evaluation.

Regarding the first point, it seems that actions of all kinds can achieve better or worse results than intended and be praiseworthy or blameworthy on that ground. Tom insulted Mary, although he did not intend to. Despite his lack of intention, the insult might be blameworthy. Ron set the world record for one-hundred meters, although he only intended to win the heat and had no thought at all of the record, before or after. Surely the race he ran should still be an object of praise and of great value in the world of track. If anything, such cases seem even more obvious in the artworld, where artworks exist as public objects to be fully appreciated in their own right. Even if we grant that artistic value lies only in what an artist achieves, uncovering such value might not lie in discovering the artist's intentions.

A related point is that intentions exist at different levels of generality. In addition to specific artistic aims, I would guess that most artists intend their works to be fully appreciated for qualities that can be found in them, indeed to be maximally appreciated. Having to accept that they might achieve less than they intend, I doubt that many would object to their works being highly praised for effects they did not specifically intend as such. Since they must accept that their works might achieve less than they intend, why would they not accept that their works might achieve more?

Then they would not intend that critics' interpretations, which might promote more valuable experiences of their works, be limited by their narrower intentions.

Imagine, for example, that Beethoven did not intend to transform compositional style in his third symphony. Suppose, presumably contrary to fact, that he simply became fascinated with the melodic transformations and variations and with the modulations in the development section of that opening movement without intending to introduce a new form. Surely we can still admire the work for its unintended historical impact and experience it appreciatively in that light. Doing something under one description may also be doing it under another, when one is aware of doing it only under the first description. But if one is unaware that one is doing something as described in a certain way, then one is not doing it as so described intentionally. The 1920s smoker might have been risking lung cancer, but he was not doing so intentionally, even though he was smoking intentionally. Attributions of intentions are not transitive across such changing descriptions of the same actions. Although Beethoven was intentionally expanding the development section of the first movement of *Eroica*, he might not have been intentionally changing the course of symphonic composition, but his work can still be positively evaluated on that score (no pun intended).

It might be objected here (as one commentator did object) that I am ignoring the distinction between appreciating a work in itself and appreciating its effects on later works or on the future history of the genre. The former, it can be claimed, the work in itself, is still limited to what the artist successfully intended, even if the latter, the effects of the work, could not be or were not in fact anticipated or intended. But I still maintain that a proper understanding and certainly part of a full appreciation of Beethoven's third symphony, to stick for a moment with that example, lies in grasping its musically revolutionary form, its power to transform subsequent symphonic composition, whether Beethoven intended to do so or not. Understanding this potential effect, later actualized, is part of fully appreciating the work.

Or, to return to the race example, there is no distinction to be drawn there between appreciating the race and appreciating its effect, the breaking of the record. The race *is* the breaking of the record, although the runner, while intending to run the race, was not aware of and had no intention of breaking the record (just as the smoker was giving herself cancer although she had no intention to do so). We understand, appreciate, and interpret the race as a shattering of the record. And surely the runner would not object to our doing so; nor would Beethoven object to our interpreting the opening movement of *Eroica* as transformational. On similar grounds, I will argue in the next chapter that we must judge whether the characters in *The Sun Also Rises* morally develop by explaining for maximal appreciation the descriptions of their actions and thoughts in the text, whatever interpretation of those descriptions along these lines (if any) was intended by Hemingway.

That works can be praised for effects not specifically intended might explain why critics often speak of what a poem or painting says or does, instead of what the poet or painter says or does. It is true that in one sense poems and paintings don't literally say or do anything. But artworks as objects in their own right do have effects, i.e. they do such things as change the course of art history, whether their creators intended to do so or not. That their works can be praised for unintended effects on other artists or audiences might also explain why so many artists are reticent about their more specific intentions in creating them. Some artists might not be good at describing their own intentions. But authors of literary works are just as reticent about their own interpretations of them as are other artists, and surely they are not generally clueless about how to describe their mental states. So I suspect that artists' reticence about their intentions has much more to do with leaving room for unintended valuable properties in their works leading to better aesthetic experiences in audiences and positive evaluations by critics than it has to do with inabilities to express themselves in words.

Even when artists are not reticent about their own interpretations of their works, this does not prevent critics from proposing alternatives. Henry James notoriously remarked that *The Turn of the Screw* was simply a ghost story, which did not foreclose other readings of the novella. (What should foreclose them is clear textual evidence that the ghosts are real.) Hemingway remarked that there were no human heroes in *The Sun Also Rises*, but many critics have disagreed. Would it matter whether Melville saw Ahab as a heroic if futile defender of humanity against a hostile nature or as an evil megalomaniac blindly leading his crew to certain disaster? Would either intention foreclose the other reading of the novel? Even when critics themselves are professed intentionalists, their criticisms may not match their meta-theory. Richard Wollheim claims to be a strict intentionalist critic, but proceeds to offer very interesting Freudian interpretations of paintings that their artists could not have intended in their most Freudian of dreams.[4]

Another argument against strict intentionalism as a full theory of interpretation appeals to performance interpretations of musical works. Few if any would suggest that a performative interpretation should be constrained to realizing a composer's explicit intentions. First and notoriously, composers who conduct are not always the best conductors or interpreters of their own works. In my opinion, one may hear this first hand by listening to Bernstein and Copeland conduct Copeland. Second, once more composers, as others, have intentions on different levels. Bach, for example, may have intended not only that a certain passage be played on particular instruments, but that it produce a dramatic effect that may have been realizable on those instruments for his audience, but would require a larger orchestra now than any available in his time. A contemporary conductor would then have to choose which intention to honor. Only by ignoring the broader or higher-level intention would one conclude automatically that original instruments contribute to a more "authentic" performance for a contemporary audience. Third, it is clear from the incompleteness of the notations that composers use that they do not in general intend to limit interpreters of their works by very specific intentions as to performance. Tempi, for example, could be indicated far more precisely than they usually are.

It will be objected here that musical performances are not literally interpretations in the sense specified above. Conductors and performers do not simultaneously explain what they are playing, but are said to interpret simply by playing a piece with certain accents and emphases. They might be said to be interpreters only because they facilitate understanding in the way that translators of foreign languages do, by making accessible to audiences content that would otherwise be inaccessible.[5] In that case examples from performance interpretations would be irrelevant to proper accounts of critical interpretation as explanation, and this most obvious case of freedom from restriction by artists' intentions would not count in the general argument.

[4] Richard Wollheim, *Painting as an Art* (Princeton: Princeton University Press, 1987).
[5] This analogy was suggested by Jerrold Levinson in "Performance Versus Critical Interpretation in Music," in Michael Krausz, ed., *The Interpretation of Music: Philosophical Essays* (Oxford: Clarendon Press, 1993): 33–60.

In defense of these examples and their implications regarding intentions as constraints, we might first try responding strongly that a performance that is genuinely interpretive must reveal an understanding of its piece that could be made explicit in an explanation of the values realized by playing it that way. We might claim on that ground that interpretations as explanations are implicit in interpretations as performances. But that claim might be too strong. First, it is doubtful that performers who are said to be interpreters must be capable of providing explanations for their ways of playing; those ways may just seem intuitively right to them. Second, even reflective critics may not be able simply to read off explanatory interpretations from particular performances; the latter could be compatible with several different versions of the former.[6]

A safer answer to this objection uses the fact that interpretive performance requires understanding in a different way. Even if we cannot match such performances with verbal interpretations one-to-one, it is still the case that performances will be compatible only with certain verbal interpretations and incompatible with others. A performance is incompatible with a particular explanation of the values to be brought out in a piece if a competent musician who accepts that interpretation would not play the piece in that way. We then need maintain only that there can be acceptable performances of the same piece that are compatible only with incompatible explicit interpretations, and that composers cannot consistently intend incompatible interpretations, in order to conclude that musical interpretations are not constrained by composers' intentions.

The premises are indeed plausible here. One interpretation of a piece might seek to maximize its expressive qualities by explaining various passages as means to such expression. Another might seek to make the formal structure of the piece as clear as possible. A conductor of the piece may not be able to do both at once, as can be heard, for example, by listening to performances of Brahms' Fourth Symphony by Bernstein and Szell. Once more, Brahms may or may not have intended either sort of performance (he may once more have written certain passages as he did simply because they seemed right to him).

The point here is that performance interpretations are linked closely enough to explanatory interpretations that apply as well to literary works

---

[6] Levinson once more makes a similar point in "Performance Versus Critical Interpretation in Music."

to make it plausible to ascribe the same amount of freedom to both sorts. Peter Kivy has argued that readings of novels *are* performances.[7] While this might appear to be a surprising claim, there is now available a simple argument to the same conclusion, indicated in the introductory chapter. Most of us are familiar with readings of books on tapes and CDs. Surely these are performances. But then, if the reader were to give the same reading silently in his head, this too would be a performance, the same performance, only silent. But then our readings must be silent performances too. Then the same constraints, or lack of them, must apply as in the case of other performances, e.g. musical. Our intuitions are similar in both cases. Constraining a performative interpretation to what the creator of the piece intended does not seem to depend on whether the performance is public or private. In both cases we want the interpretation to be true to the text and value enhancing.

At the level of giving "deep" interpretations of a whole work, for example in Freudian or Marxist terms, or in terms of its place in a historical sequence defining a developing style, few would maintain that interpreters are constrained by artists' specific intentions along those lines. That Shakespeare could not have been capable of interpreting *Hamlet* himself in Freudian terms does not make that interpretation uninteresting or unacceptable. To switch to painting, that El Greco could not have seen himself as an early expressionist does not rule out our interpreting his works in that way. Whether we are interpreting whole works or their parts is not really important here. Interpretation of a whole literary work, for example, requires interpretation of particular passages that is coherent with the broader account. In all these cases interpreters are not limited to reconstructing artists' intentions. I don't know whether John Irving intended all the theses regarding obedience to rules that I take to be implicit in his characters' fates in *The Cider House Rules* (Chapter 7). But it does not matter.

IV

A final argument against intentionalism appeals to the multiple interpretability of most artworks, a topic that merits separate consideration. The example of musical performance in the previous section made clear also that there is room for interpreters to maximize the value of artistic works

---

[7] Peter Kivy, *The Performance of Reading* (Oxford: Blackwell, 2006).

via equally acceptable but incompatible interpretations. Artworks are typically subject to multiple interpretations, sometimes even in regard to their broadest themes, as I will illustrate in the next chapter. I will offer there incompatible interpretations of Hemingway's *The Sun Also Rises* in regard to the theme of moral development and its blockage. I claim that these interpretations are equally acceptable in enhancing different literary values not themselves jointly realizable. While artists will typically have in mind only one interpretation, if more than one may be acceptable, they cannot be limited to what the artists intend. Thus establishing that more than one interpretation of the same work can be acceptable, even when they are incompatible, at the same time argues against the constraint of intentionalism.

In arguing against multiple interpretability, David Novitz maintains that critics typically are convinced that their own interpretations are correct and those of others wrong.[8] But it seems to me that only the most naive critic in offering the fiftieth interpretation of the same work will think that she has exactly captured what the artist intended, while all previous critics failed to do so. Recognizing this thought as naive or disingenuous does not and should not prevent the critic from offering her new and different interpretation, if it newly uncovers or enhances value-relevant properties in the work.

What she cannot think is that the previous forty-nine interpretations are simply wrong, or that in order to be acceptable, all these interpretations must be compatible and intended by the artist. Both these alternatives are false to the practice of criticism and its reception by audiences. Most really good works of art are open to continuous and unending reinterpretation, sometimes in terms their artists could not have envisioned. And even when their creators possessed the relevant critical concepts and so could have anticipated the many different interpretations, it is very unlikely that they did.

Novitz argues also that if interpretations seek to uncover properties in works themselves, then they cannot admit incompatible rivals, since artworks, like any other objects, cannot have incompatible properties at the same time.[9] To assert that an object is a particular way at a particular time is to imply that it is not some incompatible way. According to him,

---

[8] David Novitz, "Against Critical Pluralism," in Michael Krausz, ed., *Is There a Single Right Interpretation?* (University Park: Pennsylvania State University Press, 2002).
[9] Novitz, "Against Critical Pluralism," pp. 104, 115.

if a work is indeterminate in regard to certain relevant properties, then pointing this out will be part of the single right interpretation. If critics are to disagree about the right interpretation, there must be a single work with internally consistent properties about which they are disagreeing.

I agree that there must be a single text that is the target of explanation for an interpreter. But interpretations fill out the fictional world of a text by adding fictional truths to those that are explicitly stated in the text. And they can do this in acceptable although mutually incompatible ways. This is not to ascribe contradictory properties to the same object, since it is not to ascribe such properties to the text itself. It is to acknowledge that the text can generate different fictional worlds, different sets of fictionally true propositions, depending on how it is interpreted. Fictional truth, what is true in the world of a work, unlike literal truth, is relative to interpretive contexts. This allows that what is explicitly stated in the text, absent irony or unreliable narrator, is true in all its fictional worlds.

I noted above that, while some interpretations are obvious and can be known to be true, more interesting ones are contestable. Not only are such critical disagreements more tolerable than in the case of noninterpretive descriptions, but the former may be interminable. The account offered here explains this fact as the result ultimately of differences in taste. (The concept of taste itself includes the recognition that tastes need not converge.) If interpretation explains elements in works as contributing to this or that aesthetic value, if it seeks understanding in order to guide perception and facilitate appreciation of various aesthetic values (ways of engaging us), if artworks can be appreciated in different ways, if they have potential values that cannot be realized simultaneously, then there will be incompatible interpretations or explanations that appeal to different tastes or preferences for different aesthetic values. Previous examples and but little reflection suggest that the last antecedent is correct—the multi-dimensionality of artworks, especially very good works, makes it rare that all their potential values can be appreciated under single interpretations. This is clear in the case of performative interpretations, where a piece cannot be played in different ways at once. But it is also true of literary interpretations.

To cite some notorious cases, Henry James' *The Turn of the Screw* can be read as a ghost story or as a psychological study of a deranged woman, or it can be read as ambiguous between the two. Blake's *Tyger* poem can be read with an understanding of the tiger as evil, as noble, or as ambiguous between the two. But in both cases the third interpretation does not simply combine the disjoined previous two readings. It cannot do so if an interpretation is intended as a guide to perception or reading and appreciation. The experience of an evil tiger as the object of the poem's vivid imagery is very different from that of a noble one, and the experience of the poem as ambiguous is once more simply distinct from the impossible union of the other two experiences. Similarly, the expressive atmosphere of a ghost story is very different from that of a realistic psychological thriller, the one engaging us more on an emotional level and the other on a cognitive level, and these qualities cannot be conjoined in a single reading of James' novella. We cannot experience the story as both supernatural and realistic at once. To read the book as ambiguous between the two is in this case to assume an analytical attitude that destroys the empathetic identification with the characters and emotional engagement with the work.

Interpretations are incompatible when they ascribe, either explicitly or implicitly, properties to a work that it cannot have simultaneously. Different interpretations need not be incompatible, but they will be when, for example, one interprets a passage as light and delicate and another as forceful, or if one interprets characters as morally developing and another sees them as mired in morally bankrupt identities. At least some great works have expressive or thematic possibilities that cannot be realized simultaneously or in compatible interpretations, but that create equally valuable experiences for audiences. Incompatible interpretations may be equally acceptable when they enhance different potential values within a work. An interpretation is acceptable when it guides an audience to an experience of a work above some threshold of value derivable from the work, and when it enhances some value in the work to a greater degree than that affordable under other interpretations.

Normally, in order to meet this criterion, the various parts of an overall interpretation must cohere with each other, and they must coherently explain the values of many different parts of the work. In interpreting novels we seek broad themes that can unify the contents and sometimes the structures of the works. But an interesting interpretation might be acceptable even while dismissing some parts of a work as mistakes on the artist's part, and different acceptable accounts might dismiss different elements of a work in that way. An interpretation of *Moby Dick* as high drama might dismiss the chapters on whales as loss of literary will on Melville's part; one which views it as a paean to the power of nature might dismiss certain supernatural elements in it instead.

It always counts in favor of one interpretation over a second, however, that the former has less need to do this. Clearly according to this theory, not all interpretations or explanations of the describable elements in a work will be acceptable, although two or more may be. Iago's famous Credo aria in Verdi's *Otello*, for example, which is a hymn to evil, can be sung as boisterously defiant or as broodingly sinister, but an interpretation of it as jovially comic would be clearly unacceptable. Similarly, more or less optimistic readings of *The Sun Also Rises* are possible, as we shall see, but to interpret it as light-hearted Woodhousean comedy is unacceptable within any critical tradition.

When we have two or more acceptable but incompatible interpretations, we cannot speak simply of a true interpretation, although we might speak of fictional truth within a world as projected by an interpretation and of being true to the work. Plausibility will not do either, since propositions are plausible when they are probably true, under some subjective concept of probability. If incompatible interpretations cannot both be true, and if they can nevertheless be equally acceptable (with no hope of eventually finding either objectively preferable or true), then they cannot be plausible. I propose that we then speak on the first level simply of acceptability.

A uniquely acceptable interpretation can be said to be true. As noted, we can also speak relativistically of truth within an acceptable interpretive scheme, and we will need to do so in order to construct and evaluate arguments from within such schemes. Interpretive propositions that are true within no acceptable interpretive schemes are simply false, or false of the work. Once more this relativism in regard to interpretation is compatible with, and indeed ultimately reduces to, the relativity of evaluation to developed tastes that is also endorsed here.

Aside from appeal to critical practice, that much art is meant to be open to a variety of interpretations is evidenced by its abundant use of metaphor and ambiguity, the incompleteness of its descriptions and/or notations, and by the multiplicity but incompatibility of the values that multi-dimensional works can afford. The toleration of incompatible interpretations differentiates this sort of explanation both from causal explanation in the sciences and from interpretation of philosophical and other nonliterary texts. In the sciences different causes may cooperate to produce an effect, and different factors may be singled out as "the cause" of an event in different explanatory contexts, but they all must fit in principle into a single complete explanation of the effect or event.

A philosophical text may be open to more than one interpretation, but ambiguity is more of a defect than a source of multiple values in nonliterary texts.

The claim that there are incompatible but equally acceptable interpretations of artworks is important in itself, and I will return to it below. It has been used here as a premise in a final argument against intentionalism. (I will also refute other arguments in favor of this theory below.) Our conclusion in this section is that the sort of explanation that we seek in interpretation is not simply causal explanation. It is rather a kind of teleological explanation. We interpret an element of a work by explaining its role in creating artistic value through its contribution to representation or thematic content, expression, or to the formal or narrative coherence of the work. We interpret a work as a whole by explaining those representational, thematic, formal, and expressive qualities that make it artistically valuable, or by explaining its place in the history of the genre or in the broader culture.

The purposes to which we appeal in offering such explanations (to create this or that value in the work) need not be purposes in the mind of the artist who creates it, but may be Kant's "purposiveness without purpose" internal to the structure of the work. We arrive at this conclusion by considering the fundamental purpose of interpretation itself: to guide perception toward maximal appreciation and therefore fair evaluation of a work. This purpose also generates the criterion of acceptability for interpretations. The best interpretative explanations are those that guide the perceptions of an audience toward maximal appreciation of a work, those that maximize its value for the audience.[10]

---

[10] A few similar accounts have been suggested in the literature. One is P. D. Juhl, "The Appeal to the Text," *Journal of Aesthetics and Art Criticism*, 36 (1978): 277–87. Juhl suggests that interpretations explain texts by appealing to authors' intentions to fulfill the value criteria of coherence and complexity. My account is not limited to appeal to authors' intentions, and it recognizes diverse sources of artistic value. A second is Jeffrey Olin, "Theories, Interpretations, and Aesthetic Qualities," *Journal of Aesthetics and Art Criticism*, 35 (1977): 425–31. He sees interpretations as explanatory theories that seek to unify works. I see unity as at most one formal aesthetic value, and my account applies to parts or elements of works as well. A third is Ronald Dworkin, "Law as Interpretation," *Critical Inquiry*, 9 (1982): 179–200. Dworkin sees as a goal of interpretation making a text as aesthetically good as it can be. I agree (taking "aesthetic" in a broad sense), and my account is closest to his. But I emphasize that the diverse sources of aesthetic value imply incompatible but equally acceptable interpretations of the same works, an implication inimical to Dworkin's general program.

V

It is clear on this account that another traditional view of interpretation, that it always consists in disclosing meanings, must be rejected as well as far too narrow. Interpretation does not always consist in revealing meanings, unless we take "meaning" in the very broad sense of significance and equate revealing the significance of a work or its parts with explaining the value of the work or the place of its parts within its broader structure. Trivially, in the case of music and visual art, there is not always semantic content to reveal. And I argued above that we need not interpret typical sentences in novels; instead, words and sentences with their ordinary meanings are data for interpretation as explanation.

Nevertheless, many older interpreters of literary interpretation, despite disagreeing over such basic issues as whether there is one correct interpretation for each text, whether author intention is relevant, and whether interpretations are to be held true or false, agreed that interpretation consists in the disclosure of meanings for texts.[11] They disagreed often about the *ground* of meaning in a text, whether it is author intention, public rules of language, conventions of an interpretive community, or creative acts by readers, but in so doing they shared the assumption that meaning is what interpreters are after. The ground of meaning is what philosophers of interpretation, like old-fashioned philosophers of language, sought.

There are many objections to this assumption. First, if interpretation were simply the disclosure of verbal meaning, then artistic or literary value would be most often irrelevant. Stating literal meanings is normally value neutral. Critics ponder which assignment of meanings makes a poem or prose passage most interesting or aesthetically best only when considering whether to interpret terms or phrases ironically or metaphorically. And even irony and metaphor rely on ordinary meanings given prior to interpretation. Second, if interpretation simply revealed meaning, then every paraphrase of a section of a literary text, no matter how short and obvious, would count as a literary interpretation. But giving the univocal ordinary dictionary meanings of the words in a simple sentence in a novel does not constitute a literary interpretation of that

---

[11] See, for example, Monroe Beardsley, *The Possibility of Criticism* (Detroit: Wayne State University Press, 1970); E. D. Hirsch, *Validity in Interpretation* (New Haven: Yale University Press, 1967); Stanley Fish, *Is There a Text in This Class?* (Cambridge, MA: Harvard University Press, 1980).

sentence. Once more, we need not interpret such sentences; we simply read them or grasp their meanings right off, much as we perceive trees in an 18th-century landscape painting without having to interpret the colored shapes as trees. Such disclosure of meaning is description, not interpretation.

I have granted that stating meaning, say of some obscure lines in a poem, can constitute at least partial interpretation of those lines. It does so when there is an implicit claim that they contain the terms and phrases that they do in order to convey that meaning, that their value in the poem lies in conveying that meaning. Stating meanings will rarely constitute a complete interpretation of a text or its significant parts, since in literary art the way meanings are conveyed or presented is almost always relevant to the value of the work, and hence part of the explanation for the way it is constructed. But certainly words and passages sometimes have value in a text largely because of the meanings they convey. This is especially true in the case of poems, where meanings are most often controversial, and so it is no accident that those who see interpretation as a matter of revealing meaning concentrate almost exclusively on poetry. In none of the novels I will consider in later chapters is there any need to interpret the meanings of the sentences in the text. One can grasp all those meanings and still not appreciate in the least the novels themselves. And while the sentences do have meanings, it makes little sense to talk of the meanings of the novels.

Perhaps in order to avoid the sort of objection just raised to ordinary paraphrases as interpretations, Monroe Beardsley construes interpretation as reconstructing the meaning of a whole text or large segment from the ordinary meanings of its parts, its words and sentences.[12] But this account ignores the fact that words and phrases can be interpreted too. And as just indicated, I am not sure what the meaning of a whole text would be, unless it is given in a long paraphrase. If that is what is meant, then it implies that a simple paraphrase of a whole work is the paradigm interpretation of it. But it is most likely not an interpretation at all. Finally, the account fails to indicate any connection between interpretation of literary and nonliterary arts, those which lack semantic content. The connection is that artistic interpretation as an aid to understanding and appreciation is always explanation of the aesthetic values served by the data in the artwork that is being interpreted. Even in regard to a difficult

---

[12] Beardsley, *The Possibility of Criticism*, pp. 38–9.

poem, to say what the words mean in context is only the beginning of a full interpretation, and such preliminary explanation will be guided by a fuller understanding of the significance or theme of the poem.

Before turning to other philosophers with competing views of interpretation, I should consider a broad objection that is certain to arise to the view defended here. There may appear to be clear counterexamples to the claim that interpretations of artworks aim to enhance their value or facilitate their appreciation. We might interpret a German work from the 1940s as Nazi propaganda; a feminist might interpret a work or elements within it as expressions of contempt for women; or a historian might interpret a work as indicative of a degenerative stage of a style or tradition. In each of these cases, the interpretation, while it might be acceptable as far as it goes, would seem to lower the value of the work for its audience, not enhance that value. Such accusations, if true, would seem to turn us off from a work, not engage us.

In response, it can be pointed out first that no such interpretation in itself can approach being a complete explanatory framework for a work with any significant potential artistic value. Claims such as the above may not even qualify as interpretations of such works as works of art. To point out, for example, that *The Merchant of Venice* is an expression of anti-Semitism or that *Huckleberry Finn* is racist (a more controversial, less plausible, but perhaps more interesting claim) is hardly to begin to interpret such works as literary art. Second, there are several ways in which such claims might indicate value or significance in the works to which they refer, or at least valuable ways to view those works. Part of the significance of a work may lie in its being a symptom of or symbol for social attitudes prevalent at a certain time and place, however objectionable those attitudes might be. That certain elements in a work express such attitudes may, in explaining their presence there, also render explicable or comprehensible what is otherwise inexplicable, increasing the coherence if not the overall appeal of the work to its audience. Interpreting a work as an instance of a degenerating style at least indicates the sorts of aesthetic values one might seek in the work (while indicating also that an overall negative evaluation is the most one could hope for).

Interpretation, we said, links description to evaluation, and, while trying to facilitate appreciation, must sometimes dismiss or explain features of works as defects in order to generate honest evaluations. Interpretations must reveal works in their best light, but they must also be true to their character and content. They must be built on accurate descriptions. Thus, the claim that interpretations of works ought to give them the best run for their money is compatible with the admission that final evaluations of them can be strongly negative and can show that others overrate them.

VI

The account of interpretation as inference to value-enhancing explanations captures both the fact of incompatible but equally acceptable explanations (given different ways to enhance value) and the fact that not all interpretations are equally acceptable or acceptable at all. Other philosophers have seen interpretation as either more or less objectively constrained. Whereas the dominant view among analytic philosophers may be that there is one correct interpretation for each text or segment of text, the current vogue among literary critics is that interpretation is not constrained by independent text at all: the only constraints are those self-imposed by readers or interpretive communities. This section will comment briefly on certain of these alternative views and their implicit criticisms of the sort of account defended above.

The denial of objective constraints from the side of the text is typified by the theory of literary interpretation of Stanley Fish.[13] He denies the database on which the explanatory account of interpretation relies. For him it is interpretive activity that creates texts with meanings. Without the contexts that interpreters supply, literary works remain indeterminate; our accepted ways of reading determine how they are to be understood. This allows, as any teacher of literature must, for better and worse readings; but acceptability here is settled by interpretive communities, by what they allow and disallow by way of interpretive strategies. To believe that texts constrain interpretations independently of such strategies is to underestimate the power of interpretive communities to license fundamentally different readings of any given work, a power evidenced both by the history of criticism and by the imaginative ingenuity of critics such as Fish.

I argued above that consideration of nonliterary arts reveals obviously the presence there of uninterpreted elements functioning as constraints on interpretation. However much interpreters may vary tempo or tone or emphasize different musical relations, they cannot

---

[13] See especially Fish, *Is There a Text in This Class?*.

ignore (at least the large majority of) the notes that confront them or alter their basic formal relations. A similar point was readily available in the case of literature. However many interpretations of Blake's *Tyger* poem may be forthcoming, all must confront and explain the fact that he centrally used a term that ordinarily refers to tigers. Surely this fact in itself renders certain interpretations more acceptable than others.

A main oversight in Fish's theory is its neglect not only of the artwork or text itself, but of the artist, who disappears from this picture of artistic creation. Not only meaning, but the significance and value of literary works seem in Fish's view to be creations of critics and their interpretive communities. It must be so if their interpretations remain unconstrained by authors' texts. Fish writes:

No longer is the critic the humble servant of texts whose glories exist independently of anything he might do; it is what he does, within the constraints embedded in the literary institution, that brings texts into being... The practice of literary criticism is not something one must apologize for; it is absolutely essential not only to the maintenance of, but to the production of, the objects of its attention.[14]

The neutral reading public may think this thesis places the bulk of the credit for great literary works in the wrong quarter, to say the least.

Fish often relies for his theory's defense on the theoretical claim that meaning is created through institutional practice rather than residing transcendentally in language or texts independent of practice.[15] This claim is not disputed. The response is that those fundamental practices that create cores of stable meanings for terms are not the practices of literary criticism or even writing literature. The writer as well as the critic uses a language that is ready-made through earlier social practice. The writer can stretch or add to the language, but only parasitically on earlier use. The critic confronts language in particular texts that use it in specific ways, and she must explain those uses. The distinction between creative artist and critic is real and sharper than Fish in his passionate defense of the critic allows.

The final complaint against his theory has to do with standards. As noted, for him interpretive communities set the standards for acceptable

---

[14] Fish, *Is There a Text in This Class?*, p. 368.
[15] Fish, *Is There a Text in This Class?*, e.g., p. 318.

critical interpretations.[16] This meta-normative thesis allows that some groups of interpreters are better at their practice than others only according to their own standards, leaving all groups with equal status, that is, without objective criteria for critical standards themselves or ultimately for acceptable interpretations. In practice, of course, no literature teacher would or should admit that a stable group of high school students with common standards and methods of interpretation for collaborating on their homework has the same claim to acceptable interpretation as the best critics.

On the other side, if, like Fish, we locate interpretive authority in the community of recognized professional critics, then we have the problem of the gifted but unrecognized amateur. What makes such a critic gifted is the acceptability of his interpretations, his offering novel explanations that show how to understand parts of the work in ways that enhance their values. Meeting this criterion of adequacy to text does not await recognition from the community of professional critics. In elevating the status of critics to artists, Fish's theory destroys their status as critics (except according to their own idiosyncratic standards and academic or publishing positions).

Among literary critics, on the other side of the spectrum from our intermediate position is E. D. Hirsch, an early champion of the intentionalist theory of interpretation. He relies mainly on the argument that only consideration of authors' intentions can make the meanings of literary texts determinate. According to his view, if there is to be a standard of correct interpretation, it must lie in the determinate meaning of the text; and if meaning is to be determinate, it must be made so by the author's intending a determinate meaning, since texts in themselves may be interpreted in radically different ways.[17] I have rejected both the claim that interpretation seeks to reveal meanings and the thesis that interpreters must reveal the intentions of artists as the criterion of the uniquely correct interpretations of their works. I rejected both the idea that there normally are uniquely correct interpretations of multi-valued works and the claim that interpreters are constrained by artists' intentions (although I accepted that seeing the world of a work through its artist's eyes or intentions is one major value among others to be derived from it).

---

[16] Fish, *Is There a Text in This Class?*, p. 347.
[17] E. D. Hirsch, *Validity in Interpretation* (New Haven: Yale University Press, 1967), chs 1, 2.

These earlier objections aside, one can dispute the degree of determinacy in ordinary discourse and expository writing, where context and conventional content normally make it quite clear what is being said by making it overwhelmingly improbable that anything else could be meant. In much poetry, however, it might seem that we must grant Hirsch his indeterminacy thesis. In the case of novels, the claim should not be that the ordinary meanings of the words or phrases used are unclear, but instead that the broader themes understood to be asserted by those words, the proper explanations for their uses in those contexts, are not uniquely determined by the texts themselves. In this sense ordinary meanings in themselves do not constrain us to a single interpretation, a thesis that Hirsch correctly shares with his rival Fish against Beardsley. Author intention, when discoverable and added to verbal context, is the means, according to him, to make texts that are indeterminate in this way determinate and to avoid the chaos that Fish's sort of theory entails. Assuming for the moment that interpreters do seek to specify meanings in this broader sense, is intention the key to such specification?

One might first accuse Hirsch and other intentionalists of confusing utterance meaning with speaker's meaning. This is now a common distinction in philosophy of language, and it is implicit in the possibility of failed linguistic intentions on the part of speakers. Speakers can fail to say what they intend to say if they use words improperly, and then their meanings, what they intend to convey, will not match the meanings of their utterances, what fully competent listeners would construe them as saying. The extreme result of ignoring this distinction entirely is the Humpty Dumpty theory of meaning, according to which speakers can make their statements mean whatever they like. Hirsch is not guilty of this extreme, silly theory, since he allows that semantic conventions constrain what can be conveyed or meant by the use of words.[18] But there is still a confusion in this vicinity in Hirsch's main argument.

The intention of a speaker cannot in itself alter her utterance meaning, and so we cannot, as Hirsch implies we should, make utterance or textual meaning determinate by taking into account author intention, if that meaning is otherwise indeterminate. We can, however, substitute author (speaker's) meaning for textual (utterance) meaning, if the latter is indeterminate and the former is independently discoverable. This would not in itself make

---

[18] Hirsch, *Validity in Interpretation*, p. 27.

the text a satisfactory work, if determinacy in its meaning is required for that; but it might make the experience of the work more satisfactory, and we might now charitably interpret Hirsch as advocating this move.

I argued above, however, that constraining interpretations within the bounds of artists' intentions denies to audiences certain values that may be derivable from works although not explicitly foreseen or intended by their creators. This is certainly true at the level of explaining the significance of various events as described in a work or at the broadest level of choosing an overall explanatory framework. If *The Turn of the Screw* makes an interesting work under a naturalistic (as opposed to supernaturalistic) framework, or if *Hamlet* can be understood and explained in detailed Freudian terms, these interpretations would not be ruled out by the recognition that their authors did not or even could not have intended them. The same point holds in regard to the significance of particular words and phrases in such texts. In fact, the narrower point follows from the broader claim, since interpreting entire texts in different ways will entail interpreting some of their parts differently. By contrast, the ordinary meanings of the terms even in abstruse works are ordinarily determinate enough, or, if ambiguous in context, remain so whatever the intentions of their authors.

Thus, Hirsch's appeal to author intention as a constraint on interpretation is often either useless or pernicious if heeded. We do not ordinarily use speaker's meanings to get at utterance meanings, as Hirsch (implicitly) suggests that we should in understanding literary art. Normally it is the other way round: we use utterance meaning as determined by semantic conventions to grasp what a speaker is trying to convey to us. We do the same in reading literary texts if we are interested in capturing an author's intentions or point of view. But, as argued above, this is only one value to be derived from reading a novel.

VII

The most recent and in my view the most plausible arguments for an intentionalist theory of interpretation are those of Noël Carroll.[19] Although unlike Hirsch, he does not see interpretation as a quest for

---

[19] All the arguments considered below are contained in Noël Carroll, *On Interpretation* (London: Routledge, 2009).

meanings, he also defends intentionalism as the only way to achieve objectivity or determinateness in the interpretation of texts. He points out that audiences must appreciate artistic works as they are, not seek pleasurable experiences from free-floating associations prompted by the works or from false views of what the works contain. If the object of criticism is not whatever the audience does with the work, or however they might react to or experience it, then, he argues, it must be what the artist did, whether he succeeded in doing what he intended to do. Critics must focus either on audience experiences, whatever those might be and however they can be made most pleasurable, or on artistic productions and achievements, and again, only the latter focus produces objective criticism.

But my position represents a third alternative. Critics and audiences can focus on the works as they are, as they are properly described, both in terms of what their artists intended and independently of such intentions. I refer here again to texts with standard meanings, as well as to accurate descriptions of what is in musical scores, what is on canvases, and so on, descriptions that can be given prior to interpretations. Everyone can agree that audiences must appreciate artworks as they are, not as the audiences might fantasize them to be. But the needed constraints can consist in the paint on a canvas and what it obviously represents, the notes in a score, or a text and the fictional events in its story as written.

When our experience of a piece of music or of a picture is made more pleasurable by some personal association, we do not take the music or painting itself to embody additional value available to others. The value of artworks lies not just in any good experience they might prompt, but only in authentic experience based on objective features of the works. We cannot ascribe value to a work based solely on idiosyncratic responses or free-floating associations of a single individual. But when responses are widely shared and valuable to those responding, they need not be intended by the artist. Carroll argues that critics cannot center their evaluations on audience responses, since they must first know whether the responses are merited by the works themselves. Unmerited responses do not merit positive evaluations of works. But if we respond to great or good artworks in similar ways, reflecting our motivations for attending to artworks in the first place, then works that produce those responses can be judged good independently of how artists intended their works to be understood.

Carroll uses the example of the awful movie *Plan Nine from Outer Space*, which would not be considered so awful if it were a comedic avant-garde attack on Hollywood film making. He argues that, even if critics could get a sizeable audience to think of it that way and hence experience it more pleasurably, that would not be a proper interpretation of the movie. It would not be proper because the director was trying to imitate Hollywood techniques, not attack them, although he spectacularly failed in his intention. He concludes again that it is not the job of critics to maximize the good experiences of their audiences, but instead to judge the achievement of the artist, whether he succeeded in what he intended.

I agree that we should not judge this movie to be good, even if it prompts as much laughter as a clever comedy. But that is first of all because we are not to ascribe false properties to artworks, misdescribe them, as the basis for our interpretations or evaluations. This includes relational properties. "Avant-garde attack" is a relational concept describing not only an object, but the intention with which it was produced. To describe this movie in those terms is to misdescribe it. But this does not mean that all the descriptions on which our interpretations and evaluations are based must be intentional in this sense. Interpretations based solely on accurate descriptions of properties inherent in works themselves that omit nothing of major importance in the works are suitably constrained and therefore can be acceptable. While we are not to misdescribe an artist's intentions in describing her work, our descriptions of the work in support of our evaluation once more need not be limited to what she intended.

Second, I do not agree that this movie would be better if interpreted as an intentional affront to Hollywood. To think that all deviations from established methods, even when they are intentional, indicate positive values, is to place too high a value on mere originality. Originality can add to the virtues of a work when it contains other virtues that are original, but it cannot in itself make a very poor work better. Interpreting as intentional deviations features of a film that appear to be mistakes precisely because they make the experience of it so unsatisfying would not make that experience any better.

Carroll's second argument in favor of intentionalism points out that critics find value in properties of works not experienced by the audience, properties such as originality and historical impact. He uses the point as an argument for intentionalism because he sees it as the only alternative to focusing criticism solely on the value of the audience's experience, as I do (with the rider that the experience must be rooted in the work as it is). According to him, a perfect forgery affords the same experience as a genuine work, but it does not have the same value since it is not original and lacks the same historical significance. If the value of artworks lies solely in the experiences they afford, we have to judge the forgery as having the same value as the original. If the value of artworks does not lie in the experiences they afford, then, Carroll assumes, it must lie in what the artists have intentionally accomplished.

I have already argued that what artists and others accomplish may be more than what they intentionally accomplish, so that focusing on achievement is not necessarily focusing on intentions. But I also think that the present argument appeals to an impoverished view of aesthetic experience. Such experience is more than bare sensory experience of the patches of paint, heard notes, or read words. Just as emotional engagement with expressive qualities is integral to the experience of artworks, so is cognitive engagement with a work's relation to other works and to its tradition. And that cognitive engagement can alter the ways we perceive the work. Contra Carroll, we do not experience a forgery in the same way as its prototype once we learn that it is a forgery. Education and repeated experience of works change the ways we perceive them, in keeping with our emphasis on the interaction of mental capacities in appreciating artworks.

When we learn that a purported picture by Van Gogh is a forgery, we no longer see the brushstrokes as agitated or vibrant. Instead, they begin to look mannered. When we learn of the way that the opening movement of Beethoven's Eroica transforms composition in the classical style, we experience it differently, paying closer attention to its many transformations of melodic and harmonic elements. Such properties as originality and historical impact, while not experienced directly, affect the ways we experience artworks. So does recognition of the historical context of a work. Recognizing the historical context of Huckleberry Finn affects whether it appears racist to us, hence affects our emotional and moral engagement with it as we read. Hence focus on these properties by critics does not refute the thesis that criticism aims to facilitate the most valuable experience of artworks in audiences and so should not be restricted by artists' specific intentions regarding the significance of their works.

Carroll's third and perhaps central argument is that artworks are vehicles of communication between artists and audiences. Artists communicate with their audiences via their artworks. If the artwork instantiates an act of communication, it ought to be interpreted as are other acts of communication. In general, when we interpret what other people communicate to us, we are inferring from their words or acts what they are intending to say or communicate. If interpretation in general aims to uncover communicative intentions, it should be no different with interpreting artworks. Furthermore, unless the communicator was sloppy or negligent in her choice of words or other media, we wrong her, and so artists, when we attribute to them meanings they never intended. Intentionally misinterpreting what people mean or intend is like lying to them, the only difference being the direction of the communicative misrepresentation.

In reply, I have implied that artworks are something more than acts of communication. They are produced as public objects for aesthetic appreciation, and this distinguishes them from ordinary ways of communicating. In ordinary acts of communication, the particular words chosen are insignificant, as long as they communicate what is intended. We look through the words to grasp their intended meanings. And we grasp these meanings straight off, without having to interpret the words if we are native speakers. Not so with artworks. We never simply look through the media or formal structures to grasp the intended content, however expressed.

To borrow a phrase that only slightly exaggerates, in art the medium is the message. And we do interpret literary artworks, not in the sense of disclosing meanings, but in the sense of seeking themes, characters' motives, formal relations, all of which has nothing to do with ordinary conversation. This opacity in the artwork itself once its creator releases it into the artworld leaves it open to the multiple interpretations that critics will provide in trying to uncover all the value it might contain. Again, no such animal exists in regard to ordinary conversation. Critics no more wrong artists in offering their different interpretations of their works than we wrong Ron the runner when we grant that he has broken the record even though he had no intention of doing so.

What makes the context of art different from ordinary contexts of communication to which Carroll assimilates it is the intention and need to have works appreciated in addition to having artists understood. This difference is why the manner of communicating is always as important as the content communicated in art. The appeal to intention as a constraint does not err in forcing us outside the work in search of its proper interpretation. We must in any case view the work in its proper historical context to interpret and appreciate it fully. Nor is it the problem that artists' intentions are inaccessible. We must ascribe intentions to others all the time in interpreting not only their language, but their behavior in general. The problem is only that the appeal is too limited and ascribes too much importance to certain inferred specific intentions on the part of artists. Recovering such intentions is a way to access one, but only one, value that artworks can provide. But interpretation, I have maintained, is a guide to experiencing a work so as maximally to appreciate its values, so as to be maximally engaged by it.

My account neither grants to readers as interpreters the freedom to compose their own texts from associations prompted by the actual texts before them, nor makes literary and other artworks the exclusive mental property of their creators. It recognizes that, when artworks leave their creators' hands, they enter the public domain demanding recognition and explanation as they are. The account maintains the line between explaining the value of a work as we encounter it and creating a new or different work. It avoids the intellectual chaos that results from ignoring the demand to be true to the work in acceptable interpretations, the confusion of substituting the critic for the artist, without substituting the artist for the work. It recognizes the value of seeing as the artist saw and the challenge to our cognitive powers to appreciate that value without elevating it to absolute status in aesthetic contexts. Most important, it accommodates the diversity of interpretive activities and acceptable interpretations without abandoning standards of adequacy to text or work.

VIII

I have said that interpretation of novels takes place partly at the level of imaginatively filling out what is explicitly stated in the texts so as to create broader fictional worlds. Once we have in mind this fictional world, we can search for unifying themes, character developments, and so on. One further test for theories of interpretation, then, is their implications for filling out worlds of fictional works, for determining which propositions not explicitly stated in those works are nevertheless true in those worlds. It is (fictionally) true, for example, that Sherlock Holmes has an obsessive personality and also true (to borrow an example from David Lewis) that he lives closer to Paddington than to Waterloo Station, although neither proposition is stated explicitly in the texts of the stories. When we read a fictional work, we expand the text into an imaginary world by adding imaginatively to what we are explicitly told. The question is how we do this, according to what principles.

The answer again, I believe, is that we follow our best explanations for the text as it is written. The first statement about Holmes made above, for example, is a straightforward interpretation of his character, while the second, although probably not explicitly part of any acceptable interpretation and therefore not entertained by any reader save Lewis, follows from the text and its acceptable interpretations, specifically, from the proposition that Holmes lives on Baker Street and from the interpretive claim that the London portrayed in the text is the real London of the time.

We can then test a theory of interpretation by seeing whether propositions held true in various fictional worlds according to interpretations of the texts that are endorsed by the theory are plausibly held true in those worlds. My claim is that the most plausible ways to expand upon texts (and representational paintings) follow from the theory of interpretation defended here. Other principles have been proposed, but are easily found wanting. Let us compare their capacity to capture examples against our theory's implications.

Two principles first proposed by David Lewis have been widely considered. One has us fill out what is explicitly stated in a fictional text with truths from our real world. Roughly, what is true in the world of the fiction is what is true in the closest possible world to ours in which the story is told as known fact.[20] The second principle fills out fictional worlds to be consistent not with the real world, but with what their authors and intended audiences believed, so that, for example, it is fictional in a medieval work that the world is flat. The second principle allows us to view the world of a work through the eyes of its author, while the first makes that world more familiar to us.

These principles are first of all too rich in the worlds they generate. The worlds of fictional works are only partial (compared to the usual sense of "possible worlds"). In incorporating truths in accordance with these principles, we consider only propositions that are explanatorily

---

[20] David Lewis, "Truth in Fiction," in *Philosophical Papers*, v. I (New York: Oxford University Press, 1983): 261–80, p. 270.

linked in some way to those in the text. In incorporating truths from the real world, for example, we do not consider it true in the world of Bertie Wooster that the invention of the cotton gin antedated that of the radio by 103 years (nor false in that world either). But it is true there, although not explicitly stated in the Wodehouse texts, that Cannes is a resort city in the south of France and Harrods a department store in London. These propositions are true in that world because the best explanation for the use of these names in the text is to refer to the real city and store in question. Thus, it appears already that a deeper principle appealing to explanations of the text is at work.

Second, even if these principles were jointly sufficient, in that fictional truths not explicitly stated were derived only from the real world or from beliefs of authors and their intended audiences, it seems we would still need a deeper principle to tell us when to use one or the other. Holmes lives closer to Paddington than to Waterloo even if Conan Doyle and his audience were ignorant of the geography of the London underground system. We use the truth from the real world here because, as maintained above, it is explanatorily linked to the text via its acceptable interpretations. By contrast, a Russell's viper can climb a rope in the world of Sherlock Holmes (as it cannot in the real world) not simply because Conan Doyle believed that, but because it is necessary to Holmes' really having solved the case of the speckled band, to the obvious interpretation of the denouement of that story.

Third, these principles are not sufficient. What is true in the world of fantasies or supernatural tales is what is consistent with the best readings of those works as fantasies. Such worlds may be distant from the real world and from the beliefs of authors and intended readers. There may be ghosts in the world of *The Turn of the Screw*, even though there are none in the real world, and neither Henry James nor people literate enough to read him believe in them. There are ghosts in that world (under some acceptable interpretation) if the interpretation of relevant passages as referring to or implying their presence enhances some major value of the work, say its atmospheric or expressive power. Once more, whether we ascribe fictional truths that are not explicit in texts in accord with these principles depends on interpretive, value-enhancing explanations.

Similarly, in some fantasy novels impossible propositions are asserted. These first of all give rise to "imaginative resistance," since it is questionable whether we can imagine to be true propositions that cannot possibly be true.[21] In my view, as noted earlier, we do not in general so much actively imagine a fictional text to be true as we simply suspend disbelief in its propositions (although, as emphasized in this section, we do fill out a text's fictional world, which might involve more active imagination). More to the point here, Lewis Carroll's criteria once more do not work in such contexts. Even if we are not dealing with logical impossibilities, there is no clearly closest world to the real world in which smiles can appear without bodies, caterpillars smoke pipes, and playing cards walk and talk. Who knows what the laws of physics would have to be for these things to be true in the real world? Is there any possible world in which smiles appear without bodies? Nor can we tell which world in which these things are true is closest to what Lewis Carroll believed, since he certainly did not believe what he wrote in *Alice's Adventures in Wonderland*. By contrast, we can imaginatively fill out the fantasy world of Alice in various ways consistent with the text, although surely not with the imaginative flair of a Lewis Carroll.

Borrowing another example, this time from Nicholas Wolterstorff, it may be that in the real world a relationship such as Mark Twain describes between Huck Finn and Jim would include homosexual activities. But it is not true in their world that their relationship is homosexual:[22] we do not apply the Reality Principle, as Kendall Walton calls it. Why not? Not because Twain or his audience did not believe in homosexuality. Instead, we do not ascribe in accord with the Reality Principle because it is no part of a best explanation for the descriptions of the relation in the text that these descriptions indicate sexual preference. Such an explanation would be inconsistent with the moral tone of the work and its broader themes. It would complicate those themes, introducing a distracting foreign element that would detract from most readers' experience of the work.

Kendall Walton provides a final example in which our ascriptions of fictional truths accord with neither principle. He cites a Conrad story in which the reader concludes that a character has committed suicide from

[21] For sample discussions of imaginative resistance see Tamar Gendler, "The Puzzle of Imaginative Resistance," *The Journal of Philosophy*, 97 (2000): 55–81; Kathleen Stock, "The Tower of Goldbach and Other Impossible Tales," in M. Kieran and D. Lopes, eds, *Imagination, Philosophy, and the Arts* (London: Routledge, 2003).
[22] Nicholas Wolterstorff, *Works and Worlds of Art* (Oxford: Clarendon Press, 1980), p. 120.

subtle clues in the text, when no one in real life, either in Conrad's time or at present, would draw that inference or be warranted in doing so on such slim evidence. Walton concludes from the insufficiency of these principles that we require a multiplicity of divergent principles without any overarching meta-rule for determining when to use them.[23] He offers a Wittgensteinian response to the question of how we can operate with such a divergent set to arrive at agreement on what is true in various fictional worlds. The response consists in pointing out that many concepts must be applied without governing rules.[24]

But the concept of fictional truth is not like the concept of red in this respect. The former is not a concept that we see immediately to be applicable in such a way as to rule out rational debate. To settle such critical debate, we need a guiding rationale, and our theory of interpretation provides it. Walton's example provides further evidence of this. We infer to the suicide of the character in Conrad's story because that is the only explanation for the clues in the text being placed there at all.

The theory also explains why many of the questions characterized by Walton as silly do not arise for literary or other representational works. We do not ask why Othello, a Moorish general, speaks such fine English poetry because the purpose of or explanation for his lines being written in that way is not to represent his style of speaking. Thus it is not fictionally true that he speaks in that way. Similarly, the explanation for artificial poses and positions of figures in Renaissance paintings most often appeals to formal beauty and expressive power, not to representational accuracy. That is why we need not ask why Leonardo's diners at his *Last Supper* are all lined up on the same side of the table.

One other more recently proposed principle for generating fictional truths should be mentioned here, that of Gregory Currie. According to him, when we read a work of fiction, we make believe not only that the story is true, but that someone is telling it to us—a fictional author. What is true in the story is what the fictional author believes. This figure is to be distinguished from a narrator, who is fallible, and from the real author, who does not believe what is written in the text.[25]

---

[23] Kendall Walton, *Mimesis as Make-Believe* (Cambridge, MA: Harvard University Press, 1990), p. 169.

[24] Walton, *Mimesis as Make-Believe*, p. 185.

[25] Gregory Currie, *The Nature of Fiction* (Cambridge: Cambridge University Press, 1990), ch. 2.

There is once more much overlap between the application of this test for fictional truth and the ascription of such truths in accord with value-enhancing interpretations. If we posit a fictional author, then we will normally seek to make the beliefs of this figure coherent, for example, and coherence is also normally an aesthetic value in a fictional work. But there are also cases, including some of those mentioned above, where these criteria come apart, or where there seems to be little if any room in our make-believe world for the fictional figure that Currie builds into his principle for generating fictional truths there.

An author, fictional or not, intelligent enough to write *The Turn of the Screw* would not believe in ghosts. Hence Currie's criterion would once more wrongly rule out reading the novella as a ghost story. Sherlock Holmes lives closer to Paddington than to Waterloo whether or not Conan Doyle, his audience at the time, hence a fictional author of that time, were ignorant of geography. It is fictionally true in the Holmes stories that the highly fallible Watson is telling them. Conan Doyle really tells them. Is there room for us to make believe there is a third teller of the stories, and is it plausible that we utilize such a complex scheme in generating the fictional truths of Holmes' world? Our best readings or interpretations of the works are readily available, by contrast, since we are always interpreting as we are reading. In other fictional media, such as movies, it is often doubtful that it is fictionally true that anyone is telling us a story: we simply see the (fictional) events unfold before us. If we were to imagine learning of these events only second-hand, this might lessen our direct involvement in the world in which they take place, a directness that is an aesthetic virtue of this particular medium.

We may conclude that our theory of interpretation generates fictional truths in accord with our actual practice, as opposed to other proposed principles. These truths are consistent with value-enhancing explanations for relevant passages in fictional works. We have used the criterion for fictional truth as a test for the theory which views interpretation as a means to the appreciation of aesthetic value. That it passes this test helps to show once more that interpretation aims at full appreciation and is indeed the link between description and proper evaluation of artworks.

3

The Sun Also Rises
Incompatible interpretations

In the previous chapter I suggested that there can be incompatible but mutually acceptable interpretations of art and literary works. The most obvious case was performative interpretations of musical pieces. Closer to novels are interpretations of characters in plays on stage. Once more no one disputes that actors can and do interpret the same characters in different ways. It would be inexplicable if, despite this, readers could not acceptably interpret characters in novels in different ways. In this chapter I will demonstrate this directly. The example of James' *Turn of the Screw* having grown somewhat stale, I begin with a different one, much debated by literary critics[1] but absent from the philosophical literature. My opposing interpretations will not only view main characters differently, but will offer contradictory interpretations of a main theme, that of moral development or its lack.

I

Interpretation 1. In Hemingway's *The Sun Also Rises*, the lead characters morally develop over the course of the novel. At the beginning, the narrator and lead male character, Jake, has not come to grips with the

---

[1] For a sampling of critical articles on this novel, see James Nagel, ed., *Critical Essays on Ernest Hemingway's "The Sun Also Rises"* (New York: G. K. Hall, 1995); Harold Bloom, ed., *Brett Ashley* (New York: Chelsea House, 1991); Linda Wagner-Martin, ed., *New Essays on "The Sun Also Rises"* (Cambridge: Cambridge University Press, 1987); A. Robert-Lee, ed., *Ernest Hemingway: New Critical Essays* (Totowa, NJ: Vision and Barnes & Noble, 1983). I have drawn freely from many of these essays and others in what follows. The illustrative interpretations are not novel, although I have combined claims from different sources.

person that his war wound has left him. Despite his impotence, he harbors illusions of a long-term romantic relation with Brett, the lead female character. Near the beginning of the story, his picking up the prostitute Georgette and his attitude toward the homosexuals who accompany Brett in her first entrance underscore his ambivalent sexual identity, a theme involving several of the characters in that early scene. Throughout most of the story he is reluctantly at Brett's beck and call, finding relief only in the male bonding of the fishing trip he takes to Burguete. The low point of his life as a human punch bag comes in Pamplona after his pimping for Brett with the bullfighter Romero. He has betrayed the code of the bullfighters he so admires. Like Romero, he pays by being beaten up and knocked unconscious by Robert Cohen.

He is awakened by a carafe of water being poured on him. Nature symbolism abounds in this book, and water is the motif for Jake's rebirth and development toward self-realization. After his awakening, everything looks new to him: "everything looked new and changed. I had never seen the trees before . . . it was all different."[2] At the same time he begins to awaken from the unreal dream of Brett. But the process will be slow; transformation takes time. He wants a bath, but the water will not run. In one of his rare philosophical moments at the Pamplona fiesta, he begins to think he can change and find a new identity. Of course the thought is typically understated: "Perhaps as you went along you did learn something."[3] His full awakening awaits his solitary trip to San Sebastian, the return to nature and his long swim there. Unable to swim in the open sea, he nevertheless dives deep, plumbing the depths of his psyche as he dives to the bottom of the lake. He is now cleansed of his former illusions, and when he swims to the shore, he sees more clearly.

When summoned by Brett, he is willing to return to Spain despite the challenge. He does respond to her by returning, but their relationship in Spain has changed. Formerly under her control, he now becomes the controlling figure. He chooses their restaurant; he keeps drinking, without becoming drunk, despite her protest; and he finishes his dinner (their former relationship?), though she wants to leave. He decides on a cab ride, tells the cab where to go in order to show her the city, and in the famous last line corrects her seeming illusion, refusing to blame their

---

[2] Ernest Hemingway, *The Sun Also Rises* (New York: Scribner, 1954), p. 196.
[3] Hemingway, *The Sun Also Rises*, p. 152.

failed relationship on his sexual incapacitation. In their earlier cab ride it was Brett who pulled away from his embrace, but not now. He is now controlling the course of his life, as the policeman, his alter ego in that very last scene, controls the movement of the cab. He can now stoically accept his situation and become master of his life in the difficult times he continues to face.

The novel is largely about Jake's search for a new identity following his devastating war injury. The last line indicates that he has finally come to terms with his altered self. The change has been subtle but real, as indicated by scenes, such as the cab ride, that are nearly repeated but subtly different. This way of developing the theme of moral development is in keeping with Hemingway's understated style.

Brett has also developed. Drunk, broke, and highly promiscuous, wavering between traditional and liberated new female roles throughout much of the novel, she too is changed at its end. Always a willing drinking partner before, at her last meeting with Jake she no longer drinks and urges him not to. She breaks up with Romero, both for his own good and for hers. She has admitted to losing all self-respect in going after him. She is fifteen years older than he is, and for that reason among others, she realizes that their relationship cannot last. She would become an embarrassment to him and herself, a consideration that would not have curbed her sexual desires earlier. Furthermore, he wants to conform her to his confining image, wants her to grow her hair long and become the traditional wife and woman from which she has struggled to liberate herself.

Romero is her counterpart in the novel, as is evident from the descriptions of his good looks, his isolation even in crowds, his tight clothes and the way he wears his hat, all reminiscent of Brett, and the way that others dance around him in the bull ring, as they danced around Brett earlier at the festival. As her lover and a real Hemingway man, he helps her to shed her facades and become a real modern woman, despite trying to keep her in the more traditional role. For once, she controls her sexual desires and need for attention by convincing him to leave so that they can get on with their separate lives. She has earlier damaged Cohen and Mike by failing to exercise any self-control, but she finally shows strength of will in relinquishing Romero.

Her final statement to Jake is not an expression of continuing illusion but a recognition of time wasted with so many other men and a recognition that they could have had a better relationship. Water and vision, or sight, are the central symbols for Brett's states of mind, as they are for Jake's. Throughout most of the story she is always wanting to take baths, to cleanse herself of actions she probably regrets without admitting so. She is often described as squinting her eyes, seemingly smiling, but also blocking clear vision of the world around her. At the end of the novel, however, she wants to see Madrid, to see the world around her clearly, with eyes wide open. Like Jake, she is finally able to see the world and her role within it as they are, to accept the difficult times, the loss of innocence and psychological wounds of the war, and to make the best of her role as a new woman. Despite the dark times, the sun will rise and allow them to see their way through to the altered moral identities they have been struggling to achieve.

Interpretation 2. The lead characters in this novel do not develop, and their inability or failure to do so is a major theme. The structure of the novel is cyclical, emphasizing the tragic and monotonous repetition in the characters' irreparably damaged lives. The only villain in this novel is the war, the only hero the world that continues on despite it (as Hemingway wrote). But the characters one and all are the victims of the war, and their wounds, physical and psychological, will not heal. The very title of the novel and the biblical passage from which it is taken underscore the theme of monotonous repetition without end, the natural cycles of the world continuing endlessly and obliterating all human attempts to effect real change.

Jake ends where he begins. When things look different to him after the climactic beating by Robert Cohen, this is only a temporary effect of his concussion. When he temporarily refrains from drinking himself into oblivion, this is only to return to his former ways. At the end of the story, after his brief respite in San Sebastian, reminiscent of his earlier fishing trip in Burguete, he returns to Brett and to drinking. He is still at her beck and call and still without prospect of a long-term and exclusive relationship between equals. The taxi ride at the end also recalls the taxi ride at the beginning. Once more Brett presses close to him, the substitute for the sexual fulfillment they cannot have. His last line recognizes the hopelessness of their relationship, but arguably he has recognized it all along. This is why he arranges affairs with other men for her despite later hating himself for doing so. At the end of the story, Jake faces the prospect of more drinking and fishing, as Brett faces more meaningless sexual encounters and relationships.

Brett plans to return to Mike, and one cannot picture their relationship being any different from what it was before. She does not predict any change, saying they will continue to "look after each other," and undoubtedly they will continue to do so badly. She has dismissed Romero just as she has dismissed all her other lovers, backing out when the relationship threatened to become long term, and clinging to the illusion of meaning and self-sacrifice. Her dismissal of Romero is no different from her dismissal of Cohen, except that Romero is better able to handle it. Although she is depressed each time she ends an affair, she remains incapable of lasting relationships, except the mutually destructive one with Jake, whom she summons as usual to rescue her from the latest fiasco.

Her words to Jake in Madrid recall her words when they first reunite in the book, complaining as always about how miserable she is and how she can't help doing whatever she does. Even the first time we hear her complain to Jake, he has the "feeling of going through something that has all happened before…a nightmare of it all being something repeated."[4] In Madrid she stays at the Hotel Montana, recalling the Hotel Montoya in Pamplona. The names are repeated several times, calling attention here, as elsewhere, to the repetitive form of the narrative.

The one character in the book who personifies notions of development over time, commitment, obligations, and responsibility for lasting consequences of his actions is Robert Cohen, detested equally by Hemingway and his narrator. Probably, in Hemingway's anti-Semitic caricature, these archaic concepts are linked to that of Jewish guilt. In any case, Cohen is mercilessly ridiculed for clinging to these romantic trappings by the other characters in the book, Hemingway's postwar sophisticates. Brett in particular cannot stand Cohen's assumption that their affair could have lasting consequences ("He can't believe it didn't mean anything"[5]), while the other characters find it alternately amusing and extremely annoying. Cohen is an outsider, an overgrown adolescent, a hanger-on where he is not wanted, a mediocre writer, a dreamer who has unrealistic and clichéd dreams, and his faith that his affair with Brett could develop into a loving relationship is the object of only ridicule. Brett's off-and-on lover Mike speaks for the others

[4] Hemingway, *The Sun Also Rises*, pp. 70–1.
[5] Hemingway, *The Sun Also Rises*, p. 185.

to Cohen: "I know when I'm not wanted. Why don't you know when you're not wanted?"[6]

Finally, an analysis of style supports the claim of cyclical, nondeveloping repetition. Critics have noted two dominant styles in this book: One is very simple and repetitive, with short sentences and repeating words, what one critic calls a "staccato" style.[7] Thematically, this style is associated with and suggestive of boredom, monotony, and the lack of purpose in the lives of the characters. The second style is flowing, rhythmical, with long sentences, suggesting freedom, movement, and, most of all, the beauty of nature. Significantly, the book ends as it begins, in the former style. The tone, when not describing nature or bullfighting, is relentlessly cynical, certainly not optimistic. The large form of this novel is one of repetition with minor and insignificant changes in names and places, repetition of both content and style. The minor character, Count Mippipopolous, expresses most explicitly what is true of all the characters in the novel: "Doesn't anything ever happen to your values?" Brett asked. "No, not any more."[8] In all their travels, these characters are going nowhere.

II

The characters' attempts to forge new identities in the face of earlier traumas and difficult times make up a major theme of this novel. And yet we have seen that the theme can be interpreted in opposite ways. The two interpretations just offered have roughly equal textual support. As noted in both, several of the events and locales in this novel are repeated with slight variations. The first of these interpretations emphasizes the variations, such as Jake's telling the second cab driver where to go. The second interpretation emphasizes the repetitions, which in any case could not be identical. Some critics have taken the view that one of these characters, the real hero of the novel, develops, while the other does not, and the possible permutations of the above, together with their supporting evidence, are easy to work out.

---

[6] Hemingway, *The Sun Also Rises*, p. 146.
[7] Harold Mosher Jr., "The Two Styles of Hemingway's *The Sun Also Rises*," *Fitzgerald/Hemingway Annual* (1971): 262–73.
[8] Hemingway, *The Sun Also Rises*, p. 67.

I prefer the second of the above interpretations, not because I believe the text better supports it, but because I think it better fits the overall hard-nosed, cynical atmosphere of the novel, despite its interludes of lyrical descriptions of landscapes. It underlines the theme of moral malaise in the postwar generation that one can feel in Hemingway's prose. But others might prefer the more optimistic theme of coming to terms with hard times, and the psychological complexity that that theme implies. Not only are the characters more complex on this reading, but the events in the plot take on more significance as contributing to and mirroring their development, perhaps adding formal structure to the novel as well.

Thus one interpretation enhances one set of literary values, and the other, a different set. This, together with equal textual support, makes them equally acceptable. Instead of continuing to debate the merits of these opposed interpretations, I want now to raise philosophical questions about interpretation that appeal to this example will help to answer. First, are these interpretations really incompatible or contradictory? Second, must we rest content with the answer to this first question? And third, can any interpretation be true, if incompatible ones can be equally acceptable?

Addressing the first question, the clear answer is yes. Although characters in the novel may be indeterminate in regard to certain key properties until filled out by an interpretation, such filling out to create the fictional world of the work is clearly called for. Characters in this expanded fictional world of *The Sun Also Rises* either have the property of morally developing or they do not; they cannot both develop and not develop. Interpretations can be incompatible in assigning properties that cannot be simultaneously possessed, even if these readings do not maintain explicit contradictions. If, for example, one interpretation claims that Jake morally develops and another claims that he reacts in the same ways and maintains the same relationships throughout, these would be incompatible in virtue of having contradictory implications.

Addressing the second and third questions, that these interpretations are contradictory does not imply that they cannot be equally acceptable, although it does imply that they cannot both be true. But don't we need the notion of truth for interpretational assertions, so that we can, for example, derive implications from them and use them in arguments? Philosophers who answer this last question affirmatively might seek to avoid or resolve the contradictions that block assignments of truth values to interpretations as a whole. They might, for example, claim that the interpretations assert only that the book can be read in one way or the other: we can see Jake as developing, and we can see him as not developing. The latter two assertions are not contradictory.

But to make this move is to confuse statements about interpretations (that one or another is possible) for interpretations themselves. The first interpretation, for example, does not say, "You (the reader) can interpret Jake Barnes as morally developing"; it says that he does develop, and supports this assertion with textual evidence. We can interpret Jake as developing, but actually to do so is to read his actions as having a certain significance, a significance that directs our readings of other episodes and descriptions and constrains other interpretations. Interpretations guide us toward the appreciation of certain aspects of the world of a work— for example, the psychological complexity of its characters or its consistently cynical atmosphere—and perhaps exclude the appreciation of certain other possible aspects. Potential interpretations, the ways we can read works so as to bring these worlds to life, remain inert until actually adopted.

A second and more interesting way to avoid the contradictions is to say that *The Sun Also Rises* is simply ambiguous or indeterminate on the question whether the characters develop. More broadly, it might be claimed that equal textual support for each of two opposing interpretations shows not that they are both acceptable, but that a third interpretation of the work as ambiguous or indeterminate on the matter in question is always preferable. Indeed, isn't it simply implied by equal textual support that the work must be indeterminate in this respect? Isn't that interpretation then mandated?

If interpretation aimed simply at true description of a work, then this implication would hold. But the paradigm of a correct or good interpretation would then consist in an explication of the meanings of the words of the text in their textual context. As argued in the previous chapter, this is not an interpretation at all, although many philosophers seem to have been confused on this matter. The two partial interpretations of *The Sun Also Rises* offered above are not concerned at all with the meanings of Hemingway's words, all of which are perfectly clear to any competent speaker of English. They are concerned to go beyond what the text literally asserts, to fill out the world of the work so as to make determinate answers to questions the text may raise without answering in any obvious or explicit way. They are, as indicated, to guide the reader to a rewarding experience or reading of the work, one that enhances some of the literary values it might afford.

Here it can be argued that a reading of the novel as ambiguous on the point in question is not as rewarding an experience as the other two readings. The world of the novel loses some of its impact, the feeling of the plight of characters caught in meaningless endless repetition or overcoming a hostile world in their own ways. To read the novel as ambiguous between these two is to call attention to the novel as novel at the expense of its projected world, accessible through interpretation, in which the characters either do or do not develop. There is no world in which they do neither. Such self-referential reading hinders the reader from getting caught up in the story, from projecting herself into its fictional world. It sacrifices the feeling of subdued but determined optimism, or that of consistent hard-nosed cynicism or nihilism. In short, it sacrifices emotional engagement with the work.

On the other side, it might be argued for this one novel that an interpretation of it as ambiguous is acceptable, as supported, for example, by the ambiguity of its concluding line, which might express both Jake's recognition of his limitations and his continuing desire to dwell on illusions. Here the actions of the characters themselves within their world, including even the seemingly heroic Romero, are seen to be morally ambiguous. He, after all, has a kind of girlish beauty, is, like Jake, beaten up by Cohen, runs off with Brett in apparent violation of his own code, and cannot keep her. Even the best candidate for moral hero in this novel is therefore far less than that, although his being so makes him a more believable character. The other characters share his moral ambiguity: Jake as both supportive and accurate observer struggling to overcome his devastating wound and forge a new identity, and as pimp; Brett as liberated woman and as drunken nymphomaniac; Cohen as a Romantic with principle and as an annoying intruder.

But whether or not this interpretation flies, the point remains that it is not mandated by the textual support for the other two. It requires independent, indeed opposed, textual evidence, and it must apply, like the other two, to the world of the novel and not simply to its literal text.

Thus, we are left with equally acceptable but incompatible interpretations, now three. We cannot therefore speak in this case of the interpretations as a whole being true. We can, however, continue to speak of the individual statements that combine to make them up being fictionally true in the particular worlds projected by the interpretations. This is fictional truth, what we are to imagine as true (while suspending disbelief in the assertions of the text), and it is truth relative to an interpretive scheme. What is fictionally true under one interpretation may not be under another. But such truth suffices for the purposes of inference and argument for which the notion of interpretive truth is needed.

If we imagine some statements to be true, we are committed to the fictional truth of others, and on this basis many interpretive arguments can proceed. If Jake has not morally developed in the course of the story, he will continue to drink uncontrollably and to serve Brett's every whim without personal reward. If he has changed, then their relationship, if it continues at all, will also be different. The fictional truths of the antecedents in their opposed worlds require us to infer the consequents, although they do not entail them. Unlike real people, who either have certain properties or do not have them, Jake as a fictional character is indeterminate until filled out in relevant ways by interpretations. And we have seen that there are different ways to do so, providing different explanations of his actions and thoughts as described in the text. But once we have filled out the worlds in relevant ways, we think of him as if he were a real person: he has either developed or not (or, under the third interpretation, less satisfactory in my view, he is morally ambiguous and, as might be the case with a real person, we cannot determine if or how he has developed).

III

Other philosophical questions immediately arise, however, once we grant that the incompatibility of equally acceptable interpretations cannot be eliminated. Do such cases require more than one work; do interpretations then create separate works? Do such cases imply that there can be no single overriding criterion of acceptability for interpretations? Do they show that the only constraint on acceptable interpretations is the practice of a critical community? All these questions have been answered affirmatively by recent theorists of literature. But we should not jump to such radical conclusions too quickly.

In regard to the first two questions here, we should certainly say intuitively that Hemingway wrote *The Sun Also Rises*, not his critics or interpreters. Furthermore, we would certainly say that he wrote at least and at most one novel with that title. If one could create that novel by simply interpreting it, it would be far easier to be a great author than it is. But the book is there to be read; it does not await anyone's reading of it to become a book. Interpretation aims to enhance appreciation of the work in question, not to create a new or better one, a far more difficult task.

A bit less obvious but still eminently plausible: if interpretation is a kind of explanation, as I claimed in the previous chapter, if it must explain the characters and episodes as written, then it requires an independent explanandum existing prior to the explanations offered. If these incompatible explanations are to compete, then they must be explanations of the same object or work, a work that endures from earlier interpretations to later ones.[9] An object can endure while changing, but this requires continuity in properties that different interpretations themselves may not possess. It is also implausible to think that one could change Hemingway's novel every few seconds by successively thinking that Jake does and does not develop. Thus, it certainly seems initially that we should answer these first two questions negatively: competing explanations explain the same work differently; they do not create new and separate works.

There are nevertheless other considerations that motivate the opposing counterintuitive intuitions (oxymoron intended). Competing interpretations appear to attribute properties, indeed incompatible properties, to the work itself. One claims that Jake develops in *The Sun Also Rises*. The other claims that he does not, that is, does not develop in that same novel. I argued above that this does not mandate our interpreting Jake as neither developing nor not developing. But it seems that he cannot do both in the same story, and these interpretations, I have argued, are equally acceptable. Doesn't all this require two stories, separate narratives or novels, one in which he develops and one in which he does not? And if the permutations between him and Brett are again equally acceptable, then we seem to require four different stories just on this score.

More generally, if acceptable interpretations impute properties to characters or episodes, in a work, and if it is then fictionally true in the work that they have these properties, then incompatible, equally acceptable interpretations would require separate works, as many works as there are such interpretations. The same object cannot have incompatible

---

[9] Compare David Novitz, *Knowledge, Fiction, and Imagination* (Philadelphia: Temple University Press, 1987), p. 105.

properties at the same time. And if this is so, then there seems to be a clear sense in which interpretations do create new works, if they can ascribe incompatible properties to the same (or parallel) characters. Did I then create *The Sun Also Rises* twice by offering the interpretations defended above? Did I collaborate with Hemingway, whom I never met, or did he fail to create any novel at all?

The answers to these now vexing puzzles lie, I believe, in a set of distinctions properly drawn between levels of text on the one hand and fictional worlds projected by those texts and acceptable interpretations of them on the other. If we want to begin at the most basic level, then we might mention the physical ink marks on the paper. But no reader sees these as such, and Hemingway inscribed similar ones, of course, only because he was choosing syntactic and semantic types. The reader need never interpret the ink marks (unless his or her copy is damaged), but reads them straight off as words with standard meanings. As mentioned above, the words and sentence meanings on the next level virtually never need interpretation in Hemingway either, although there may be a very occasional ambiguity that context does not immediately resolve. Irony, metaphor, and symbolism are different matters, but these are recognized via explanations of the language with its ordinary meanings read right off.

If the literal assertions made by the text Hemingway wrote, in which we suspend disbelief, are the second level, then what is fictionally true, what we are required to imagine as true based on those assertions, is the third. Here are included all those inferences from the literal assertions of the text upon which all competent readers would agree. It is undeniable, for example, that Brett makes her entrance into the story in the company of a group of homosexuals, although they are never explicitly identified as such. It is also undeniable that Jake suffered a genital injury in the war that has left him with sexual desire that he has no means to fulfill, although once more perhaps the last vestige of Victorian prudishness prevents Hemingway from explicitly saying so.

These are interpretations based on the explicit assertions of the text, but they are epistemically unchallengeable. They therefore falsify the common assumption that interpretation is to be distinguished from description on epistemic grounds. What does distinguish it is that interpretations are inferred from the literal assertions of the text; they are inferred as explanations for what is literally asserted, explanations for the descriptions of characters and events that can be understood as such without interpretation.

What is fictionally true in a story, based both on the explicit assertions of the text and on those inferences on which all competent readers would agree, constitutes what can be called the narrow world of the work. The inferences in question include not all implications of what is explicitly asserted (if the latter contains a contradiction, for example, then everything would be implied), but only those statements that are uniquely related as parts of best explanations for, or as best explained by, what is literally asserted. The only fictionally true explanation for the way Jake's injury is explicitly referred to is that the injury is as I described it above; the only fictionally true explanation for the way Brett's escorts in her opening scene are described is that they are gay. This narrow world of the novel leaves indeterminate not only all those propositions that do not contribute one way or another to our understanding or appreciation of the novel, for example whether Jake has a sister, but also many propositions that do so contribute, answers to questions that naturally arise, such as whether he morally develops. These answers remain indeterminate in the narrow world because they are the subjects of interpretive disagreements.

Contestable interpretations, further explanatory inferences that fill out the world of the text in ways necessary to full appreciation, then constitute the fourth level. Here we begin to see multiple worlds of the novel (we might speak of a universe of worlds), and they begin to diverge: for example, one in which the characters develop and one in which they do not, one in which Jake breaks free from Brett or begins a new relationship with her on equal terms and another in which he continues to subserviently serve her every whim and mood change, one in which Romero remains an untarnished hero, having dodged a bullet in Brett, and another in which he ends up like Belmonte, his older, much maligned and disillusioned colleague, or like Vicente Girones, gored and dead "just for fun." While the third level, also in large part a product of interpretation, still contains only fictional truths that the text requires us to imagine as true, the fourth level is made up of propositions that the text permits us to imagine as true, although some such imagining is required for maximum appreciation.

We expand the narrow world of the work to create a richer, more aesthetically satisfying, if not more real, fictional world. Here the reader does begin to collaborate with Hemingway in creating fictional worlds, to use the author's rich material for the much easier task of expansion.

Here interpretation remains anchored to text by explanatory links, but there are several possible best explanations. The expanded worlds remain incomplete, in that there remain countless propositions—for example, that Jake has a sister—that are neither fictionally true nor false, but these worlds are richer to just the degree that there are contestable, that is interesting, interpretations that add fictional truths to the work's narrow world, that fill out the best explanations of the text as written.

We can see now that distinctions between texts, objects of interpretation, constraints on interpretations, interpretations themselves, and fictional worlds cut across one another. The text consists of what is explicitly asserted, as determined by the literal meanings of the words at the time of the writing. There is very little interpretation at the level of the text in *The Sun Also Rises* and most other novels. There are exceptions, such as *A Clockwork Orange*, in which one must often infer what the words of the futuristic language mean. But these are exceptions. There is much interpretation, though uncontestable, at the level of the narrow fictional world, which consists in those universally agreed-upon fictional truths that the text requires us to imagine without explicitly asserting. The object of contestable interpretation is this narrow fictional world, as well as the text (especially its stylistic elements) that projects it. These constrain contestable interpretations, which must explain them in such a way as to enhance their values for readers. As we have seen, one acceptable interpretation might enhance one set of literary values, while an incompatible but equally acceptable interpretation might bring out a different set, when these values cannot be jointly maximally realized.

IV

We may now turn to our as yet unanswered questions. Whether we say that interpretations create works depends on where we locate the work in this scheme. If we locate it way out on the fourth level, identifying it with the complete story as supplemented by contestable interpretations, then *perhaps* interpretations do indeed create separate works, the author only supplying the raw material for them. The hedging word is included because, even on this very broad understanding of what the work is, we can still maintain that there is a single work with different relational properties, where these relations include responses of different readers or interpreters.

There could be a parallel here to an artwork's aesthetic properties. Aesthetic properties, I have argued elsewhere, are relative to the tastes of different competent critics.[10] Thus, Hemingway's style, a feature of his text, might be terse and crisp to one critic and monotonous to another. The text would then have both these relational properties, which is not inconsistent because it would have them relative to these different critics. This might seem to have the counterintuitive consequence that there is no critical disagreement here. But there remains a difference in response, and indeed an implied disagreement about which response is appropriate. Nor does this imply that the text is not an independent object, as long as it also has nonrelational properties. My house has relational perceptual properties, for example colors, but it remains an object independent of my perception. In like fashion, Jake might both develop and not develop in the same work, relative to different acceptable interpretations of it. His developing would then be a relational property, although, like terseness as a property of writing, it does not appear to be relational.

However, in the case of properties ascribed by contestable interpretations, as opposed to evaluational aesthetic properties, there is no pressing reason to make this relativizing move. The only reason to locate the work on the fourth level is the temptation to say that whatever properties the characters have, indeed whatever is fictionally true, must be fictionally true in the work. The characters must either develop or not develop in *The Sun Also Rises*, in that very work. But this is not a conclusive reason. It is just as intuitive to say that the characters develop in the world of the work, more generally, that what is fictionally true is true in the world of the work.

The work itself is more intuitively identified with the text or, at the outside, with its narrow world. The text, remember, is what is literally asserted; the narrow world is what we are required to imagine as true based on the text and incontestable inferences from it. What is literally asserted is not necessarily what we are to imagine as true, since there may be irony or fallible narrators involved, and in any case we need not actively imagine what we simply read straight off, as opposed to suspending disbelief. The work can then be the text or its fictional content, that is, what is fictionally true based directly and only on what is asserted. Or it can be its narrow world, what is fictionally true based on what is

---

[10] Goldman, *Aesthetic Value*, ch. 2.

asserted plus incontestable inferences from it, that is, what is universally agreed to be in the story, its universally accepted content.

Thinking of comparisons with other artistic media, perhaps the narrow world is most intuitively identified with the work as the object of interpretation. A painting, it seems, is not just pigments on a canvas, but a rural landscape, a still life, or portrait, its universally recognized representations. This suggests that a literary work too should be identified with its agreed content. There may seem to be a problem, however, with identifying a work with the narrow world that the text projects instead of with the text itself, at least if we want to claim that we do not create or change the work itself by interpreting it. If a work is identified with what is universally agreed to be true in the story, then it seems that as soon as someone disagrees, the scope of the work diminishes; hence the work changes. The way around this problem is to maintain that the disagreement must be reasonable, must be that of a fully competent critic. What can be a reasonable topic of disagreement is fixed before anyone actually disagrees. Hence the work can remain fixed as well.

Nevertheless, there is still something more to be said for identifying the work more narrowly with the text. Doing so maintains a clear distinction between the work and the world of the work, narrow or broad. And it identifies the work precisely with what the author wrote. Perhaps to maintain the parallel with other artworks it would not be too counterintuitive to identify a painting with the colored shapes, what it represents being the world of the painting. Of course, the artist chooses the pigments and shapes partly in order to project a particular world, but so does the author choose his words in that way.

The decision between these two identifications in either medium is largely a verbal matter. The main point here is that on either of these construals, there is a single novel. There is a single text and a single narrow world. Opposing interpretations do not create separate works. What they do create or pick out are additional worlds of the work, broader worlds filled out in different ways. These broader worlds will be determinate in respects, such as the characters' developing, in which the work itself remains indeterminate. Even the broader worlds will remain indeterminate in other respects irrelevant to the stories, which is why they cannot be identified with possible worlds in the philosopher's sense. We might identify fictional content with sets of possible worlds in light of this indeterminacy. But this strikes me as no longer an intuitive equation, only an ad hoc attempt to save a possible worlds account (since possible worlds are not indeterminate in their properties).

I have already noted the answer to the third of our latest set of questions. Both the unambiguous text and its narrow world constrain acceptable interpretations that fill out this world by explaining or being explained by its contents. The practice of the community of interpreters is neither necessary nor sufficient as a constraint; indeed, it is largely irrelevant to the acceptability of new interpretations. The meaning of the text itself is, of course, determined by practice, but this is the practice of the linguistic community upon which the author draws at the time of writing, not the practice of interpreters later; and in any case we noted that such meaning is not normally what interpretations aim to reveal. The best interpretations at given times often contradict prevalent interpretive practice in order to generate fresh readings. Their acceptability does not await their influence on that practice. It is determined instead by their ability to enhance literary values only latent in the work previously.

Our last question was whether the equal acceptability of incompatible interpretations implies that there is no single overriding criterion of acceptability. The obvious answer as to implication seems to be no, since it certainly seems possible for the application of a single criterion to generate ties among different interpretations. But we need to show more concretely how this possibility is actualized. On my view the criterion for good interpretations, like many other criteria of goodness, follows from the function of the practice. If, for example, the function of interpretation were to allow the reader to take part in a conversation with the author, to understand what the author is trying to say, then correct interpretations would reveal authorial intentions. There would then be a single correct interpretation for each work, assuming a single consistent set of authorial intentions. Our initial interpretations could not then have been equally acceptable, except in a weak epistemic sense, if we were not able to find out what Hemingway intended.

In fact Hemingway did offer a few statements on the matter, the most relevant being his pronouncement that there are no human heroes in this novel.[11] This would support the thesis that the characters do not develop since his characters seem not to be heroic when first introduced.

[11] Cited in Arnold E. Davidson and Cathy N. Davidson, "Decoding the Hemingway Hero in *The Sun Also Rises*," in *New Essays on "The Sun Also Rises*," ed. Linda Wagner-Martin, p. 104.

Jake might be thought a war hero for having been wounded, but wounds in that war were typically inflicted by bombs or machines impersonally and at a distance, not in heroic hand-to-hand combat, and that was part of their damaging psychological effects. In any case, I do not take Hemingway's pronouncement to be definitive, indeed to be very strong evidence in favor of our second interpretation. The reason, as I argued in the last chapter, is that the function of interpretation is broader—instead of merely aiming to understand the author, aiming to guide the reader toward the fullest appreciation of the work and the values it can afford.

As also noted in the previous chapter, seeing the world of the novel, and ultimately the real world, through the eyes of the narrator, and ultimately the author, is certainly one value that may be pursued in reading a novel. But it is not the only one, and it does not always override others, for example, in our case, appreciating the psychological complexity of characters who can take on a life of their own in the world of the novel. Given this broader goal of inferring explanations from the text or narrow world as presented that enhance the value of the work for the reader, it is clear why we can derive multiple interpretations from this single criterion of maximizing the value of the text as written. Different values that cannot be simultaneously realized, in our case cognitively engaging psychological complexity versus emotionally engaging, consistently building atmosphere, imply this possibility of multiple acceptable interpretations. New and different interpretations can lead us to see elements in a work that we had previously missed and to integrate these elements in aesthetically more fulfilling ways in the new interpretations (even though these interpretations cannot themselves be combined or integrated).

The intentionalist might respond that, if the constraint of author intention is dismissed as too restrictive of satisfying experiences of the work, there is similar reason to dismiss the work itself as a constraint, as more radical theorists do. Why should we not ignore or alter large sections of a work if a more interesting reading can be generated by doing so? The simplest answer is that rewriting the text in this way might be a valuable exercise for a clever writer if such improvement could be made, but the result would be a new, albeit largely plagiarized, novel, not a new interpretation. Most often, of course, plagiarizing authors such as Hemingway would not result in better works or more satisfying experiences for readers. It is generally more satisfying to try to understand Hemingway's works than to try to rewrite them.

This does not mean, however, that we should be prohibited from find-ing motives in the characters, for example, that Hemingway did not explicitly intend when he brought them to (fictional) life. As once more noted earlier, we find a similar mixture of constraint and freedom in interpreting other artistic media. Acceptable interpretations of a musical composition, critical or performative, cannot make major alterations in the notes as written, but neither are they limited to bringing out expres-sive qualities in the music explicitly intended by the composer. Altering tempo or accent does not create a new musical work, but it might create a different musical world with different formal and expressive properties. Similarly, different interpretations of *The Sun Also Rises* create different fictional worlds with different formal relations and traits of character, all of which must nevertheless remain true to Hemingway's work.

V

I have spoken so far of interpretations that fill out the fictional world of a work, that create fictional truths suggested but neither stated nor implied by its text. There are also other sorts of explanations for why the text might be written as it is or why the narrow world of the work is as it is described by and inferred from the text, explanations that speak of the structure, style, or themes of the work without adding fictional truths to it. Thus, when Brett makes her entrance into the story in the company of a group of gay men to whom Jake reacts with hostility, this might be seen to introduce the fictional truth that they are both confused about their sexual identities. But it can also be explained as beginning to develop the theme of futility in sexual relations or as creat-ing parallels or contrasts among the main characters, that is, as adding structure to the novel, and so on.

These are all interpretations, albeit of different sorts, because they all explain why the episode might be described as it is, what literary value this adds to the text or its world. Furthermore, these different sorts of explanations or levels of interpretation can interact. What we take to be fictionally true obviously affects what we see as both the themes and the structure of the novel. I also noted above how an analysis of the style of the text can support an interpretation of what is fictionally true in its world. Hemingway's terse, staccato style expresses the frustrations and cynicism of his characters.

In defending my own account of what the two initial interpretations of the Hemingway work show, I have along the way criticized the intentionalist view as too narrow and restrictive and the no-textual-constraint view as too permissive. There is another prominent compromise view that might be criticized briefly in closing. This account also aims at a position between the two extremes, although I believe it is less intuitively motivated and more ad hoc than the explanatory account that I have defended. I refer to hypothetical intentionalism. According to its criterion of correct interpretation, interpreters seek the intentions of the author that would be attributed to him by an ideal intended audience, whether or not the actual author had such intentions. This allows for richer readings than those foreseen by an author.

But what of the case in which there is good evidence that the actual author intended a reading different from and incompatible with the richer one being contemplated? In our example, for instance, we have Hemingway making a statement that indicates that he does not see Jake or Brett as the hero of this novel. That certainly indicates that he did not intend an optimistic conclusion to the novel,[12] in which their having developed sufficiently to have overcome their histories and the difficult times presages a better future for them. I have held nevertheless that the interpretation of them as developing remains a live option. This seems to make a perfect test case for differentiating the value-enhancing explanatory account from any intentionalist criterion, hypothetical or not.

Surprisingly, however, defenders of hypothetical intentionalism rule out authorial pronouncements as to their intentions as definitive, indeed as any evidence for the ideal audience.[13] The motive once more is the praiseworthy one of maintaining some autonomy for the work and its critics, presumably in order to allow more satisfying readings. Jerrold Levinson, a main proponent of this criterion, writes:

Works of literature thus retain, in the last analysis, a certain autonomy from the actual mental processes of their creators during composition . . . It is this small but

---

[12] Although at another time Hemingway is said to have commented that *The Sun Also Rises* is not a pessimistic novel. Cited in Frederick Svoboda, *Hemingway and "The Sun Also Rises"* (Lawrence: University Press of Kansas, 1983), p. 108.

[13] See, for example, Jerrold Levinson, "Intention and Interpretation in Literature," in *The Pleasures of Aesthetics* (Ithaca, NY: Cornell University Press, 1996), p. 208. Levinson even allows the attribution of allusion when it is clear that the author had never heard of its target, p. 211.

crucial dimension of distinctness between agent's meaning and work's meaning—even when the latter is understood as roughly an optimal reader's projection of the former from the text-in-full-context—which is obliterated by actual
intentionalism but safeguarded by the hypothetical variety.[14]

The idea behind appealing to hypothetical intentions is to steer a middle
course between the rigid constraint of actual intentionalism and the free-
for-all of the critical community standards view:

> A virtue of hypothetical intentionalism stands out clearly, which is to mediate
> between a position, actual intentionalism, which gives just a little too much
> to authors as persons, and a ludic position such as that of Shusterman (or, more
> extremely, Rorty, Barthes, or Derrida), which gives altogether too much to
> readers, and threatens to undermine the motivations of authors for upholding
> their end of the implicit literary contract.[15]

My main criticism of hypothetical intentionalism is similar to my criticism in the previous chapter of Currie's positing of a fictional narrator:
namely, that this highly theoretical device is at best superfluous. We do
want an account that allows for interpretations of a novel's episodes,
characters, and their motives that were unintended by their authors, that
allows these events and characters to speak for themselves in their fictional worlds in ways their readers can maximally appreciate. We also
want an account that is true to the text and the narrow world of the work.
We can have the latter while allowing for the former without pretending
that we are still bound by authorial intentions of any sort. The artificial
notion of hypothetical intentions is entirely dispensable. If the aesthetically best explanation of Jake's behavior and thoughts at the end of the
novel is that he has morally developed, then either Hemingway's hypothetical intentions must match that explanation, or they are as irrelevant
as his real intentions, which he was properly loath to reveal.

I have held therefore that hypothetical intentions are *at best* superfluous. But there is yet another criticism of this criterion for proper interpretation from my point of view, in that it appears to diverge from my
criterion in one sort of case. If we cannot ascribe hypothetical intentions
to an author that he could not possibly have had at the time he wrote, the
Freudian readings of *Hamlet*, for example, would be ruled out (assuming
that Shakespeare could not have intended an earlier version of Freud's

---

[14] Levinson, "Intention and Interpretation in Literature," p. 194.
[15] Levinson, "Intention and Interpretation in Literature," p. 199.

theory). But there is no good reason to prohibit such readings, if Hamlet displays symptoms of Freudian neurosis and interpreting him as such makes for an interesting and insightful experience of the play.

Authors, like composers, ought to welcome the most rewarding interpretations of their works. Since they must accept that their works may fall short of their intentions, they should also accept that their works may exceed in value what they originally envisioned. Indeed, they should intend that this will happen. They should insist only that their texts be respected as they wrote them. Having created the single object that stands to be explained but that can afford multiple literary values under different and sometimes incompatible explanatory schemes, they can leave it to their readers and critics to provide such schemes in the service of their appreciation of the work. A single object of interpretation, such as *The Sun Also Rises*, under a single criterion of acceptable interpretation, which allows the author's work to stand on its own without disappearing, can provoke a rich variety of interpretations that reward the reader in different ways.

4

The appeal of the mystery

I

In the previous two chapters I defended a theory of interpretation and tested one of its main implications by an extended example. Here I want to test the theory of value for art and literature that I defended in an earlier book,[1] again by example. That theory focuses on the sort of effects that the best works in any genre have on us. Given ultimate differences in taste even among the most competent critics and the ways that contexts affect the values of different properties in works, we cannot usefully generalize about intrinsically good-making properties of art or literary works. What is good in one context or for one critic is not in another context or for another critic. And it might seem that the effects of even the best works are equally diverse: some depress us, others cheer us up; some spur us to action, others have a serenely calming effect, and so on. But there is one common sort of effect. All the best works afford us rich perceptual, cognitive, affective, and imaginative experience, and therein, I claim, lies their value.

The value of such works lies in their capacity to challenge and continuously engage us on all these levels simultaneously. The worth of any artwork is measured by its tendency to engage fully and interactively all our mental capacities—cognitive, emotional, imaginative, and perceptual. Such complete engagement with the work as it is constitutes appreciation of it. Other kinds of objects, of course, engage us in several of these ways as we interact with them in the course of pursuing our practical goals in the real physical world. But when we are so fully and satisfyingly involved in appreciating an artwork, we can be said to lose our

---

[1] *Aesthetic Value* (Boulder, CO: Westview, 1995).

ordinary, practically oriented selves in the alternative world of the work. Our physical bodies disappear from consciousness, and our fully engaged mental capacities focus only on this other world.

A major goal and effect of great artworks is to so fully challenge and engage our mental capacities operating together as to seem to create alternative worlds for us to occupy, however briefly. When isolated in a dark theater or reading room easy chair, we escape the practical world to which we are at best satisficingly attuned into the alternative, more perfectly crafted worlds of art and literature. This effect is most obvious in the case of literary works and the fictional worlds they create. The reward of losing ourselves in such worlds is first the intense enjoyment of being so challenged and engaged, especially when the challenge is successfully met, when, for example, perception makes sense of complex form and cognition uncovers subtle thematic content; second, there is the expansion of our experience in many dimensions, including moral; and third, the comparisons afforded to the real world and what we can learn from these comparisons.

In the appreciation of artworks, our several mental faculties interact to grasp rich layers of relations among the representational, symbolic, narrative, or thematic, and formal and expressive elements in the works. These faculties and the different facets of appreciation in which they are engaged not only operate simultaneously, but interactively, so as to become indissolubly united. Imaginative identification or empathy for fictional characters, for example, emotionally engages us and allows us to cognitively interpret their motives, which in turn creates formal relationships with other characters and settings, grasped perceptually or by visual imagery. Such interaction and complete engagement implies experience more intense than usual, and this intensity is increased by the highly condensed temporal sequences we experience in reading. In reading a novel we can vicariously experience complete emotional changes, indeed lifetimes, in a matter of hours. This felt intensity both results from and in turn reinforces our complete engagement in the fictional worlds of the best literary works.

A crucial test for this or any theory of aesthetic or literary value is its ability to explain the value of particular works, or even better kinds of works, especially those that have been very widely appreciated over a significant course of time. In music, for example, the theory of value should be able to explain the wide use and appeal throughout the classical and romantic eras of the sonata–allegro form for large-scale movements.[2] In literature, the most widely read genre for more than a century has been the mystery or detective novel,[3] and its widespread appeal calls for explanation as well if we are to understand the nature of literary aesthetic value. My aim in this chapter will be to explain the source of appeal of such fiction, which lies in the kind of aesthetic or literary value the better examples provide. I will attempt to show how the theory of aesthetic value just summarized can explain the appeal of mystery novels, the most popular kind of novels ever written, in a detailed way that other theories, for example the claim that aesthetic value lies in the intrinsic value of the experience that artworks produce,[4] cannot.

II

It will be objected immediately, as it has been by literary critics on one side of a debate, that mystery novels are merely part of popular culture, not true literary works of art. In its most dismissive form this claim sees such "escapist" literature as worth no more aesthetically than mindless television fare. But reading detective novels has been a passion of academics and other consumers of canonical literature, while mindless TV is not (not to suggest that all TV is mindless). If such sophisticated readers seek only escape from intellectual toil or challenge in mysteries, it must at least be escape of a different kind from that of mindless diversion, in fact not mindless at all. And, as I will argue, the sort of mind engagement many mysteries provide is an indication of aesthetic merit.

But critical dismissals must be addressed first. Philosophers may be quite comfortable with attributing real aesthetic value to popular art forms. In recent years aestheticians have given serious attention to such genres as horror films and rock and rap music. But of the literary critics who have addressed detective fiction, several of the more prominent have been largely dismissive, and their criticisms are serious and need to be briefly answered before an explanation of the appeal of the genre in terms of the great aesthetic value of its members will be initially plausible.

---

[2] For my explanation, see *Aesthetic Value* (Boulder, CO: Westview, 1995), pp. 82–91.

[3] Michael Cohen, *Murder Most Fair* (Cranbury, NJ: Associated University Presses, 2000), pp. 13, 174.

[4] Malcolm Budd, *Values of Art* (London: Penguin, 1995).

More specifically, mystery novels have been dismissed as having shallow, cardboard, stereotypical characters and little atmosphere; flat style or no style at all (especially Agatha Christie);[5] formulaic, repetitive, or conventional plots; emotional disengagement; and moral smugness or one-dimensionality, with pat defenses of the social status quo and little or no investigation or implication regarding the social causes of crime.[6] Some of these charges are of course true of the worst members of the genre, as they are true of the worst members of any literary genre. But some, such as the extensive use of conventions, are not artistic vices at all; those that are literary defects do not apply with anything approaching universality and apply as well to other works considered serious and worthwhile literature; some apply to one type of mystery novel but not to another; and some are simply not true even on average.

These counterclaims will be substantiated below in explaining the wide appeal of good mystery novels in terms of their aesthetic value, but I can expand in a preliminary way here in order to indicate at the start why such an explanation is in order. Of course, as in almost any genre, there will be good and bad instances. It is therefore rather easy to refute those critics who attack the entire mystery genre or the majority of those writers with broadest appeal within it. I will argue further that mysteries typically cognitively engage us more readily than works in other genres by the type of interpretive challenge they typically present.

But I reply first to the more specific dismissals. Consider them in the order stated above, beginning with characters and atmosphere. Once more, some characters, especially minor ones, are indeed one-dimensional, and their moral natures can be immediately inferred from their physical descriptions or even names. They only fill slots in plot developments and neither answer nor even raise real questions about human nature. But the same is true of characters in Dickens' novels, for example, and such simple stereotyping may reflect the way most people view others to whom they are not intimately related. Dickens' skill in

---

[5] See especially Edmund Wilson, "Who Cares Who Killed Roger Ackroyd?," in *Classics and Commercials* (London: Allen, 1951).

[6] Stephen Knight, *Form and Ideology in Crime Fiction* (Bloomington: Indiana University Press, 1980), pp. 67, 117; Marty Roth, *Foul and Fair Play* (Athens: University of Georgia Press, 1995), p. 133; Geoffrey Hartman, "Literature High and Low," in Glenn Most and William Stowe, eds, *The Poetics of Murder* (San Diego: Harcourt, Brace, Jovanovich, 1983), p. 224.

vividly sketching a character type in a short paragraph is a literary merit, not defect, and Christie, who is widely criticized for such sketches, is only slightly less adept.

By contrast, in regard to depth of characterization and memorability, how many better characters in all of fiction than the archetype detective, Sherlock Holmes? We remember him more for his habits and obsessions and his skewed but immense body of knowledge than for his feats of detection. And just as Holmes is far more than a thinking machine, so the American archetype, Raymond Chandler's Philip Marlowe, is far more than a tough guy cynic. We return to the same authors repeatedly as much for their main characters as for the ingenuity of their plots. Multi-dimensional characters include not only detectives, but culprits or villains as well, as Chandler's Vilma, for example, a multiple murderess, proves to be morally complex at the end of *Farewell My Lovely*. Among prominent contemporary mystery writers in the British tradition, P. D. James is arguably better at characterization and atmosphere than puzzle or plot. And few contemporary writers are better at creating emotionally charged atmosphere than the American mystery writer Thomas Cooke.

In regard to style, no one accuses the classic American writers, Hammet and Chandler, of its lack. Chandler's terse and staccato dialogue and action sequences, and his creative, wisecracking, and cynical similes and metaphors are a perfect fit for the surface-tough but more subtle romantic idealism of his hero and first-person narrator in his violent and corrupt urban setting. But then Christie's much criticized simple and somewhat flat though elegant and gently humorous prose makes an equal fit for the atmosphere of English country life she describes. And her lack of emotive crescendos helps to mask her casual droppings of crucial clues in the complex games she plays with readers. Likewise, Georges Simenon's straightforward and understated French vernacular perfectly describes the character of Maigret and the Parisian neighborhoods he patrols.

I earlier compared Christie's character sketches with those of Dickens. But although Dickens' characters may be morally transparent and one-dimensional, his novels certainly contain penchant social criticism of the consequences of industrial progress. By contrast, as mentioned earlier, it is a standard criticism of detective fiction that it is uninterestingly ideologically conservative in its defense of the social status quo, in its assumptions that crime results only from individually bad characters, who fortunately are always purged from society by the unquestioning and unquestioned upholders of justice. But this criticism too is simplistic if not outright false of much good and popular mystery fiction.

Police, as the official defenders of the social status quo, are most often portrayed as bumbling if not corrupt. Even when the detective heroes are themselves police, as are Maigret, Morse, and Hamish Macbeth, there are conflicts with less competent underlings or superiors, or the police hero himself is somewhat corrupt and incompetent, as is Michael Dibdin's Aurelio Zen. It is true that there are competent police who work well with detectives, such as Evanovich's Joe Morelli, and somewhat more common, aristocratic police and detectives, such as Marsh's Roderick Alleyn, Sayers' Peter Wimsey, as well as those with aristocratic tastes, such as Dexter's Morse. But the earlier examples are among the more numerous, and thus the generalization regarding social conservatism is more than suspect. Equally to the point, detectives themselves often bend or break the law. Both Sherlock Holmes and Hercule Poirot let murderers go free after solving their crimes. While mysteries are accused of assuming pat moral attitudes, they actually challenge our moral sense when such paradigm detectives break the law, or when, at the opposite end of the spectrum, they turn in their lovers to the police, as does Sam Spade, another early paradigm.

As early as Sherlock Holmes, detectives treat the aristocracy with the same or greater disdain as socially lesser clients. This tradition too certainly continues across the Atlantic. Philip Marlowe's rich clients are effete and/or corrupt, and the novels are not misdescribed as literature of social protest.[7] Marlowe may eliminate a single killer, but violence and corruption continue to pervade his world, similar to the Italy of Aurelio Zen. Then there are other contemporary British and Scandinavian writers, such as John le Carré, Peter Hoeg, and Stieg Larsson, who attack the evil influence of big business with Dickensian fervor. The criticism of detective fiction as too socially conservative fails on all these counts.

Turning to the next dismissive objection, it is true that mystery plots tend to be somewhat formulaic and that they rely on certain relatively fixed conventions. I shall have more to say about specific conventions below, but it can be noted here that classical tonal musical composition relies even more heavily on conventional formulas, such as sonata–allegro or theme and variations, but is never criticized on that ground alone. By a kind of

---

[7] Dennis Porter, *The Pursuit of Crime* (New Haven: Yale University Press, 1981), p. 169.

Shenkerian analysis of mystery plots we can uncover nearly universal bare bones plot outlines: a detective, often retired or on vacation, is hired to look into some problem such as a missing person or blackmail; a murder ensues that initially either seems unsolvable or points to an obvious culprit; further events and more murders refute the initial hypothesis; an insight based on some previously overlooked fact occurs to the detective, who does not yet reveal his suspicion; the full solution is revealed and fully explained. But, as in listening to music in the classical style, we look for and derive pleasure from the way such formulas are varied, infused with original elements, or violated to create surprise. A tradition of formal conventions can be used to stimulate an author's imagination and originality instead of stifling it.[8] This objection can be dismissed as well.

It will finally be objected to an explanation of popularity in terms of aesthetic value that the Golden Age of the mystery novel, roughly 1920–60, has long passed and that a properly historically oriented but contemporary aesthetic theory will therefore not concern itself with the genre's appeal. The British tradition is seen to culminate in Christie, Dickson Carr, and Ngaio Marsh, and the hard-boiled American tradition to end with Ross McDonald.[9] It is also claimed along these lines that post-modern mystery writers such as Jorge Luis Borges and his counterpart Umberto Eco signaled the death of the genre in their deconstructed versions of it. Detectives in mystery novels seek the truth and the restoration of social order in the face of crime. If, as in the post-modern versions, the search for a single truth and the preservation of or quest for a rational social order are doomed along with these detectives to fail, then the necessary presuppositions of the mystery novel are exposed as pure myth. Then only such comic spoofs of the genre as are found in the likes of Janet Evanovich or Carl Hiaasen could continue the otherwise moribund literary tradition.

But a quick glance at the space of any present commercial bookstore will show that debunking authors and critics no more killed off the mystery novel than Richard Rorty killed epistemology (as opposed to offering a different version of it). Along with such recent offshoots as the feminist detective novels of Sara Paretsky, Sue Grafton, or Patricia Cornwell,

[8] J. W. Krutch, "Only a Detective Story," in Howard Haycrat, ed., *The Art of the Mystery Story* (New York: Simon and Schuster, 1946), p. 180.
[9] Julian Symons, *Bloody Murder* (New York: Warner Books, 1992), pp. 205, 302.

the classic British who-done-it and American hard-boiled forms survive and thrive in contemporary form in such writers as Colin Dexter, P. D. James, and Ruth Rendell on one side, and Elmore Leonard, Robert B. Parker, and James Lee Burke on the other. Detective anti-heroes such as Aurelio Zen or Charles Willeford's Hoke Moseley continue the tradition in another way instead of undermining it. Together with feminist, black, and Continental detectives, we now have pathologists, computer geniuses, and others trained in new technologies of evidence gathering to add to the list. It is the post-modern disdain for truth or hard fact that has come and gone as a philosophical style, while the appeal of the mystery remains to be largely explained by a theory of aesthetic or literary value (which is not to deny other sorts of value).

At the same time there are contrasts between mystery novels and other literature deemed more serious that I will attempt to elucidate. The ways that we are cognitively and emotionally engaged with mystery novels are different. I will claim that these contrasts indicate a difference in the type of aesthetic value produced and not in the quantity. Our conclusion so far is simply that there are no obstacles to explaining the great appeal of mystery novels in terms of their aesthetic value. Before providing that explanation and as a final preliminary, we might note the diverse explanations offered in passing in the critical literature on mystery fiction. That literature has been mainly concerned with the history, structure, and ideology of these novels, but critics, in noting their popularity, have offered brief explanations. Some of these mirror the dismissive criticisms of the genre, while others are more positive.[10]

They include the following: mystery fiction provides relaxation through intellectual games or puzzles much like crosswords, or like magic tricks when the puzzles cannot be solved;[11] it relieves anxiety by showing that justice prevails; it provides an exciting escape from humdrum reality; it exhibits narrative purity and intelligibility, having fully coherent stories with clear beginnings and closure at endings, in contrast to other modern fiction;[12] it affirms the power of reason, symbolizing the knowability and lawlikeness of the world, the existence

---

[10] Since it is literary critics and not philosophers who have attended to mystery fiction, it is once more the former to whom I am mainly reacting in this paper.

[11] W. H. Wright, "The Great Detective Stories," in *The Art of the Mystery Story*.

[12] Marjorie Nicolson, "The Professor and the Detective," in *The Art of the Mystery Story*, p. 114.

of hard facts, and the power of scientific reasoning or inductive inference, ubiquitous in mental life but clearly exhibited here;[13] it bridges
the gap between obscure scientific method and the layman, showing
that the former can serve moral purposes;[14] it legitimates and reaffirms
the values of the social status quo or privileged class by segregating
the criminal, at the same time exorcizing guilt from upper-class readers;[15] it provides a vicarious outlet for violent, homicidal, or sadistic
impulses, simulating voyeurism of the criminal class. I omit more
bizarre Freudian explanations. Of the ones mentioned, I have already
dismissed the appeal to social conservatism. Others are partially true,
but only very partial parts of the total explanation, as will be made
clear below. Still others apply to one kind of mystery fiction but not to
another.

I have been appealing to the standard distinction among kinds: the
classic British who-done-it versus the American hard-boiled kind.
This distinction is not hard and fast: John Dickson Carr and Rex Stout,
for example, are Americans who write in the British tradition (Nero
Wolfe being a near clone of Dickson Carr's Gideon Fell), while Dick
Francis is a Brit who writes in the tough guy American style, even
when his novels are set in the racetracks of England. And there are more
contemporary offshoots that combine traditions or fit neither. But the
contrast is nevertheless real. The English country house contrasts with
the mean American urban streets; the orderly society with the violent and corrupt; the intellectual master of observation and inference
with the tough man of action. The British who-done-it moves backward from a crime to its reconstruction; the American detective story
moves forward to crimes as they occur.[16] The explanation cited above
in terms of violent impulses therefore fits the American type but not
the British, where violence is downplayed. The explanation in terms
of an intellectual puzzle or game fits the British but not as well the
American kind.

---

[13] Michael Cohen, *Murder Most Fair*, p. 110; H. P. Rickman, *Philosophy in Literature*
(Teaneck, NJ: Fairleigh Dickinson University Press, 1996), p. 161.

[14] J. K. Van Dover, *You Know My Method* (Bowling Green: Bowling Green University
Press, 1994), p. 24.

[15] Nicholas Blake, "The Detective Story—Why?," in *The Art of the Mystery Story*,
pp. 399–401.

[16] Noted by Ross Macdonald, "Introduction," *Great Stories of Suspense* (New York:
Alfred A. Knopf, 1974), p. ix.

But I claim that there is a broader and deeper explanation for the mystery's appeal that applies to both kinds. For these typical differences, while real, are differences in emphasis and setting, and the different emphases mask important commonalities. Sherlock Holmes, the archetypal intellectual detective, acts when he needs to, does not shrink from danger, and is tough when he needs to be. Philip Marlowe, the tough man of action, finds out crucial facts by "stirring things up" through violent actions from which inferences about who did what to whom follow naturally. But while his inductive thought processes may be less explicit, they are there and they uncover many complex entanglements of secrets. Marlowe may follow hunches initially, but in the end he provides a full explanation of what happened and why. The British story may move backward from an initial murder, but other murders invariably follow. The murder in the American story may not be in focus in the beginning, but it will have happened well before the end. A central crime must always be reconstructed from clues often uncovered in the ongoing narrative, and it is in the reader's experience of this reconstructive process that the value of the mystery novel largely lies.

III

According to the theory of interpretation defended in Chapter 2, interpretation of a work is a kind of explanation of its elements. Critics explain why those elements occur in the work as they do, that is, how they contribute to the aesthetic value of the work (since, I take it, they occur in the work in order to enhance its value). Interpretation itself then aims to enhance or maximize the value of a work, to make it comprehensible so that it can be completely engaging, its value fully appreciated. This theory of interpretation contrasts with both that which limits it to uncovering meanings in the usual sense, and with that which limits it to uncovering what is explicitly intended by an author. But in the case of mystery novels, as we shall see, correct interpretation is more circumscribed than it is in other genres. Here too, however, interpreting a work, necessary to its appreciation, is also part of its appreciation since it is a large part of our cognitive engagement with it, so that a work that is richly interpretable, all of whose elements can be seen to contribute in one way or another to its overall value, is to that extent a good work.

Such cognitive engagement, however, must lead to engagement in other mental dimensions as well.

To explain the broad appeal of mystery novels in terms of their aesthetic or literary value[17] is thus to explain why works of this kind tend to engage our mental capacities in all these ways. We may consider the tendency of such novels to stimulate each mental capacity in turn. As mentioned, cognitive engagement consists mainly in attempts to interpret. In explaining how the elements of a work relate to each other so as to contribute to its value, interpreters often seek sources of unity or overall coherence in the works they interpret. Often the unifying principle lies in a single or several overarching themes. Such thematic content will be examined in relation to several novels in the second half of this book. In the case of mystery novels, however, themes and the symbols that often point to them may be minimal. The right interpretations will nevertheless still seek to uncover the unifying principles in the novels. Here, unlike in the case of other literary works, there will be single right interpretations, in each case consisting in a fully coherent narrative into which all the events and descriptions in the novel fit.

This correct interpretation emerges at the end and is put by the detective in the form of an argument as to why and how the crucial events took place. The correct interpretation is the full solution to the crimes and its complete explanation. This is the correct interpretation because every described event and character trait in the novel will be either a clue to how and why the crimes were committed, a red herring, or part of a sub-plot that ties into the crimes but delays their ultimate solution. The world of the novel will be constructed so as to be ultimately maximally interpretable in this way. Everything will fit the final explanation of the crimes. Every element will bear interpretation as a clue to the solution or a detour on the way to it. This is what Edgar Allan Poe's often cited line about an author's constructing a mystery backwards refers to. The detective's final inferences as he organizes scattered effects into a single causal chain will prove correct, at least in standard mystery novels, and the reader's interpretation of events and descriptions must be measured against this final coherent narrative.

---

[17] I am once more using "literary value" to refer to the kind of aesthetic value that works of fiction have. They engage us as do other types of art, but by different means and with different emphases.

The detective will reason as a scientist—observing, applying knowledge of causes and causal laws, inferring to best causal explanations, eliminating initial hypotheses by further observational testing, and arriving in the end at the single coherent narrative that captures all the data. The reader will be mimicking this process as she reads, but in actuality her inferences will not be causal in the usual way, but aesthetic. Like the detective, she will be matching clues or physical traces to testimonies. Like him, she will be constructing explanatory hypotheses from an initial set of clues to be tested against further evidence, trying to separate real clues from misleading evidence that the author in the guise of the criminal throws her way. But unlike the case of ordinary causal inference, here the most obvious explanation of the most prominent facts will invariably turn out to be wrong. It will be the seemingly insignificant and offhand remarks that will point the way to the correct interpretation. The reader is inferring to the narrative that makes the best mystery, not to the one that is most probable in terms of ordinary causal laws in the real world. Hence she is engaged in literary or aesthetic interpretation. Like the author, she seeks a coherent, all-inclusive narrative that is surprising and aesthetically pleasing, not one that is realistic and prosaic. The detective's final reasoning pattern, of course, is really that of the author, and therefore the aim of the reader's reasoning as well will be to construct the aesthetically best solution to the mystery.

The main point here is that a reasonably well-written mystery will literally force the reader to engage constantly in this interpretive activity. Like the detective hero, the reader must pay close attention to even seemingly insignificant details (*especially* to such details), attempting always to fit them into a coherent explanatory narrative. As Miss Marple notes, "The point is that one must provide an explanation for everything."[18] And Sherlock Holmes adds, "It has long been an axiom of mine that the little things are infinitely the most important."[19] Initial clues will point to more than one interpretation; but ultimately only one, and not the first suggested, will prove to be correct, and it is this interpretation at which the reader constantly aims. All novels present interpretive problems of disambiguating initially ambiguous signs in aiming at completion or

[18] Agatha Christie, *Murder at the Vicarage* (New York: Dell, 1958), p. 195.
[19] Arthur Conan Doyle, "A Case of Identity," *The Adventures of Sherlock Holmes* (New York: Franklin Watts, 2007), p. 50.

closure, but mystery novels do so most insistently, posing interpretive questions to readers directly. The aim here is not to find the meaning of obscure language, an often tedious task, but to find a place in the final overall narrative for all the elements described.

All elements of the mystery novel—events as described, characters' motives as inferred, background histories as described and inferred, and so on—are made meaningful or significant by this interpretive activity, relating to past crimes or their future solutions. The reader is constantly projecting backward and forward, predicting future developments from interpretations of past events. The process is two-stepped: clues must first be identified (corresponding to observation by the detective) and then explained. Everything that happens calls for interpretation, and so the reader is cognitively engaged on every page, seeking ordered narrative patterns in the textual data.

Thus the explanation of the mystery's appeal in terms of an intellectual puzzle or enjoyable game played between author and reader is partially correct, since the author is always challenging the reader to develop a correct interpretation of the story as a whole. This challenge or competitive game can be more or less complex, the puzzle solvable by the seasoned reader, as in most Agatha Christie novels, or not solvable by the reader (namely, me), as in mysteries by John Dickson Carr or Colin Dexter. In the latter cases the trick is to understand the final explanation offered by Gideon Fell or Morse and to appreciate the ingenuity involved in putting all the pieces together. But even when the reader, if reasonably astute, can solve the mystery before the detective does, the aim is not simply to know the solution to the puzzle. What the reader wants to know is not simply who did it, but how the detective determines who did it and the extent to which her, the reader's, inferences match those of the detective.

The detective's final narrative is not simply the solution to a complex puzzle, but an explanation of how it was solved, and the reader wins the competition with the author (or detective) to the extent that she anticipates that explanation in her ongoing interpretations. What we readers enjoy are not solutions to puzzles or what they represent or symbolize (the triumph of justice, preservation of order, or affirmation of reason), but the process of interpreting as we read, with all the obstacles placed in our way. This cognitive process requires attention to detail, inferential ability, memory, and imagination. There may be interlocking narrative lines and disjointed positive and misleading clues to be ordered into a coherent pattern. Sometimes the final pattern emerges only after an ingenious twist that reverses initially plausible hypotheses, as in the contemporary stories by Jeffrey Deaver. Only in the mystery novel is this interpretive process a competitive game. It comes to a head when the detective announces that he knows the answer to the crime puzzle but delays revealing it, challenging the reader to complete the interpretive process.

The detective is in the end an infallible interpreter of the clues, but the seasoned reader has one advantage over him in their competitive game. The detective, of course, has experience in (fictional) crime solving. But the reader's advantage lies in knowledge of the narrative conventions used by the author in other novels and those used by other authors in similar novels. These conventions guide the overall process of interpretation and also allow for shorter partial games, for example predicting who will turn up dead next. Once they are well established, they can be reversed to create surprise or complication, becoming variations on themes. They derive mainly from the genre's traditions, the author's style, or aesthetic considerations, but also partly from conformity to the real world, for example the fact that detectives are usually hired to investigate lesser crimes than murder.

Some of the more widely used conventions are the following:[20] an early apparent solution to the crime will be false, especially if put forth by the police; the initially most obvious suspect will be innocent; a missing person will turn up dead, as will anyone other than the detective who announces he has knowledge of the crime without revealing it; if something strikes the detective as not right, it will turn out to be a significant clue; anything mentioned in passing without apparent reason, especially if mentioned more than once, will be a significant clue; an unidentifiable victim will be identified but will not be the obvious one; an undecipherable dying message will be deciphered and will be a significant clue; the culprit will be among the known suspects, although they will all claim that the culprit is an outsider; all these suspects will have had different

---

[20] Some of these are mentioned by George Dove, *The Reader and the Detective Story* (Bowling Green: Bowling Green State University Press, 1997), pp. 21, 33, 84; some others not mentioned here are noted by David Lehman, *The Perfect Murder* (Ann Arbor, MI: University of Michigan Press, 2000), p. 212.

motives for killing the unlikeable victim who will have wronged most of them; a vociferously feuding couple will really be cooperating; seemingly unrelated characters will turn out to be related, often by past events or obscure family ties; physical description will match moral character; an apparent intended victim who survives may well be the culprit. As in tonal music, these genre-specific literary conventions facilitate the reader's following and predicting overall structure while allowing for original variation. Giving readers a competitive edge in their interpretive games with detectives and authors, they further explain why readers repeatedly return to the same authors.

I have said that solving the puzzle posed by the author, engaging in the competitive interpretive game, is a large part of our cognitive engagement with mystery novels. Thus those who locate the appeal of the mystery in the attempt to solve its puzzle are partially correct. But cognitive engagement is only part of the story, and the interpretive process challenges us on other levels as well. I have also said that the right interpretation will take the form of an all-inclusive narrative, encompassing all the described events, with emphasis on the crimes. This narrative will constitute the underlying form of the novel as well as its content, although the more superficial form consists in the events of the investigative process as it unfolds. As hinted at earlier, the latter will resemble sonata–allegro form in music: the posing of the problem, an initial seeming solution, complications, insight, and confirmation with revelation. The best mysteries will in the end exhibit a deeper formal structure that satisfies Aristotle's criterion for good form in art generally: closure when it comes will surprise at the same time as seeming to be necessitated by the parts that make up the form.

In interpreting, the reader must try to anticipate this completed and closed form in imagination, thinking in quasi-perceptual ways (*quasi*-perceptual because large-scale form is inferred rather than directly perceived, quasi-*perceptual* because form is imaginatively perceived with visual images rather than simply being conceived or described). She must anticipate how all the narrated parts will fit into the whole that makes up this formal structure. She will try to imagine the most aesthetically pleasing structure into which the already experienced elements fit. Here the detective's causal explanations will finally coalesce with the reader's sense of aesthetic form. Thus the interpretive process already engages the reader imaginatively and even perceptually, as well as cognitively. But there are more obvious imaginative and perceptual processes involved in appreciating novels that mystery novels are especially apt to elicit. We will turn to those, along with emotional engagement.

IV

We noted that in interpreting a mystery novel a reader must imagine possible reconstructions and outcomes. An equally or more important role for imagination to play in appreciating fiction consists in imaginative identification with the fictional characters and with the author's point of view. By so doing one expands one's experiences and outlooks and develops empathy and sympathy for different character types, a major value to be derived from reading fiction. Novels themselves have value to the extent that they facilitate such imaginative identification, even with less admirable characters, at least to the extent of thinking as they do, since there is still value to be gained by understanding their motives. We identify with characters when we share their emotions, thoughts, or motives, when we imagine facing the situations they are in and the decisions that must be made in those situations. We identify with fictional characters when we imagine being those characters in the situations they face. This is easiest when we share some of their needs, desires, challenges, and frustrations.

There is another consideration, however. Identification is easiest when a character is most like the reader, but then there is less value to identifying with the character since the reader's experience and viewpoint will undergo little expansion. What is most engaging to our imaginations and most broadening of our horizons is to be able to identify with or think like characters very different from us. This is normally difficult, but it is exactly what mystery novels encourage. Novels in general encourage such identification through the use of such stylistic devices as first-person narration, free indirect discourse (in which the author mimics a character's thoughts in third-person narration), present tense, and explicit description of narrative contexts, especially suspenseful contexts in which we easily empathize with the characters' negative emotions (generally more conducive targets of empathy). Mystery writers make ample use of such techniques.

It is true that the detective hero is on first appearance very different from us. He or she is almost invariably an outsider, something of a loner, being unmarried, divorced, or widowed, and either near infallible in observing and reasoning or super tough and sardonically witty: a unique combination of Enlightenment rationalism and Romantic heroism. The British version will lean toward the former and the American toward the latter, but both will combine both features. The archetype, Sherlock Holmes, is an eccentric bohemian, a violin-playing, cocaine-using, obsessive manic-depressive. Even when later detectives are policemen, they are far from ordinary, being published poets, like Adam Dalgliesh, or alcoholic opera lovers, like Morse. Other amateurs are obese curmudgeons, like Gideon Fell and Nero Wolfe, or strange anal little foreigners, like Hercule Poirot. Whether artistic bohemians like Holmes, man-of-the-people tough guys like Marlowe, Lew Archer, or Spenser, or life-risking, wisecracking female bondspersons like Stephanie Plum, they are always out of the mainstream. Their most notable features will almost surely differentiate them clearly from most readers.

On the other side, while empathy or identification is facilitated by similarity, it is not necessary. We can empathize with animals in real life and with characters in fantasy fiction. To some degree, however small, we automatically react with empathy to other conscious beings,[21] especially to those in distress, as characters in mystery novels often are. And, as emphasized earlier, in playing our interpretive game we must try to match the detective observation for observation and inference for inference. Both she and we attempt to read the culprit's mind, predict his future actions, and reconstruct his crime by inferring from traces he left. Sharing projects as well as emotions facilitates fuller identification.

In assuming the detective's task and imaginatively engaging in his actions to fulfill it, in empathizing with him and assuming his interpretive role, we naturally tend to identify with him, to imagine ourselves possessing his other traits. And of course we all want to identify with him as the defender of loyalty, truth, and justice. The often present bumbling sidekick or corrupt colleague will strengthen our desire to put ourselves in the detective's place, if anyone's. And despite what was noted above, this imaginative identification of reader with detective will be easier for the type of reader who is a likely devotee of the more sophisticated

---

[21] Suzanne Keen, *Empathy and the Novel* (Oxford: Oxford University Press, 2007), pp. 69–70.

examples of the genre, especially the academic, who often engages in complex inductive reasoning.[22]

Professors are not as different from detective heroes (especially those in the British tradition) as other readers might be. Although there may be little similarity in physical prowess, the mental activity at the heart of identification through common interpretive endeavor will be familiar. I noted earlier that inference to the best explanation is ubiquitous in mental life. Sherlock Holmes describes it as "systematized common sense." It occurs even at the perceptual level and includes as well the most complex levels of scientific reasoning. But the detective and the professor utilize specialized forms of such inference more often than others do.

One critic who has written on this scholarly audience for detective fiction describes academics as "detectives of thought," obsessed with creating mental order out of puzzling or chaotic data.[23] Neither the professor nor the fictional detective is in it for the money, but, at least in part, for the love of the intellectual challenge. Like Holmes, both are obsessed with the search for truth and with mastery of their subject matter, and both are outsiders to normal society in some sense. It is easiest and most pleasant to identify with characters who are somewhat like us but better. Fictional detectives are very different from us in some ways and like us in others, but we would all like to have the mental acuteness of Holmes, Fell, Poirot, or Wolfe, or the toughness and wit of Marlowe, Spenser, Plum, Robicheaux, or Morse. We celebrate our individuality, rationality, and moral integrity in imaginatively identifying with these detectives.

Our imaginative activity of this type does not end there. The fictional detective, we noted, must get inside the culprit's mind, must try to identify with the criminal, or at least think like him, in order to decipher his actions. In playing the role of the detective, then, so must we. To solve the crime, we must think like the criminal, as must the detective, so we imaginatively identify with the fictional criminal's mind as well. But the criminal's relationship to the detective parallels the author's relationship to the reader, since the author, like his creation, the criminal, both constructs the crime and throws misleading evidence in the way of its solution.

---

[22] The emergence of numerous detective heroines, such as V. I. Warshawski, Kinsey Millhone, Kay Scarpetta, and Stephanie Plum, undoubtedly facilitates such identification by women readers. But I have emphasized the genderless mode of reasoning as the main source of identification with detectives.

[23] Marjorie Nicolson, "The Professor and the Detective," pp. 125–7.

The reader must think like the detective and the criminal, but ultimately like the author in trying to find the right interpretation.[24] In trying to construct a coherent final story from what has come before, the reader assumes the task of the author, and based on her knowledge of the author's style and use of conventions, she anticipates what remains to be written. Just as she must imagine why the culprit would have acted as he did, so she must imagine why the author would have mentioned certain (fictional) facts in the places and ways that he did.

The reader must reconstruct the thought processes and therefore possibly imaginatively identify with both the culprit and the detective, but at least equally with the author in trying to anticipate the outcome of the aesthetically best mystery that fits as much as she has read. In thinking the author's thoughts while she is reading, she must also reconstruct his past thoughts and those about the future denouement of the story. Once more it is mystery fiction above all other kinds that forces so much imaginative activity on the reader as necessary to the activity of interpretation. Cognitive engagement in interpreting these novels is indissolubly linked to imaginative identification with both characters and authors.

I can be briefer in regard to emotional engagement, which is yet more immediately apparent and obvious. The explanation of the appeal of mysteries in terms of vicarious excitement again clearly captures part of the truth. Some critics have nevertheless pointed out that mysteries instead promote emotional detachment by discouraging pity for the murdered victim, who is almost never a well-developed character, and to the extent that he is adequately described, is almost always thoroughly dislikeable. He may be characterized in this way in order to give all the other characters a motive for doing away with him, but perhaps also partly to make the reading experience more relaxing and less threatening to the reader's state of mind.

But the absence of felt tragedy certainly does not entail the absence of exciting and often violent action, and lack of strong feelings of pity are certainly offset by the excitement that comes from suspense and threats to the hero and to other innocent potential victims. Even in the more intellectual varieties of the genre, such dangerous threats are ever present.

---

[24] John Irwin, *The Mystery to a Solution* (Baltimore: Johns Hopkins University Press, 2000), p. 414; Heta Pyrhönen, *Mayhem and Murder* (Toronto: Toronto University Press, 1999), p. 15.

Fear no less than pity signals emotional engagement, and vicarious fear without real threat can be an enjoyable kind of excitement. The most obvious emotional stimulus from these novels produces this excitement through the sense of danger, suspense, and surprise and from the depictions of fast and violent action. Imaginative identification with characters in peril is at the same time empathetic or emotional engagement with them, just as it involves sharing cognitive tasks.

Much has been written on emotional engagement with fictional characters, and I can indicate only briefly here my own view and place in this debate. The seminal stimulus for this literature was Kendall Walton's claim that it is make-believe that we feel genuine emotions in this context, in that we are only to imagine having the emotions.[25] One main reason for this claim is that our feelings in reading fiction lack some of the features of ordinary emotions. The "quasi-fear" (Walton's term) that we feel when we identify with the detective in danger, for example, lacks the belief that we are really threatened as well as the disposition to physically flee. But I believe that a proper account of emotion concepts negates the need to deny that such fear is real.

Following the contemporary literature in psychology, we should recognize that concepts of emotions are cluster concepts, having clusters of criterial properties none of which is necessary or sufficient for the application of the concepts.[26] Paradigm or prototypical emotions include within the cluster of criterial properties judgments about their objects, physiological symptoms and sensations, directions of attention, pleasant or unpleasant thoughts, as well as motivations or behavioral dispositions. But less prototypical instances can lack some of these elements. Phobic fears, though genuine, lack belief in danger, and anger that the weather is bad lacks the disposition to attack it. Thus there is no reason to deny that emotional engagement with fictional detectives takes the form of genuine (but not paradigmatic) emotions. Usual judgments and behavioral dispositions can be lacking from genuine emotions. Thus we need not claim that we have only imaginary emotions in the context of reading mystery fiction,

[25] Kendall Walton, *Mimesis as Make-believe* (Cambridge, MA: Harvard University Press, 1990), ch. 7.
[26] See, for example, Beverly Fehr and James Russell, "Concept of Emotion Viewed from a Prototype Perspective," *Journal of Experimental Psychology: General,* 113 (1984): 464–86; J. M. G. Williams, *Cognitive Psychology and Emotional Disorders* (Chichester, UK: John Wiley, 1997), pp. 5–6.

but can recognize real emotions when we imagine ourselves to be in the detective's dangerous world.

I have been describing the obvious emotions we experience when caught up in a mystery story. There is also a more subtle kind of emotional engagement deriving from and more closely tied to the form of these narratives. I refer here not to the deeper narrative form of the final interpretation that reconstructs the crime and its preceding and ensuing events, but to the surface form of the reading experience as it occurs. Once more an analogy to musical form is apt. In tonal music there is a guarantee of ultimate resolution of tension from tonal dissonance in the final cadence of the piece, but its occurrence, and more important, its anticipation is more satisfying and enjoyable for its being prolonged and delayed. In like manner we are emotionally engaged by the building tension in the prolongation of the final solution to the crimes in mystery novels. All devotees have felt the compulsion to keep the pages turning late at night, and it is this feeling to which I refer.

This is a reaction to a different kind of suspense derived from form and added to the suspense that derives from the content of the story. The reader's interpretive projection or expectation of the final deeper form creates the suspense of awaiting confirmation or surprise, and this is heightened by the sub-plots, purely descriptive passages, and twists in the main plot as they occur in the surface form. Emotional engagement of this sort is thus closely connected to cognitive and perceptual activity (in so far as apprehension of form is quasi-perceptual). Such simultaneous and interactive engagement is the mark of aesthetic value in my account.

Finally, there is in my view yet another kind of emotional engagement in the stimulation of our moral sensibility, which, according to many recent accounts of moral judgment, is emotional in nature.[27] Critics, we noted earlier, disparage this literature as morally pat or even corrupt in its unthinking defenses of the social status quo. But I disputed this claim, pointing to negative depictions of state officials or police and of upper-class clients. More to the point, we noted the very many instances in which detective heroes themselves bend or break the law, to the extent of letting known murderers go free, as do the supposedly staunchest

---

[27] See, for example, Jesse Prinz, *The Emotional Construction of Morals* (Oxford: Oxford University Press, 2007); Shaun Nichols, *Sentimental Rules* (Oxford: Oxford University Press, 2004); Bennett Helm, *Love, Friendship, and the Self* (Oxford: Oxford University Press, 2010).

defenders of social conservatism, Holmes and Poirot. Other detectives, such as Hammet's Sam Spade, are more clearly morally ambiguous, leading us to reflect on their motives and the ethical status of their actions. Loyalty to client (or in Spade's case to a strongly disliked dead partner) seems often to trump other virtues or moral requirements, but this priority, while prevalent in professional ethics generally, should itself be a source of moral reflection and questioning.[28]

In general, it is the personal morality and anti-authoritarianism of the loner and outsider detective that is celebrated in these novels, not the norms of a socially stratified society. Not that there are not also morally objectionable assumptions underlying some typical character and action portrayals, for example, the depiction of lead liberated female characters as nymphomaniacal or homicidal psychopaths, as well as the celebration of sadistic violence, in the hard-boiled American classics. And just as the initial murder will fail to evoke pity for the victim, so it will fail to evoke moral outrage, as opposed to interest in the narrative. But on the whole, it is the detective's somewhat idiosyncratic ethical code, as well as our imaginative identification with characters both better and worse than we are, that will prompt moral reflection and engagement of the morally reactive emotions in the sensitive reader.

Once more much has been written on the aesthetic implications of moral perspectives assumed in fiction. One main question at least since Hume has been whether objectionable moral stances are aesthetic defects. Following both Hume and the theory of aesthetic value assumed here, my view is that they are aesthetic defects when they turn readers off instead of stimulating moral reflection as another level of engagement. Moral ambiguity, in such classic characters as Hamlet or Ahab, or in Sam Spade or Aurelio Zen, can therefore be a literary virtue, while straightforward advocacy of the viewpoint of a patently evil character would be a defect. We are stimulated by being placed along with fictional characters in moral quandaries without simple answers, not by moral preaching, even if sound, or by obvious debauchery. And detective novels have their share of such morally challenging situations.

The final mode of engagement, most prominent in other art forms but less so in literature, is perceptual. Although somewhat subtle, there

---

[28] See Alan Goldman, *The Moral Foundations of Professional Ethics* (Totowa, NJ: Rowman & Littlefield, 1980).

are nevertheless two types of perceptual involvement with novels: apprehension of formal structure and feel for the writing style or texture of the language. I have pointed to a distinction between two levels of form in the mystery novel: the form of the final narrative that reconstructs the causal sequence leading up to and through the crime to its consequences, and that of the story as written and experienced in reading.[29] We noted that the reader must constantly anticipate the former in interpreting the fictional events as described, and she will experience the latter forcefully in terms of building tension and its resolution. Thus she will be strongly engaged in this quasi-perceptual way, connected to her cognitive, imaginative, and emotional engagement.[30]

I earlier disagreed with those critics who dismiss mystery fiction as lacking interesting prose style. The writing of the better authors in the genre is a perfect match of style to content. This includes not only the terse, witty vernacular laced with wisecracks and similes of the Americans, but the much toned-down prose styles of Christie and Simenon that simply and directly relate dialogue and action. Both traditions, the simple elegance of the British and highly stylized rhythms of the American, have their contemporary masters in such writers as P. D. James and James Lee Burke. Appreciation of these textural qualities in the language and of their fit with settings and action constitutes the reader's more clearly perceptual engagement with this literature. Here there is literal perception of the language and its texture, the feel of the sounds and rhythms, as opposed to the quasi-perception of the overall form of the novel through visual images as well as conceptual maps. The prose style of the better writers in this genre, as in others, has a distinctive feel that relates positively to content and promotes another level of engagement with their works.

V

I have explained the appeal of mystery fiction in terms of its genuine literary or aesthetic value, where that value consists in the full simultaneous and interactive involvement of all our mental capacities. It will be

---

[29] Critics standardly draw a similar distinction between the time sequence of the investigation and that of the crime.

[30] Again, quasi-perceptual in involving visual imagery instead of direct perception.

emphatically objected here as at the beginning that this explanation cannot be accurate in failing to distinguish this escapist literature from more serious kinds. In reply, although I see all literature, indeed all art, even of the socially critical kind, as escapist in relation to the real or non-imaginary world, I do not wish to deny a distinction between mystery and other literature deemed more serious.

In fully occupying us in fictional or imaginary worlds, art allows us to escape our more mundane concerns, even where these fictional worlds invite comparison to the real one and suggest reform. We escape the real world by fully participating in art's imaginary worlds, and therein lies at least part of its great value for us. It provides an alternative outlet for our mental activities, one often richer and more intense than our ordinary daily endeavors. The more complete our engagement in these fictional worlds, the more complete our escape, and the better the art, given the value for us of the creation of such alternative nonreal worlds. Dismissing mystery fiction as escapist therefore has little bite.

But mystery fiction is indeed different from other kinds to which professional literary critics have traditionally paid more attention. The difference does not lie simply in having larger-than-life near super-heroes, although that too distinguishes this genre from some other kinds. The main difference, which explains why critics pay more attention to other genres, lies in the interpretive task that has been at the center of our discussion. So-called serious literature keeps critics endlessly in business because of its multiple and sometimes inexhaustible interpretability, as illustrated in the previous chapter. Most fairly complex novels admit of equally acceptable but incompatible interpretations that bring out or enhance different valuable aspects of the novels, and this possibility of different interpretations by different readers invites creative cognitive engagement with the works.

By contrast, we have seen that mysteries admit in the end of only one correct interpretation, although they will invariably suggest others along the way. This is why we do not as often reread individual novels, as opposed to authors, in this genre (at least I don't). We have also seen that the lack of multiple correct interpretations in this case does not lessen the reader's cognitive engagement (although it would on a second reading). If anything, interpretive activity is more constant here and practically forced upon the reader, even though at the end the story will interpret itself and refute all rival interpretations.

Some questions may nevertheless remain in the end about morals and motives, but in the main all loose interpretive ends will be tied up. All elements of the story will have been related to the central crime, even if only as a digression or red herring. As in much good art, we will be left with an ultimately coherent picture, but one in the appreciation of which all our mental capacities and efforts will have cooperated. We return to this literature so often for this challenging and pleasurable exercise.

PART II

Philosophy in Novels

5

Moral development in *Pride and Prejudice*

Earlier chapters on philosophy of novels offered accounts of interpretation, appreciation, and literary value. Interpretation, I claimed, aims to maximize such value by explaining how elements of works contribute to it, facilitating full appreciation or engagement of our intellects, emotions, and imaginations. Part of our cognitive and emotional engagement with novels results from challenges to our moral sensibilities that many good novels present. Philosophers, prominently including Martha Nussbaum, have described one important use of novels in moral education in sharpening our powers of moral perception and discrimination. In presenting morally charged situations in their fully complex history and detail, novels can teach us to attend to all morally relevant features of such situations, features typically overlooked or undervalued when simply applying general rules in making decisions. I do not deny such use, but I will illustrate extensively in this second part that, contrary to what some other philosophers maintain, we can also learn important general truths about ethics from novels.

This is especially true in regard to facts about full moral agency as the culmination of moral development, as well as the opposite of moral development—character disintegration. Novels often depict such development or negative change in narrating extensive periods in the lives of their characters, something that other art forms cannot do. All the novels I will examine here focus squarely on the theme of moral development or change. This chapter will address this topic explicitly and exclusively in one of the great novels that thematizes it centrally, *Pride and Prejudice*.

First, it will be helpful to present briefly some more contemporary views of the subject, in order to see more clearly just how perceptive and prescient Jane Austen is in this regard.

I

Assuming that we begin life with few or no genuine moral capacities, we can tell what is required in the development to full moral maturity by specifying the capacities exercised in fully mature moral judgment. Such judgment, if it is to be translated into action, requires three distinct but interrelated types of competence: cognitive–perceptual, emotional, and volitional. In order to judge accurately, we must above all perceive, i.e. recognize, the morally relevant factors in a situation and determine their weights or priorities among them when they conflict. Often in order to do this, we must empathize and sympathize with those potentially affected by our actions, since what is morally relevant is what affects their interests, and their interests are relative to their emotions and desires. The emotional capacity to empathize is necessary for accurately predicting the consequences of our actions or their effects on others. After identifying interests at stake in a situation, one must weigh them. When interests conflict and the priorities among them are not yet clear, moral judgment requires comparing the situation in question with others in which the priorities among similar interests are more clearly established.

To feel and judge in the right way, one must also have an accurate self-image, a healthy sense of one's own fallibility and biases. This will prevent overly hasty and self-centered judgment based on false analogies, superficial appearances, and relations only to one's own interests. It will also prevent ascribing one's own feelings and desires to others whose emotional makeup may be different. Such self-centered, superficial judgment is the mark of the morally immature or stunted, and empathy that is not fully developed assumes that all feel as one does oneself in similar circumstances. Mature judgment, by contrast, appreciates the feelings and intentions of others, adopts their perspectives.

A realistic sense of one's fallibility involves knowing when to defer personal judgment to social rules, which are generally good rules of thumb for successfully coordinating actions among agents not intimately related. Part of moral development therefore consists in internalizing such rules that facilitate efficient interaction. At the same time, since morally relevant factors can arise unexpectedly and can interact unpredictably, so as to prevent their being completely captured in a set of rules simple enough to be of use, full moral maturity includes the ability to rise above social rules of thumb and violate them when morally necessary. Such violations of socially accepted rules are justified, however, only when it is clear that personal judgment is morally superior to the application of the rules. Again, full moral maturity involves the ability to make such judgments. According to the psychologist Lawrence Kohlberg, the highest stage of moral development, which he calls "post-conventional," includes an ability to adopt this critical attitude toward the conventional rules of one's society.[1]

Finally, a morally mature person must not only judge correctly, but must also be motivated to act on the moral judgment. This may again require acting outside accepted social convention or acting against one's narrow self-interest or the interest of one's group. While more sophisticated moral judgments are more likely to be acted on than are more immature judgments, the ability to judge develops somewhat independently from the tendency to act on moral considerations.[2] Studies vary on the correlation between moral judgments and actions,[3] but there is a developmental pattern. When given the opportunity, children will typically act in their self-interest even while judging it wrong to do so. At later stages, agents will seek greater psychological consistency, being true to their values and acting in keeping with their judgments.[4] But acting on one's moral judgment requires not just moral motivation, but resoluteness, the ability to overcome distraction, temptation, and frustration and to delay satisfaction and absorb costs to one's own interests and the interests of those one might otherwise favor.

To develop such motivation and have it override more primitive or natural narrower interest, one must develop a self-identity that includes

[1] Lawrence Kohlberg and Daniel Candee, "The Relationship of Moral Judgment to Moral Action," in W. M. Kurtines and J. L. Gewirtz, eds, *Morality, Moral Behavior, and Moral Development* (New York: John Wiley & Sons, 1984), p. 62.

[2] Anne Colby and Lawrence Kohlberg, "Invariant Sequence and Internal Consistency in Moral Judgment Stages," in Kurtines and Gewirtz, eds, *Morality, Moral Behavior, and Moral Development*, pp. 53–4, 58.

[3] Elliot Turiel and Judith Smetana, "Social Knowledge and Action," in Kurtines and Gewirtz, eds, *Morality, Moral Behavior, and Moral Development*, p. 265.

[4] Augusto Blasi, "Moral Identity: Its Role in Moral Functioning," in Kurtines and Gewirtz, eds, *Morality, Moral Behavior, and Moral Development*, p. 129.

moral considerations as major components. The self can be defined in terms of properties without which one would not see oneself as the same individual. These self-defining properties can come to include moral attitudes. Morality can be seen by the individual as part of her self-conception or identity, or as an external constraint that blocks pursuit of her central interests. Again there is a typical developmental pattern. The concept of one's self develops independently from the capacity for moral judgment, but they become integrated typically in middle to late adolescence.[5] Without a moral identity one can still make moral judgments, but moral considerations will have no bearing in themselves on important decisions, actions, or emotional reactions to situations.[6] A sense of responsibility will be lacking. The adolescent acquires this sense when he becomes concerned with his reputation, with how he appears to others. He then begins to identify with his social roles, defining himself by how he interacts with peers rather than by his physical characteristics and capacities, the self-identifying features for the child earlier.[7] At a yet higher stage, if it is achieved, he will act on ideals independently of how this might appear to others or affect his reputation. (As we will see, such action marks the culmination of the moral development of Darcy in *Pride and Prejudice*.)

Thus, the resolve to act on one's moral judgments is a third distinct capacity in the fully mature moral individual, in addition to the emotional capacity for empathy and the cognitive ability to recognize and correctly weigh morally relevant factors in complex and conflicted contexts. The morally mature individual must simultaneously recognize her fallibility, yet have the ego strength and resolve to act on her reflectively confident moral judgments. Mature moral judgments and actions are combinations of emotional involvement, reason-guided perception, and volitional commitment. All these capacities are acquired gradually and interdependently over the course of moral development. Such development takes one from an initially self-centered perspective to full appreciation of the perspectives of others. This happens as the subject encounters

---

[5] William Damon, "Self-understanding and Moral Development from Childhood to Adolescence," in Kurtines and Gewirtz, eds, *Morality, Moral Behavior, and Moral Development*, p. 116.

[6] Blasi, "Moral Identity: Its Role in Moral Functioning," p. 122.

[7] Damon, "Self-understanding and Moral Development from Childhood to Adolescence," p. 118.

and is forced to acknowledge those other points of view, typically initially in family members and then in ever-widening groups of respected peers.

Identification with the interests of family members and then friends is an important step toward broader moral concerns, but it can also hinder further steps as individuals tend to separate into in-groups that oppose out-groups.[8] Full moral development requires the widening of these initially narrow perspectives. Eye-opening encounters with those from different groups can occur through initial confrontations or from the need for cooperative endeavors that benefit all. In both contexts, dialogue that brings to light shared and opposing interests in solving problems can lead to reciprocal respect. The process can be stunted by lack of beneficial interactions in such ever-expanding circles.

I have briefly described the capacities acquired in the course of moral development by noting what full moral maturity requires. Psychologists, of course, do not use this method to describe the process of moral development. Instead, they typically relate parables or describe morally problematic interactions to children and adolescents to see how their interpretations and the lessons they draw from these stories differ at different ages. The major psychological theories, like the emotive and cognitive meta-ethical theories, have emphasized either the cognitive or emotional side of moral development, although more recently there have been some attempts to combine them.[9] Cognitive theories emphasize judgments of reciprocity or fairness, while theories of moral emotional development emphasize empathy as prompting benevolent responses.

Empathy, or consideration for others based on shared feelings, is indeed distinct from the concept of fairness or distributive justice, as well as from a sense of duty. Even mature empathy occurs more easily in relation to people perceived as similar to oneself. It therefore remains somewhat biased, as opposed to the impartiality definitive of a true sense of justice or fairness. The moral resolution of conflicts can therefore require impartial judgment as well as feeling for the interests and needs of the parties

---

[8] H. Tajfel et al., "Societal Categorization and Intergroup Behavior," *European Journal of Social Psychology*, 1 (1971): 149–77.

[9] See, for example, John C. Gibbs, *Moral Development and Reality* (Boston: Allyn and Bacon, 2010). Despite much strange metaphysical musing, this is the best example of a combined theory. See also Martin Hoffman, "Empathy, Its Limitations, and Its Role in a Comprehensive Moral Theory," in Kurtines and Gewirtz, eds, *Morality, Moral Behavior, and Moral Development*.

that might need to precede such judgment.[10] Cognitivists thus point to a concept of fairness somewhat independent of empathy that also explains the motive to punish immoral acts independent of sympathy for victims. Both kinds of theory see immature judgment, as I described it above, as self-centered and superficial, focused on one salient property most often related to oneself. Mature judgment, by contrast, understands, identifies with, and integrates diverse viewpoints and takes all situational factors, both external and internal, into account.[11]

Cognitive theories, beginning with Piaget and then Kohlberg,[12] focus on the ability to attend to multiple properties and perspectives and respond to less superficial cues, a "decentration" of attention that parallels a like development in the purely cognitive realm. Piaget's initial centration (conservation) experiments involved pouring a liquid from a short, wide container into a long, narrow one. Young children focus on either the height or the width as the salient property and therefore judge the volume to change, while older children can attend to both properties as the change in one compensates the change in the other. Likewise, in the moral realm young children tend to focus on salient overt action and not intention, tend to see immoral behavior as any that is punished by adults, and they focus on only one side in situations of conflict. Children at a slightly later stage rely on simple rules and generalizations. More mature judgments can focus on and balance opposing interests and take into account less superficial properties such as intentions.

On the emotional side, infants appear to be wired with a primitive kind of empathy, in that they will cry when others do in a kind of imitation. Such primitive empathy expands by conditioning and association, but in early stages the child will respond only to overt signs of distress, will seek comfort or relief from its own empathic distress instead of seeking to relieve the affliction of the others who cause it, and, as mentioned earlier, the child will ascribe his own feelings to others who may be feeling differently. Children assume that others will feel what they would

---

[10] Hoffman, "Empathy, Its Limitations, and Its Role in a Comprehensive Moral Theory," p. 297.

[11] Compare Colby and Kohlberg, "Invariant Sequence and Internal Consistency in Moral Judgment Stages," p. 41.

[12] Jean Piaget, *Moral Judgment of the Child* (New York: Free Press, 1965); Lawrence Kohlberg, *Essays on Moral Development: Vol. 2, The Psychology of Moral Development* (San Francisco: Harper & Row, 1984).

feel in similar situations. At later stages, empathy is cognitively and verbally mediated, the subject responds to more subtle cues, comes to respond to more distant individuals and groups with different values, and directs help to their conditions and painful feelings. At first there is simply spread of affect without differentiation of self from others; then the self is distinguished but assumes emotional states in others like its own and seeks its own relief; then empathy with more complex states is verbally prompted; and finally, the subject can empathize with the chronic distress of distant groups.[13]

What is perceived as moral or immoral behavior, as well as responses to moral and immoral behavior as perceived in others, also develop over time. As noted, immoral behavior is seen at first as what is punished, then as what society or one's group condemns, as its rules are internalized. Subjects at intermediate stages of development will seek to reciprocate perceived benefits or harms to themselves, the motive being to get even, not to treat others kindly or as they would want to be treated, and not to foster meaningful relationships. Fully morally mature individuals accept social norms self-consciously and critically, making exceptions when circumstances morally require them. Their self-identity incorporates a moral identity with a strong sense of personal responsibility to avoid harm and provide help even to those at some distance, physical or social.

As noted, such maturity comes about through interaction with ever-expanding circles of individuals considered as equals even though differing in perspectives or values. If those considered peers or equals comprise only a tightly knit group hostile to outsiders, this restriction can stunt moral development. Morally stunted individuals fail to empathize broadly, instead generalizing classes of people as threats. They also suffer cognitive distortions: mislabeling revenge as justice, blaming others for their own shortcomings, seeing themselves as victims. They typically lack social skills as well, being overly aggressive or submissive. They fail to adopt others' perspectives, remaining focused on their own, or they consider other perspectives only to further their own aims. Finally, to the extent that they judge moral requirements correctly, they lack the will to act on their moral judgments.

---

[13] Hoffman, "Empathy, Its Limitations, and Its Role in a Comprehensive Moral Theory," pp. 285–7.

II

I have noted two ways of revealing the changes that occur in the course of moral development. There is a third way. While psychologists generally interview different subjects of different ages, moral development itself might be best charted by single extended narratives of the same characters. This can be done in novels, and Jane Austen's *Pride and Prejudice* is one of the best, if not the best, examples.[14] The entire text of the novel traces the extended moral development of its two main characters, while the minor characters represent various stages of stunted moral development. This brings out what is not always obvious from the psychological studies of children—that many or most adults fail to judge and act in ways reflective of complete moral maturity (although Kohlberg notes that only about fifteen percent of young adults are at his post-conventional stage).[15]

Austen's main characters are young adults, and the novel ends with a marriage that for them marks the culmination of their moral development. Their actions at earlier points in the novel, as well as the actions of the minor characters, mark the various ways in which moral judgments fail to reflect full maturity. And it is clear from their deficiencies that Austen is aware of all the distinct capacities required for fully mature judgment: empathy, decentrated discerning perception, self-knowledge and recognition of fallibility, a proper attitude toward rules, and the will to act on one's reflectively endorsed judgments made in exercise of these other capacities. While her main characters achieve full moral maturity by the end of the novel, all the others are defective in one or more of these ways. So I shall argue in the remainder of this chapter.

It is perhaps necessary first to offer some excuse for adding to the corpus of Austen critical literature, already a lifetime's worth of reading, and especially for adding to commentaries on this, her most popular novel. The excuse is the lack of adequate treatment of our topic. The vast majority of that critical literature concerns the novel's language, efficient narrative structure, relations to earlier and later works and authors, and social stance. Regarding the latter, most closely related to moral themes, critics over time have been more or less evenly divided as to whether the

---

[14] Jane Austen, *Pride and Prejudice* (New York: Bantam Books, 1981). Page references in the text are to this edition.
[15] Colby and Kohlberg, "Invariant Sequence and Internal Consistency in Moral Judgment Stages," p. 47.

novel is radical or conservative, focusing either on Elizabeth's character or on her marriage to Darcy. Is she a revolutionary early 19th-century female, or does her marriage signal capitulation to the social status quo (even if that status quo reflects the recent rise of the bourgeois class)?

Criticism that revolves around that question tends to see the novel's characters simply as representatives of their social classes. But, as will be clear below, they are far more complex, better seen as individuals, although subject to social stereotyping (a vice recognized by Austen) by others and themselves. Of the philosophers who have written on Austen, most do not focus on *Pride and Prejudice*, and they are most concerned with arguing whether she is best seen as an Aristotelian, a Humean, or a Kantian in general moral outlook.[16] (Not surprisingly, there are elements of all three in her characters, as in all of us.)

Thus, although the theme of moral development is as clear as could be in *Pride and Prejudice* and is noted by many critics, none has described its detailed dramatization in the novel in full and correct terms. Most criticism views the novel as dealing with very limited subject matter in a literarily masterful way, or as interesting in content only for its controversial political or social stance. Critics find no interesting universal moral truths here, only defense of certain (disagreed upon) class and gender values.[17] Jane Austen herself famously described her novel as "too light," and it is the least didactic in style, if not content, of her works.[18] Its famous first sentence indeed sets the tone for the whole: "It is a truth universally acknowledged that a single man in possession of a good fortune must be in want of a wife." The opening clause could come straight from Berkeley, Smith, or Hume, portending philosophical depth to follow; but what follows, setting the amusing ironic tone on several levels, plunges us back into the most mundane of contexts. The double irony lies in the fact that it is the single women who are in want, and, more pertinent for us, in the contrasting clauses that surely warn us not to look for deep philosophy here.

---

[16] The most sustained argument is in E. M. Dadlez, *Mirrors to One Another* (Malden, MA: Wiley-Blackwell, 2009).

[17] See Johanna Smith, "The Oppositional Reader and *Pride and Prejudice*," in L. C. Lambdin and D. T. Lambdin, eds, *A Companion to Jane Austen Studies* (Westport, CT: Greenwood, 2000), p. 27.

[18] So characterized also by Marylin Butler, *Jane Austen and the War of Ideas* (Oxford: Clarendon, 1975), pp. 197, 217.

Such humorous irony continues throughout the novel, both in plot construction and style. The plot, while a conventional Cinderella-type story, turns on ironic reversals in which characters' actions have effects the opposite of what they intend. For example, Elizabeth's barbed attempts to repel Darcy attract him; Lady Catherine's attempt to prevent their union promotes it. Stylistically, whatever profound truths we are to find must be gleaned from informal witty conversations in the context of this wholly conventional plot. But profound truths about moral development are indeed to be found in this novel, its astonishing accuracy in regard to moral development only partially captured in much later diverse psychological studies and philosophical analyses. Beyond the commonplaces that we should strive for self-knowledge and not judge others too quickly, the details of the characters' paths to moral maturity are easily clouded behind the downright funny apparent comedy of manners.

Austen writes of no earthshaking events or larger-than-life heroes. Her characters are unremarkable people in circumstances like ours (albeit in a different historical–social context). Momentous events in their lives are not violent or life-threatening, but such as marriage refusals or letters explaining misunderstood motives. Their personal relationships are the foci of their moral judgments and behavior. This allows us ordinary readers to share their judgments and more easily identify with their developing perspectives. At the same time, their being fictional characters affords us access to their thoughts with a kind of unbiased detachment, which is accentuated by the light touch of the humorous tone (the proper use of humor being itself thematized in this novel, as we shall see).

At the beginning of the story none of the characters has attained ideal or full moral maturity; all are morally lacking in one way or another. The minor characters remain so, each illustrating moral defects that together show Austen's awareness of all that is required of a morally mature person. In regard to the two main characters, Austen does not so much describe their development as reveal it through their changing judgments and actions, allowing us to relive our own process of maturation through their experience, without the extensive superfluous noise and years of real life. Our emotions are engaged, but, as noted, not so strongly as to block clear vision of what is happening, if we reflect carefully enough on this central theme.

III

The narrator's and reader's viewpoint almost throughout is that of Elizabeth Bennet. Wickham is introduced, for example, not by a description of his character, as are her parents before we meet her, but in terms of what she sees in him—his looks and manner. We share her emotional reactions to the other characters, feeling embarrassment for her mother's behavior, amused contempt for Mr. Collins, and resentment at Lady Catherine's slights. Having access to her thoughts, we initially share her mistaken judgments too, delighted by her and her father's acerbic wit, often exercised at the expense of other characters. Judgment of character is the moral focus, and Elizabeth, although priding herself on her ability to so judge, displays all the characteristics of immature moral judgment noted by cognitivists.

Her initial judgments are based on superficial salient appearances and centered on properties related to herself. She judges Wickham, who is handsome, pleasantly mannered, and attentive to her, to be of good character, and Darcy, who declines to dance with her, negatively. Of Wickham she says:

There was truth in his looks... He is, beyond all comparison, the most agreeable man I ever saw... A young man whose very countenance may vouch for being amiable... His countenance, voice, and manner, had established him at once in the possession of every virtue. (65, 108, 61, 154)

Clearly she is focused on superficial appearance as the key to character. With Darcy in conversation she is witty, but also overly aggressive and defensive, as in a conversation during their first dance:

I have always seen a great similarity in the turn of our minds—We are each of an unsocial, taciturn disposition, unwilling to speak, unless we expect to say something that will amaze the whole room, and be handed down to posterity with all the éclat of a proverb. (69)

The verdict after first meeting Darcy mistakes his reserved manner for pure disdain and snobbery, and is based on his inadvertent insult to her appearance and her resentment of his stereotyped social class: "I could easily forgive *his* pride, if he had not mortified mine" (13). And speaking negatively of him to others both assuages her wounded pride and, as she later admits, provides "such a spur to one's genius, such an opening for wit to have a dislike of that kind" (168), again self-centered motives.

She admits that in making Darcy the constant brunt of her humor, "she meant to be uncommonly clever in taking so decided a dislike to him, without any reason" (168). She constantly misjudges his motives, misperceiving his interest in her as intent to ridicule. Finally, she blames him for the shortcomings of her relations, for judging the behavior of her family members negatively, when such judgment is warranted. She is once more guilty of the immature cognitive errors of mislabeling, having a narrow self-centered perspective, and failing to take adequate account of motives and intentions.

Having rushed to judgment of Wickham and Darcy, she persists, remaining selectively biased in taking in evidence, failing to note inconsistencies in Wickham's hostile testimony regarding Darcy (he says he would not speak ill of or avoid him and then does both). She refuses to blame Wickham or change her positive opinion of him even after learning of his pursuit of the recently rich Miss King:

A man in distressed circumstances has not time for all those elegant decorums, which other people may observe. If *she* does not object to it, why should *we*? (115)

And she continues to misjudge Darcy's motives even after changing her opinion of him, thinking, for example, that her sister Lydia's elopement will separate them when it actually helps to bring them together.

But, as noted, Elizabeth is not a child, nor is she a simple character. Her reactions and judgments are more complex than those of a child, and when she is not personally involved with another character, her judgments are more accurate, and her behavior reflects some already acquired moral values. She quickly sees through Caroline Bingley's hypocrisy, as her sister Jane does not, and she immediately recognizes Mr. Collins as the pompous yet sycophantic fool that he is. Her rejection of his marriage proposal demonstrates a refusal to place material comfort over personal integrity, and even her rejection of Darcy's first proposal shows that her judgment of his moral character, however mistaken, is more important to her than great wealth. She is equally shocked by her friend Charlotte's marriage for money and Lydia's elopement for sexual passion. And she knows in the abstract that knowledge of character requires long and careful unbiased perception. She notes that Jane's having known Bingley for two weeks is insufficient for such judgment of character:

She has known him only a fortnight. She danced four dances with him at Meryton; she saw him one morning at his own house, and has since dined in company with him four times. That is not quite enough to make her understand his character. (15)

She expresses this ironically to Jane in praising his handsomeness as an accomplishment or moral virtue:

He is also handsome, which a young man ought likewise to be, if he possibly can. His character is thereby complete. (9)

Yet, as indicated, she cannot help judging Wickham and Darcy in just the way she disinterestedly condemns. When personally involved, her judgments remain self-centered and focused on salient appearances and stereotypes, the cognitive marks of moral immaturity. As noted, she fails to note contradictions in the statements and attitudes of both Wickham and herself (she is embarrassed by the behavior of her family members but cannot recognize Darcy's criticisms of them as warranted), and she cannot balance Darcy's good qualities against his shortcomings. Emotionally, we find similar symptoms. While she feels strongly for those within her narrow circle, empathically sharing the pleasures and disappointments of her sister Jane and feeling sympathy for her friend Charlotte, she misreads both her own feelings and others' and projects her emotional perspective onto others who do not share it. She projects her own values onto Charlotte and therefore cannot imagine her acceptance of Mr. Collins, mistaking Charlotte's encouragement of him as kindness in distracting his attention from her. She ascribes her own feelings to Charlotte despite the fact that, unlike her, Charlotte is plain and completely lacking in other prospects for escaping a life of loneliness and material want.

In relation to Darcy, her misperceptions of his character are matched by misreadings of both his feelings and her own. Feeling both antagonism and attraction to him, she is unaware of the attraction and projects her antagonism onto him, refusing to recognize his attraction to her, perhaps out of fear of disappointment. Thus, she is completely shocked by his proposal of marriage:

Her astonishment, as she reflected on what had passed, was increased by every review of it. That she should receive an offer of marriage from Mr. Darcy! that he should have been in love with her for so many months! So much in love as to wish to marry her in spite of all the objections which had made him prevent his friend's marrying her sister, and which must appear at least with equal force in his own case, was almost incredible! (145)

Thus, early on in the novel we find all the marks of both cognitive and emotional moral immaturity in Elizabeth, and the typical interaction between the two types of moral deficiency. Self-centered misperception and social stereotyping lead to lack of empathy, which blocks correction of the misperceptions. And her attitudes toward rules of socially acceptable behavior are equally mixed and mostly immature. She implicitly knows when such rules must be violated for more weighty moral reasons, but her acknowledgment of their force on other occasions is less than ideal. Her long walk to tend to her sick sister justifiably ignores norms of the time, but at other times her barbed wit exceeds the bounds of etiquette (while entertaining the reader). The sharp sense of humor, along with the ability to quickly perceive weaknesses in others which she can attack with sophisticated irony, she inherits from her father (and from Austen). What she cannot internalize from her parents is proper respect for social norms, since they themselves lack this component of moral maturity. Missing the usual parental rules as guidance, her moral development must be fueled by other sources.

IV

Before describing what those catalysts are in Elizabeth's case, we may note again the complex abilities involved in mature moral judgments, especially judgments of other people's characters, the focus here. I have said that we experience Elizabeth's moral growth in tending to share her early judgments (although we may well have an inkling of the outcome early on). We, along with her, must engage in the difficult task of interpreting the behavior of the other characters, including prominently their judgments of each other, to discern the morally relevant features of their behavior. We must judge them by how they judge others, and this again requires both empathy and fine-tuned perception. The process is well illustrated by our reaction to the lively exchange between Elizabeth and Darcy on the character of Bingley (37). Darcy criticizes his friend for being too pliable. Elizabeth interprets this trait in Bingley as sweetness and praises him for it, while Bingley himself wants only to end the

dispute. We react to their assessments of Bingley's easily persuadable disposition and assess them accordingly, as they react to each other's assessments and Bingley reacts to them.[19]

As these characters are themselves complex, our developing assessments
of them cannot be black and white. When Elizabeth rejects Darcy's first
proposal, for example, we must feel ambivalent toward both: anger toward
her for continuing to misjudge him, approval for rejecting him on principle, and sympathy for seemingly losing a chance at great happiness; anger
at him for continuing to express snobbery in the proposal itself and for
being confident of her acceptance, sympathy for being rejected, and satisfaction that his supercilious attitude has been brought home to him, however painfully. As these mixed feelings guide our judgments at this turning
point in the novel, we recognize the difficult task faced by the characters in
developing the capacity for mature and accurate judgment themselves.

Large steps in the developmental process are often initiated by momentous events in a life, especially those that challenge a person's self-image,
reveal major errors in earlier judgments, or broaden the circle of those
demanding respect. So it is in this novel. Darcy's letter to Elizabeth following her rejection of him has all three effects, although the developmental process it prompts is slow and extends over the second half of the
novel. Indeed, the initial effect is to slow her usual judgmental process. In a break with her previous practice, on a solitary walk she reflects
long and carefully on the letter itself, reinterpreting earlier events (as we
reinterpret the earlier text) and beginning to correct its earlier narrative, especially regarding the relation of Darcy to Wickham. Once more,
moral perception involves interpreting actions and language in order to
judge character, so that Elizabeth's moral maturation is epitomized in her
changed judgment of Darcy's character.

The complete reversal is brought about gradually through a series of
events and new perceptions following the letter: her perception of the
unpretentious beauty of Pemberly in contrast to the ostentation of Lady
Catherine, the testimony of Darcy's housekeeper as to how he treats
dependents, his changed manner toward her aunt and uncle, and finally
his humbling actions in the Lydia affair. Sharp verbal challenges to her earlier perspective are complemented by his role in this implicitly cooperative

---

[19] Compare Jan Fergus, "The Comedy of Manners," in Harold Bloom, ed., *Jane
Austen's Pride and Prejudice* (New York: Chelsea House, 1987), p. 123.

endeavor. By taking account of this broader base of evidence, expanding her perspective beyond its initial focus on his reserved appearance and insult to her, she comes to consider and better appreciate his motives and justifications for criticizing her mother and younger sisters and separating Jane and Bingley:

Neither could she deny the justice of his description of Jane. She felt that Jane's feelings, though fervent, were little displayed ... When she came to that part of the letter in which her family were mentioned, in terms of such mortifying, yet merited reproach, her sense of shame was severe. The justice of the charge struck her too forcibly for denial. (156)

So we see the marks of moral maturity emerge: the ability to weigh conflicting evidence, overcome stereotypes, and take into account hidden motives and intentions. But again the process is gradual and proceeds in steps. Having changed her feelings toward Darcy, gradually becoming concerned for his interests, she must still learn to infer motives more accurately and to act on her moral perceptions. As noted earlier, she continues to misjudge his reactions to Lydia's elopement, thinking that he will certainly end their relationship:

Her power was sinking; everything *must* sink under such a proof of family weakness, such an assurance of the deepest disgrace ... never had she so honestly felt that she could have loved him as now, when all love must be vain. (205)

Likewise, she badly misjudges his reaction to Lady Catherine's interference:

It was certain that in enumerating the miseries of a marriage with *one*, whose immediate connections were so unequal to his own, his aunt would address him on his weakest side. With his notions of dignity, he would probably feel that the arguments, which to Elizabeth had appeared weak and ridiculous, contained much good sense and solid reasoning. (270)

Finally, having learned of Wickam's true character, she fails to act on her knowledge by warning her family to avoid him, a failure she later bitterly regrets:

"When I consider," she added, in a yet more agitated voice, "that *I* might have prevented it!—*I* who knew what he was. Had I but explained some part of it only—some part of what I learned to my own family! Had his character been known, this could not have happened." (205)

Despite the mutual reinforcement of judgments, feelings, and actions, these are all separate steps on the path to moral maturity, as Austen dramatically illustrates. They are prompted by the necessity of recognizing the different perspective and demand for respect of another person and subsequent changing of self-image and broadening of one's own perspective.

Elizabeth expresses her own change of self-image in moral–perceptual terms:

Of neither Darcy nor Wickham could she think without feeling that she had been blind... "Had I been in love, I could not have been more wretchedly blind. But vanity, not love, has been my folly." (156)

The change in perceptions and feelings brings other changes symptomatic of greater moral maturity. She comes to know better when social rules must be adhered to and when they must be ignored. Ignoring rules of etiquette and deference to higher social class, she is unrestrained in her rebuke of Lady Catherine:

Allow me to say, Lady Catherine, that the arguments with which you have supported this extraordinary application have been as frivolous as the application was ill-judged. (267)

She seeks to find out Darcy's secret role in the Lydia affair when she knows that it is not socially permissible to seek such confidential information. Yet she restrains herself when Bingley's sister continues to provoke her in the presence of Darcy and his sister. And the aggressive wit that amused us in the first half of the novel when used as a weapon becomes much toned down in the second half:

how heartily did she grieve over every ungracious sensation she had ever encouraged, every saucy speech she had ever directed towards him. (243)

This makes for a less charming remainder of the novel but for a more morally responsible character.

V

As noted, Darcy undergoes a somewhat similar transformation, although from the opposite social perspective. I can be briefer here, since his development, as opposed to Elizabeth's, takes place mostly offstage. We see his transformation through her eyes, our evidence of his change being his letter to her and his actions toward her family. Because we see it only second- or third-hand, it is likely to seem somewhat less believable than the change in her. His initial judgments are, like hers, self-centered, superficial, based on stereotypes, and defensive, in his case an excuse for social ineptitude based on natural reserve and shyness. Blinded by her social class, he cannot see Jane's true good nature or motives. Thinking her a social climber, he keeps Bingley from her, blind also to the consequences of his action. He finds country people boring. When Elizabeth speaks of studying character, he responds:

The country can in general supply but few subjects for such a study. In a country neighborhood you move in a very confined and unvarying society. (31)

Despite early attraction to Elizabeth, his disdain for her family prevents his seriously considering her a possible match:

Darcy had never been so bewitched by any woman as he was by her. He really believed that were it not for the inferiority of her connections, he should be in some danger. (38)

When he does come to consider a proposal to her, he cannot conceive that he might not be accepted.

He admits that while, unlike Elizabeth's parents, his parents taught him rules of proper conduct, they never encouraged empathy with those of lower social classes:

As a child I was taught what was *right*, but I was not taught to correct my temper. I was given good principles, but left to follow them in pride and conceit...my parents...allowed, encouraged, almost taught me to be selfish and overbearing, to care for none beyond my own family circle, to think meanly of all the rest of the world. (276–7)

He clearly comes to recognize, and we therefore see, that knowing what is right and internalizing social rules are not sufficient for moral maturity: we must also feel for those affected by our actions and act accordingly.

But, like Elizabeth, he has even before his transformation some rudiments of sound moral character, as we see from his embarrassment at his aunt's treatment of Charlotte: "Mr. Darcy looked a little ashamed of his aunt's ill breeding, and made no answer" (130). He is, like Elizabeth, a young adult, partially socialized but still requiring further moral development. He is less quick to judge character than is Elizabeth from the beginning, ending the discussion of Bingley's character by pointing out that correct judgment of an action requires full knowledge of motives and circumstances:

Will it not be advisable before we proceed on this subject to arrange with rather more precision the degree of importance which is to appertain to this request, as well as the degree of intimacy subsisting between the parties? (37)[20]

It is his empathic feeling for others different from him that most needs maturation. He immediately contrasts with Wickham, having a rougher exterior but better interior character, but his character too is not fully developed until the end of the novel.

His perspective, initially limited to a narrow circle of upper-class family and friends, begins to broaden through the encounters with Elizabeth, who addresses him as a person and indeed as an equal and adversary, unlike the usual sycophantic language of Mr. Collins and Caroline Bingley, who sees him only as a most desirable catch. Attracted rather than repelled by his sharp exchanges with Elizabeth, his real change is again prompted by the first climactic event in the novel, his first proposal and her rejection. Although inept, ultimately insulting, and still focused on her social class and family, he shows himself in his clipped and emotion-filled language for the first time here capable of strong feeling (in clear contrast to Mr. Collins' proposal):

In vain have I struggled. It will not do. My feelings will not be repressed. You must allow me to tell you how ardently I admire and love you. (142)

Her refusal, like his letter to her, provokes serious self-reflection, and the consequent moral transformation is again a slow and somewhat painful process. Recalling the words she used, he admits:

You know not, you can scarcely conceive, how they have tortured me; though it was some time, I confess, before I was reasonable enough to allow their justice. (275)

It takes him a long time also to admit his moral error in keeping Jane from Bingley: "On the evening before going to London, I made a confession to him, which I believe I ought to have made long ago" (278). But after seeing from the Gardiners as well as from Elizabeth that members of

[20] The import of this passage is noted also by Tobin Siebers, *Morals and Stories* (New York: Columbia University Press, 1992), p. 149.

the middle class need not be coarse or sycophantic, his focus shifts from his own social status to the needs of others. Ultimately, he is willing to sacrifice his own family honor to save Elizabeth's family from disgrace.

It is a common assumption that, as in Austen's closest other novel, *Sense and Sensibility*, each of these main characters exemplifies one of the title properties: he pride and she prejudice.[21] This assumption is reinforced by their accusations to each other: "Your defect is a propensity to hate everybody" (said by Elizabeth to Darcy), "And yours is to willfully misunderstand them" (43). But in fact he also misunderstands her and Jane, and she is proud of her intelligence, wit, and capacity for quick judgment. Both early exemplify both vices, and these defects in them all derive from a morally immature, narrowly focused, self-centered, and superficial perspective. Unable to perceive inner character or motives, their judgments are based on superficial appearances and social stereotypes. Their misperceptions causally interact with their lack of empathy for those outside their narrow circles, and these are all the marks of the morally immature.

Their hypercritical judgments of other characters change as their hypocritical judgments of themselves do, prompted by at first witty and then frank and angry exchanges with each other, ultimately forcing recognition of the other's very different perspective.[22] In the climactic first proposal scene, both violate social norms of courtesy that previously partially constrained their exchanges. The shock to his self-image produced by her brutal frankness is clear: "And this is your opinion of me!" (144). The shock to her self-image comes with his letter that immediately follows: "'How despicably I have acted,' she cried. 'I, who have prided myself on my discernment!'" (156).

The transformative broadening of perspectives, aided by subsequent exchanges with other characters to whose testimony they become open, occurs, as noted, gradually, as both characters recognize. Like Darcy, speaking of her rebuke, she admits "how gradually all her former prejudices had been removed" (276). Neither immediately acts on their changed perceptions, she failing to reveal Wickham's character and he

---

[21] See, for example, Stuart Tave, "What Are Men to Rocks and Mountains?," in Harold Bloom, ed., *Jane Austen's Pride and Prejudice* (New York: Infobase, 2007), p. 39.

[22] Compare Richard Eldridge, *On Moral Personhood* (Chicago: Chicago University Press, 1989), pp. 173–4.

failing to reveal his prior actions to Bingley. Their moral journey is symbolized, as is often the case in this sort of novel, by their slow physical journeys from place to place, the low point occurring at the Netherfield ball (as its name implies), and the culmination at Pemberly. The slowness of the developmental process, emphasized by Austen, once more underlines the number of distinct capacities she recognizes to be required for full moral maturity.

VI

Austen's awareness of these distinct capacities is indicated as well by her depictions of the minor characters, all of whom remain defective in one way or another. They are not always simple caricatures, as are Mr. Collins and Lady Catherine, but even when complex, they do not change, and each represents some form of stunted moral growth. Jane is a naturally kind person, but she lacks the capacity for accurate moral discrimination, as she mistakenly ascribes her own good motives to others. For this reason she can be easily taken advantage of, as her father points out, and she might inadvertently allow others to be exploited as well. She cannot recognize the hypocrisy of Caroline Bingley, and even after it becomes painfully obvious, she attributes it to affection for her brother instead of interest in Darcy:

I pity her, because she must feel that she has been acting wrong, and because I am very sure that anxiety for her brother is the cause of it. (111)

Similarly, she cannot discern the lack of character in Wickham. She feels shame for Lydia and thinks she must be miserable when she is happy as a lark:

Jane more especially, who gave Lydia the feelings which would have attended herself, had *she* been the culprit, was wretched in the thought of what her sister must endure. (234)

Finally, she cannot even see how obviously foolish Mr. Collins is, fully defending Charlotte's choice to marry him. Benevolence or natural kindness without moral perceptiveness is shown here to be insufficient for moral maturity, as Jane could not be relied upon to defend possible victims of the unscrupulous. Even empathy must be properly discriminating if it is to lead to correct moral judgment, as Austen shows here.

Mr. Bennet suffers from a different kind of stunted moral development. He is when young all passion and no thought or perception in his choice of a wife:

Her father, captivated by youth and beauty, and that appearance of good humor which youth and beauty generally give, had married a woman whose weak understanding and illiberal mind had very early in their marriage put an end to all real affection for her. (176)

But his disastrous marriage leads later to a suppression of all emotion, the adoption of a detached, cynical attitude toward the world, and a retreat to the safety of his library. He is quick to perceive the foibles and weaknesses of others, and we delight in his ironic wit in ridiculing them, but he suffers from an acute inability to act, even to protect the vital interests of his family.

Even in the face of Lydia's potentially catastrophic elopement, he makes only a feeble effort to ameliorate the situation and withdraws with great relief. He makes light of Jane's distress and shows emotion only one time in the novel, when he believes Elizabeth to be making the same mistake that he did in choosing a spouse. His only release otherwise is the acerbic wit with which he attacks even his own wife and younger daughters. The final ingredient in full moral development, strength of will to act on one's moral perceptions, is completely lacking in Mr. Bennet.

The other minor characters make neat contrasts. While Lydia and Mrs. Bennet are all self-centered emotion and completely lacking in judgment, Charlotte and Mary judge without any feelings to animate or guide their responses. Mrs. Bennet's judgments are all based on the single motive of marrying her daughters into money, as her changing attitudes toward Darcy show. And the wealth she seeks for them is not to guarantee their security, but to acquire superficial material possessions, such as clothes and carriages. Her atrocious manners mirror Lady Catherine's from the opposite side of the social spectrum, showing that social stupidity is not restricted to any one economic class.

Lydia is described as "having high animal spirits," as "untamed, unabashed, and wild," and more significantly, as "silly" (173), the latter term indicating the moral immaturity that encompasses the other characteristics as well. Elizabeth complains of her "wild volatility, the assurance and disdain of all restraint which mark Lydia's character" (173). She is not restrained by any social conventions, not because she is critical of them or sensitive to their justified exceptions, but because she has not reached the stage of recognizing them at all.

On the other side of the emotional spectrum, Mary can only mouth inanities from the books she reads in situations that call for empathy or other moral emotions. Even in reaction to Lydia's disgrace, she can only paraphrase from her stock of moral epithets:

"we must stem the tide of malice, and pour into the wounded bosoms of each other the balm of sisterly consolation" . . . Mary continued to console herself with such kind of moral extractions from the evil before them. (214)

Her piano playing is mechanical and by rote, complementing her bookish pedantry and equally revealing of her lack of emotional development.

Charlotte is more complex. While her acceptance of Mr. Collins sacrifices all feeling to a cold recognition of her meager life prospects and therefore appalls Elizabeth, her self-perception and grasp of her situation is not unrealistic. She is physically unattractive and without economic means for the future, which does not make the prospect of sleeping with Mr. Collins any less repulsive, but does make her more of a tragic than a morally undeveloped character.[23] Her chief roles in the novel are both to condemn the social situation of women like her and to bring out the moral immaturity of Elizabeth in failing to accurately empathize with her.

The most one-dimensional characters are the highly comical Mr. Collins and Lady Catherine, and the villain of the story, Wickham. They too, of course, exemplify lack of moral development: Mr. Collins, with his obsequious, overwrought manners and language, and Lady Catherine, with her intolerable, overbearing, self-centered interference. His total lack of moral feeling is most comically portrayed in his proposal to Elizabeth, in which he lists the "violence of my affection" last among his many reasons for marrying (81). Lady Catherine exemplifies not only lack of empathy and manners, but humorously illustrates again the requirement of will and action when she declares that she would have been a great musician if she had ever learned to play (130). And both lack social skills connected with moral maturity: he being both overly

---

[23] Most critics nevertheless blame Charlotte for lack of feeling. See, for example, Susan Morgan, "Intelligence in Pride and Prejudice," in Harold Bloom, ed., *Jane Austen's Pride and Prejudice* (New York: Chelsea House, 1987), pp. 96–7.

aggressive on rare occasions (for example, in his advice never to forgive Lydia) and overly submissive more often; she being always overbearing.

Finally, Wickham is devoid of moral motives entirely, despite his polished manners and acute perceptions of others' vulnerabilities to serving his own interests. He quickly senses Elizabeth's early dislike of Darcy, knows that Darcy's character will make him reluctant to expose their history, and uses both bits of knowledge to his advantage. He acts from both strong emotions (compulsive in his gambling) and accurate perceptions, but they are entirely self-centered and narrowly focused. He also exemplifies the typical cognitive distortions of the morally stunted, seeing himself as a victim and blaming Darcy for his own self-destructive actions. Each of these characters, then, illustrates one or more symptoms of underdeveloped moral personality, making clear again Austen's thematization of the nature of full moral development.

VII

Just as the life-changing events in the lives of these characters are the sorts of events we readers experience in our lives, so for Austen the arena for moral activity is not that of heroic acts toward strangers, but the meaningful intimate personal relationships into which we enter. The most intimate and intricate of these relationships is marriage, which, despite the doubts of feminist critics, at its best makes a perfect match between a social institution and our deepest personal needs and moral capacities. *Pride and Prejudice* therefore ends with the marriage of Elizabeth and Darcy as the culmination of their moral development, the main theme of the novel. At the end we get no real description of their married life, just a brief review of their now broadened circle of friends. But we can surmise that their union will be a rare complete success, since it is based on a solid foundation: equal intelligence, shared values and mutual interests (reading, music, nature), complementary personalities, self-respect and respect for each other based on a history of reciprocal growth, and deep emotional attachment.

Austen describes this deep bond as based on "gratitude and esteem" (206). As a ground for a loving relationship, this description will sound cold and detached to readers accustomed to romantic novels. But for Austen such cognitively based emotion is deeper than sexual attraction based on appearance, and it epitomizes mutual understanding and appreciation of character, the moral foundation that for her must ground a successful relationship. Such a relationship once more marks the individuals' arrival at full moral maturity. In this novel this consummation of the moral growth of Elizabeth and Darcy contrasts with the marriage for money of Charlotte and the marriages for sexual passion of the Bennets and Lydia. The former is devoid of feeling and a symptom of the oppression of women. The latter are blind. Both are again marks of moral immaturity, absent the kind of necessity that might explain Charlotte's marriage.

Only a proper mix of knowledge-based perception and emotion, both empathic and affectionate, produces a solid basis for a lasting, mutually beneficial relationship. Only the kind of marriage founded on mutual respect and esteem, following criticism and self-examination, fulfills the highest possibility of interpersonal relationship for autonomous, morally mature individuals. Their marriage is then a fitting end to the novel as the culmination of Elizabeth's and Darcy's moral development.

VIII

I will end this discussion with a brief summary. Moral maturity, we noted, requires first, decentered or broadly focused perceptiveness that can weigh such nonsuperficial properties as intentions and distant effects; second, empathy with persons having different values and motives; third, an accurate self-image and strength of will to act on reflective moral judgments; and fourth, the critical acceptance of social rules along with the capacity to make exceptions when necessary. Morally immature subjects remain fixated on superficial properties related to themselves, ascribe their own feelings to others who might not share them, fail to obey rules when they should and obey them when they should not, blame others for their failures and shortcomings, lack social skills, and lack the resolve to do what is right at the expense of their other self-regarding interests. The moral development of the main characters in *Pride and Prejudice*, along with the deficiencies of the minor characters, demonstrate Jane Austen's awareness of all these factors, only partially captured in later theories of moral development and judgment. She is also aware of the mechanisms behind such development, principally the broadening of interactions, both adversarial and cooperative, with other persons demanding respect and calling into question one's own initially self-centered perspective.

In dramatizing throughout the novel the development in ordinary circumstances of her fictional characters with whom we imaginatively engage, Austen allows us to retrace our own moral growth and to identify contexts in which we exercise full moral maturity and those in which we fail to do so. In addition to seeing the interactions among perceptions, feelings, and will, we come to see proper pride, acceptance of social convention, and use of humor as means between morally defective extremes: pride as ego strength between self-centered vice and moral weakness, critical acceptance of rules between blind obedience and wanton lack of discipline, and humor toward others and oneself between a cynical or hostile detachment and a dull or self-important gravity. We come to see all these necessary components of moral maturity most clearly by seeing what is missing when Austen's characters act in morally immature ways. As Elizabeth most succinctly summarizes:

without scheming to do wrong, or to make others unhappy, there may be error, and there may be misery. Thoughtlessness, want of attention to other people's feelings, and want of resolution, will do the business. (102)

Reasoned perception, empathy, and will are the ends of moral development, as *Pride and Prejudice* revealed long before experimental psychology.

6

Huckleberry Finn and moral motivation

I

In the previous chapter I focused on the theme of moral development in the main characters in *Pride and Prejudice*. That theme is prominent as well in *Huckleberry Finn*, the moral development of its main character again being a major part of the story. And that development once more in the absence of parental guidance consists in the broadening of the character's perspective to encompass that of the other main character, initially negatively socially stereotyped, in this case so as to deny his very humanity. Once more, like Elizabeth Bennet with Darcy, Huck Finn is forced to acknowledge Jim's perspective through personal interactions and sharp verbal exchanges that make him see how narrow his initial viewpoint is and how humane Jim is. In one such exchange Jim berates Huck for playing a trick on him:

My heart wuz mos' broke bekase you wuz los', en I didn' k'yer no' mo' what become er me en de raf.' En when I wake up en fine you back ag'in, all safe en soun', de tears come ... en all you wuz thinkin' 'bout wuz how you could make a fool uv ole Jim wid a lie ... trash is what people is dat puts dirt on de head er dey fren's en makes 'em ashamed.

Huck responds:

It was fifteen minutes before I could work myself up to go and humble myself to a nigger; but I done it, and I warn't ever sorry for it afterward, neither.[1]

[1] Mark Twain, *Huckleberry Finn* (New York: Book-of-the-Month Club, 1992), pp. 119–20.

As in Elizabeth's case, Huck's moral transformation comes to fruition in a morally momentous situation, in this case when he is faced with the choice of turning in the runaway slave or keeping him hidden from a group of pursuers. In this situation, like Elizabeth after she receives Darcy's letter, isolated from corrupting family and social influences, Huck must assess his self-image and assert a new moral identity, although his self-assessment is not as self-conscious and deliberative as in her case. Finally, like her he comes to express a properly critical attitude toward conventional social norms, more dramatically once more since he is faced with a totally corrupt set of "moral" rules governing the ownership of slaves. His attitude, like hers, is in the service not of self-interest, but of a higher morality.

Instead of continuing to note the parallels between the two novels in articulating the theme of moral development, I will focus here on the topic of moral motivation. I noted in the previous chapter that a fully developed moral agent must be motivated to act on moral reasons of which she is aware, that a lack in this regard indicated the stunted moral growth of Mr. Bennet. Full moral maturity may require one to act against both self-interest and conventional social rules. A fully morally developed character such as Darcy at the end of that novel must identify with his moral emotions so that moral considerations can override other conflicting motives. Moral motivation is a distinct requirement of full moral development, but is it also a requirement of rationality? Must fully developed rational agents be morally motivated, as fully developed moral agents must be?

Many philosophers have claimed following Kant that moral motivation is rationally required, that rational agents must be motivated to act on their moral judgments or must be concerned for the interests of others. I will argue here that Huck Finn shows us otherwise. I will argue against several prominent interpretations that Huck is not irrational at the crucial relevant points in the novel. In one sense he is not morally motivated either, showing directly that moral motivation in that sense is not rationally required. In another sense he is morally motivated, but the nature of his motivational state is such that it is not rationally required either. The philosophically interesting conclusion is that, since Huck Finn is a rational agent who is not morally motivated in any way that is rationally required, and since there is no other normal route to moral motivation than the one he takes, such motivation is itself not required of rational agents.

In the first half of this chapter I will argue that Huck is not irrational in being unmotivated to follow his explicit judgments of rightness and wrongness. It follows, of course, that rational agents need not be so motivated. As opposed to my view, philosophers have previously judged Huck to be irrational, subject to weakness of will, in being unable to act on his moral judgment. But their interpretation rests on incorrect analyses of weak will and of the emotions on which Huck does act. I will also argue that, surprisingly, my refutation of moral judgment internalism, the thesis that these judgments must be motivating for agents, including rational agents who sincerely make them, does not eliminate expressivism as a meta-ethical theory, the theory that moral judgments express emotions. We can save expressivism in large part despite denying motivational force to all moral judgments by drawing a distinction between core judgments and others.

In the second half of the chapter I will describe the way in which Huck is morally motivated by his sympathetic feeling toward his friend, the runaway slave Jim, but will argue that such emotion-based motivation is not of the kind that could be rationally required. This will necessitate a brief examination of the relation of emotions to reasons. I will show that Huck's emotion of sympathy reflects awareness of moral reasons without itself being required by them. Having this emotion, he is inconsistent in several ways in his moral attitudes, but I will maintain that this inconsistency does not amount to irrationality. I will demonstrate as well that Huck's route to moral motivation is in an important sense the usual one, as is his view of the source of moral requirements, although the relation between the two is certainly unusual in his case. The thesis that rational agents need not be morally motivated is both philosophically controversial and interesting, as well as implied by the character of Huckleberry Finn.

II

In borrowing his moral judgments from corrupt sources, Huck Finn justifiably fails to be moved by them, although he accepts their status as reflecting genuine moral requirements. He sincerely believes in a strict moral requirement to return all stolen property to its rightful owner, and he believes that his friend Jim, a runaway slave, is rightfully owned. He therefore accepts that he has a moral obligation to return Jim to his owner. But having become Jim's friend on the raft they share, when the opportunity arises to turn him in, Huck finds himself unable to do so. He paddles from the raft toward shore with the intention of turning Jim in, but when two men approach in a boat searching for escaped slaves and asking Huck whether the man in his raft is black or white, Huck can't bring himself to tell the truth:

I see I was weakening; so I just give up trying and says—"He's white."[2]

And when they decide to check, he hints that the man on the raft has smallpox, driving them off. Returning to the raft and feeling guilty, but knowing he would have felt as badly if he had betrayed Jim, Huck renounces morality:

What's the use you learning to do right when it's troublesome to do right and ain't no trouble to do wrong, and the wages is just the same?[3]

Almost two hundred pages later, Huck is again feeling guilty for helping Jim escape, and he writes a note to Miss Watson, Jim's owner, revealing his whereabouts. But once more he finds that he cannot mail the note:

"All right, then, I'll *go* to hell"—and tore it up...I would take up wickedness again, which was in my line, being brung up to it, and the other warn't...as long as I was in, and in for good, I might as well go the whole hog.[4]

He again decides to wash his hands entirely of moral requirements as he sees them and risk an eternity in hell. Having renounced morality, it is not that his desire to help Jim overrides his motivation to follow his moral judgments: he has no remaining motivation to do what he believes morality requires. If Huck is rational in this attitude, then rational agents need not be motivated at all by their explicit judgments of rightness and wrongness.

Prominent earlier interpretations of the text by philosophers, however, see Huck as irrational in failing to turn in Jim, as a victim of weak will, a paradigm form of irrationality. If Huck's decision is irrational given his moral attitudes and judgments, then, of course, his case fails to show that rational agents need not be morally motivated. In his seminal article on the topic, Jonathan Bennett sees Huck as weak-willed in being unable to resist acting on his feeling of sympathy for Jim, as opposed

---

[2] Twain, *Huckleberry Finn*, p. 125.
[3] Twain, *Huckleberry Finn*, p. 128.
[4] Twain, *Huckleberry Finn*, p. 297.

to his considered, even if bad, judgment of what is morally required of him.[5] A bare feeling propels him to act against his moral principles, however corrupt those principles may be. Feelings for Bennett are themselves irrational (he might have better said arational), while moral reasons derive from principles that enter into deliberation about what one ought to do. Huck does not deliberate and does not view his feeling for Jim as providing him with any moral reasons. He simply cannot resist acting on his feeling against his moral judgment. The moral reasons as he sees them all lie on one side; only an irrational feeling opposes them. He is weak-willed according to Bennett in acting against what he takes to be his strongest, indeed in the circumstances, his only reasons.

In a much more recent article, Nomy Arpaly and Timothy Schroeder agree that Huck is weak-willed, albeit commendably so, in that he believes one action to be right and yet does another. He is incapable of doing what he judges to be overall right, and this meets the definition of irrational weakness of will.[6] They call his weakness "inverse akrasia," since it reflects well on his character, unlike the ordinary case. But it is still weakness of will, and therefore presumably irrational. He is "psychologically incapable of doing what he believes to be the right thing,"[7] and this psychological incapacity prevents him from doing what is rational, given his beliefs. They recognize that "Huckleberry is praiseworthy because he is averse to turning Jim in for morally significant reasons,"[8] that he is not simply squeamish or motivated by fear, but they still characterize him as weak-willed, a paradigm of irrational behavior.[9]

But this interpretation of Huck as irrational rests on a simplistic view of emotions in Bennett's case (he refers to them as "unreasoned emotional pulls"), and on an incorrect definition of weakness of will. Regarding the latter, weakness of will is not best characterized simply as failure to do what one explicitly or consciously believes one ought to do, but instead

---

[5] Jonathan Bennett, "The Conscience of Huckleberry Finn," *Philosophy*, 49 (1974): 123–34.

[6] Nomy Arpaly and Timothy Schroeder, "Praise, Blame and the Whole Self," *Philosophical Studies*, 93 (1999): 161–88.

[7] Arpaly and Schroeder, "Praise, Blame and the Whole Self," p. 162.

[8] Arpaly and Schroeder, "Praise, Blame and the Whole Self," p. 164.

[9] Despite disagreeing with their characterization of Huck, I agree with their thesis later in the paper that selves are to be identified with integrated or coherent sets of motivational states. My endorsement of this view will become clear in the final chapter. See also my *Reasons from Within* (Oxford: Oxford University Press, 2009), pp. 235–6.

as failure, usually resulting from an irresistible bare urge, to act on the strongest reasons of which one is in some sense aware. When agents suffer from this malady, they feel torn by conflicting motivations and unable to muster the courage to act on their strongest reasons or to resist the urge to take the easy way out. Neither of these descriptions fits Huck Finn. He requires courage *not* to turn his friend in, and continuing to hide him is not the easy way out for Huck or the way of least resistance to an urge.

In regard to his emotion of sympathy, it is not a bare feeling or urge. Even if we are not cognitivists about all emotions, we should recognize that intentional emotions, those directed at persons or objects, represent their objects as having certain properties. They contain implicit judgments,[10] and therefore an implicit awareness of reasons when the judgments are correct. Sympathy is such an emotion.

It is true that these judgments implicit in emotions do not typically arise from or alter in response to reasons in the way that conscious judgments or beliefs do. In fact, the adaptive value of emotions lies precisely in their bypassing ordinary rational deliberation in prompting more automatic and immediate reactions.[11] Nevertheless, these implicit judgments may be seen to reflect an awareness of reasons when the emotions are fitting or appropriate reactions to their objects. In bypassing rational deliberation or weighing of reasons, emotions can threaten or defeat rational judgment, but they can also implicitly embody the contents of such judgments.

When I fear a large snake, this fear causes me to flee immediately without deliberating about the reasons for doing so (and this may be a good thing for me). Nor does my fear necessarily disappear if I learn that the snake is not dangerous and therefore gives me no reason to flee. My belief adjusts to my altered recognition of reasons, but my emotion may not. My fear implicitly judges the snake to be dangerous, although I may at the same time consciously recognize that it is not. The implicit judgment is not the product of weighing reasons. Deliberation plays no role. However, when the judgment is correct, when the snake is dangerous and I have reason to flee, the judgment can be seen to reflect the reason

---

[10] Jenny Teichman, "Mr. Bennett on Huckleberry Finn," *Philosophy*, 50 (1975): 358–9. In this brief response to Bennett, she argues on this ground that emotions can oppose moral principles in a "rational" way.

[11] For expansion on this point and further references, see A. Goldman, "Desire, Depression, and Rationality," *Philosophical Psychology*, 20 (2007): 711–30.

of which I am implicitly aware. I flee because in my emotional state I perceive the snake to be dangerous, and its being dangerous is a reason to flee of which I am aware, although not in a consciously formulated belief, which I have not had time to articulate to myself.

Huck's guiding emotion is sympathy for his friend Jim. Sympathy contains the implicit judgment that a person needs help in light of his situation. In Huck's case this emotion is entirely fitting, and its implicit judgment reflects awareness of the reasons to help Jim escape from slavery. In reflecting such reasons, this is a moral emotion, containing a judgment about the right thing to do, although Huck does not consciously recognize it as such because of his very limited view of what morality requires. Moral emotions are those that typically prompt or reflect moral behavior: guilt, anger, and disgust, but also empathy, sympathy, and pride. They embody an awareness of moral reasons to refrain from doing or to do certain things.

In Huck's case it is clear that his trip on the river and away from the corrupt society he flees constitutes and in the novel symbolizes a moral transformation, and that this transformation is prompted by his developing emotional attachment to Jim.[12] Having developed this sympathetic relation, Huck is implicitly aware of the reasons to help Jim, although he does not conceive them as moral reasons. As a moral emotion, Huck's sympathy reflects reasons constitutive of the rightness of his action of continuing to hide Jim. The action's being right consists in its being a reaction to the injustice of slavery and to his friendship. In being implicitly aware of these reasons through his emotion, Huck is implicitly aware of the rightness of his action, although he explicitly judges it to be wrong at the same time. He is aware of the moral reasons that require him to act as he does, although this awareness is not conscious or explicit, and he does not conceive of these reasons as moral.

Although not conceiving of his moral reasons as such, in not being able to turn Jim in, Huck has what Bernard Williams has called a moral incapacity, and not simply a psychological incapacity. The latter simply causes one to be unable to act, as when vertigo prevents one from climbing a ladder, while the former is rooted in one's character[13] and involves

---

[12] One interpreter who agrees is Thomas Crocker, "An American Novelist in the Philosopher King's Court," *Philosophy and Literature*, 26 (2002): 57–74.

[13] Bernard Williams, "Moral Incapacity," *Proceedings of the Aristotelian Society*, 93 (1993): 59–70, p. 60.

an appreciation of the moral reason not to act. Williams characterizes it as the possible conclusion of deliberation.[14] In Huck Finn's case, however, we have seen that his not revealing Jim is not the outcome of deliberation: his deliberation leads him to the opposite conclusion—that he ought to reveal Jim to his would-be captors. Nor is it even the possible conclusion of deliberation by him since he lacks the moral concepts to deliberate correctly.

Citing this very example, Craig Taylor, in response to Williams, argues that Huck does not and need not recognize any reason for acting as he does, any reason for this moral incapacity.[15] Defending Williams, Michael Clark responds that a moral, as opposed to a psychological, incapacity must be grounded in a reason and therefore must be the object of possible, if not actual, deliberation.[16] But the three involved in this debate all err in assuming that recognizing a reason is a matter of its entering deliberation, actual or possible. When I flee from the snake, fearfully recognizing it to be dangerous without any time to deliberate, my fear itself reacts to the danger, the reason to flee. Deliberation is not possible if I am to survive, but fortunately my emotion reacts to the reason to flee, the danger, and saves me. Likewise, Huck Finn's emotion of sympathy implicitly recognizes the moral reasons to help Jim escape and thus explains his moral incapacity without the possibility of moral deliberation.

Rational agents are those who act on the strongest reasons of which they are aware. These reasons reflect their deepest or most important concerns at the time, although priorities among concerns can certainly shift over time. Deliberation, the conscious weighing of reasons, is not required in the normal course of rational actions. It normally occurs only on those relatively rare occasions in which agents become aware of serious conflicts among the reasons on which they could act. Normally what we do automatically reflects our concerns at the time and so reflects the reasons that indicate ways of satisfying those concerns in the circumstances. Normally we act rationally without having to think or debate with ourselves about our reasons. We remain focused on our objectives

[14] Williams, "Moral Incapacity," pp. 61, 65.
[15] Craig Taylor, "Moral Incapacity and Huckleberry Finn," *Ratio*, 14 (2001): 56–67, p. 61.
[16] Michael Clark, "Moral Incapacity and Deliberation," *Ratio*, 12 (1999): 1–13, p. 10. This article responds to an earlier one by Taylor.

and not on our reasons, which motivate us automatically by indicating how to achieve those objectives.

But if most (or all) reasons derive internally from the rational concerns we have, and if they typically motivate us automatically, we might wonder how we can ever fail to be motivated by them, how we can ever fail to be rational. The answer is that our deepest and most general concerns can fail to translate into specific desires or motivations, or those specific desires can fail to generate actions because of various interfering factors. In weakness of will the interfering factor is usually an urge that is incoherent with one's deeper and more stable concerns but is, as the term indicates, more urgently felt. One then acts on the weaker reason and in so doing defeats the stronger, thereby being irrational.

In Huck Finn's case the judgment implicit in his sympathy reflects a deeper concern than his concern for morality as he conceives it. Indeed, as emphasized earlier, he is not concerned with or motivated by morality as he conceives it at all. Usually, when an emotion opposes a considered, conscious judgment, it is the latter that reflects one's deeper and more stable concerns and the former that temporarily clouds one's more sober and rational judgment. One must then try to control or suppress one's emotion. But that is not always the case: sometimes one should instead trust one's feeling as indicative of the rational course of action. This is the case with Huck. His reasons for helping Jim are stronger than his reason for turning him in and returning him to slavery, the former reflecting his deeper and more integrated concerns.

Arpaly and Schroeder hold that Huck is alienated from his desire to help Jim instead of identifying with it.[17] They nevertheless recognize later in their paper that this desire is more integrated with his character or overall motivational set than his moral beliefs are. These two claims seem to me to be in tension at best. In fact, in renouncing morality as he conceives it, he identifies himself as an immoral person, that is, he identifies with those emotions that oppose the rules requiring him to turn Jim in.

Although Huck does not engage in moral deliberation, does not consciously weigh the moral reasons on both sides, he does act on his strongest reasons deriving from his friendship and his implicit sense of justice as reflected in his sympathetic feeling. These reasons are stronger for

---

[17] Arpaly and Schroeder, "Praise, Blame and the Whole Self," p. 167.

him because they reflect his deeper concerns. Agents can have reasons of which they are not consciously aware and be motivated by or act on such reasons without conceiving of them as such. Again, this is the case with Huck Finn. Because he acts on his strongest reasons and is implicitly aware of them, he is not weak-willed, although he may think that he is. His own description of his situation might mislead interpreters, but the description is ironic.

Indeed, as pointed out earlier, it takes strong will to risk his own freedom by continuing to hide Jim. Just as the genuine moral reasons all lie on that side, so does the danger to his own welfare, and so his action is courageous as opposed to weak-willed. He does not see himself as courageous even though he takes himself to be risking eternal damnation, but like his misguided interpreters, he simply misinterprets his own action. This misinterpretation is a large part of the irony in this part of the novel, irony that is partly missed by those who see him as weak-willed. Despite his own denial, Huck is clearly morally motivated, as we infer from his behavior. He is only not conscious of being morally motivated because he does not act on his explicit judgment that his action is wrong.

In the same way that Huck is moved by moral considerations, one who appreciates an artwork might be moved immediately by its beauty without conceiving of the aesthetic reasons to be moved as such. One would then be sensitive to and responding to these reasons emotionally without being explicitly conscious of them. Huck responds to Jim's moral status and to his morally abhorrent condition in that way. He is aware of and responding to the moral reasons he has (while not conceiving of them as such), and so he is not weak-willed. If he is not weak-willed, then he is not irrational, since this is the only form of irrationality of which the interpreters accuse him. Mark Twain himself is neither approving of irrationality here nor condemning Huck for being irrational; instead, he is being ironic in having Huck describe the incident as he does.

III

One must conclude, then, since Huck's motives do not track his judgment that his action is wrong even though he is rational and virtuous, that rational agents need not be motivated by their explicit judgments of rightness and wrongness. It might be objected that it is crucial to this example that Huck is mistaken in what he takes the moral requirement to be. If my account of Huck's mental condition is accepted, it might be claimed that he fails to be motivated by his moral judgment of wrongness because he implicitly recognizes that it is in error. Recognizing such an error, he is not rationally required to be motivated by the judgment, although he is so required to be motivated by judgments taken to be correct.

Or so it might be claimed. But in fact he does not doubt his judgment, instead fully buying into the corrupt attitude toward slaves of his society as reflecting what morality requires. That this is his view of morality is supported rather than being refuted by his wholesale dismissal of moral obligations as guides to his conduct. It is true, as I have been emphasizing, that he implicitly recognizes opposing moral reasons to help Jim escape, and that this recognition in large part explains his dismissal of what he takes to be his moral obligations. But, as I have also been emphasizing, it is important here that he does not recognize these reasons as moral reasons. That is why he does not recognize the inconsistency in his judgments or attitudes, does not see it as an inconsistency in moral judgments. Instead, he fully trusts his judgment that hiding Jim is wrong as representative of morality in general, which is why he is willing to dismiss the whole business. So he does not implicitly sense an error in moral judgment, and he is not irrational for generalizing from his judgment to the conclusion that morality itself is not worthy of allegiance. A proper inference from a false belief is not thereby irrational.

Error might be claimed to be crucial to the example in a different way that still disqualifies it from refuting a rational requirement to be motivated by one's judgments of rightness and wrongness. If an agent only falsely believes that she has a reason R to do something, then R is not a reason to do it. And if R is not a reason, then it can be claimed that there is no rational requirement to be moved by it. A daughter might believe that she has a moral obligation to do whatever her father orders her to do, but she might be rationally unmotivated to adhere to some outlandish parental demand. This would not show that she need not be motivated by awareness of genuine moral requirements. Similarly, it can be claimed that Huck is not rationally required to be moved by his false moral judgment that hiding Jim is wrong, but this does not show that agents can rationally fail to be moved by judgments that reflect genuine moral reasons.

In reply, we can point out first that Huck is relevantly different from the recalcitrant daughter. He not only fails to be moved by his judgment of what he ought to do with Jim; generalizing from this attitude,

he fails to be moved by any explicit judgments of rightness and wrongness as such, many of which will be correct. And once more, although
this attitude is based on a generalizing inference from a particular false
judgment about what morality requires, it is not thereby rendered irrational. Perhaps more relevant is that we all believe that our moral judgments are correct from the moral point of view when we sincerely make
them. Some of these judgments may well be incorrect or, unbeknown to
us, inconsistent with others that we make. But we cannot be rationally
required to be motivated only by our actually correct judgments, when
we do not know that our incorrect judgments are incorrect.

Rationality depends on our reactions to our reasons as we are aware of
them, assuming that we have arrived at our judgments of reasons in ways
that are not themselves irrational. Either we must be motivated by all our
sincere moral judgments that are not irrationally formed, or there is no
such rational requirement at all. A requirement of rationality must be
able to be followed: it must be used to guide rational agents. We cannot
be guided by a requirement to obey only our correct moral judgments.
As for Huck Finn, he may be mistaken in his belief that the demands of
his society are genuine moral demands, but he is not irrational to accept
them as such. Conventionalism may be a false meta-ethical theory, but
those who hold it explicitly or implicitly are again not thereby irrational.

Thus it does not seem to matter to the connection between rationality and moral motivation that Huck is mistaken in his moral judgment.
His case still shows that rational agents need not be motivated by their
explicit judgments of moral rightness and wrongness. But we are not free
yet from objections on grounds of meta-ethical considerations. Moral
judgment internalists can still offer their standard reply to lack of motivation: that agents who are not moved by their moral judgments do not
make genuine moral assertions but only judge in an inverted commas
sense. Huckleberry Finn's judgments simply mimic those of his corrupt
society, they will point out. In simply mouthing his society's moral principles, he is quoting their morality without sincerely adopting it as his
own. Hence he is not making genuine moral assertions, and that is why
he is not, and need not be, motivated by them.

But this appeal to pseudo-moral judgments is an ad hoc invention of
the defenders of moral judgment internalism, of the claim that rational
agents must be motivated by their moral judgments, as the case of Huck
Finn again makes clear. The only evidence possible for the claim that his

judgment of wrongness is not genuine is his failure to be motivated by it. Citing this as evidence is, of course, circular or question begging. Huck's explicit moral assertions are borrowed from his society and his religious education, but then so are the moral judgments of most people. That the judgments derive from these sources does not begin to show that they are not ordinary or sincere. These are the only moral beliefs that Huck knows as such, and he is entirely sincere in taking them to be expressions of what morality requires. As noted in the previous paragraphs, that they are wrong or corrupt is irrelevant to the question of whether, in sincerely believing them, Huck ought to be motivated by them.

IV

Moral judgment internalists are most often expressivists: they take moral judgments to be intrinsically motivating because they take them to express positive or negative attitudes or emotions, and these attitudes or emotions are themselves motivational, including within them dispositions to certain behaviors (as well as implicit judgments, as emphasized earlier). If expressivism is the correct meta-ethical theory, then all agents are motivated by their sincere moral judgments, and the question whether rational agents need be so motivated is moot. Does the Huck Finn example, then, refute expressivism? Surprisingly, not entirely.

I have said that Huck's sympathy implicitly involves the judgment that Jim ought to be helped. Huck is implicitly aware of the rightness of helping Jim; he implicitly judges it right to do so, although he does not consciously accept this as a moral judgment. Despite not conceiving it as moral, he also implicitly recognizes this to be a stronger reason than any reason he might have to turn Jim in, as it reflects a deeper concern and he is motivated to act on it. Despite not tracking his explicit moral judgments, Huck's motives do track his concrete judgment about what is owed to his friend. We can therefore characterize these emotional judgments as core moral judgments for Huck, as opposed to those moral beliefs borrowed from his society that fail to motivate him. His core moral judgments express the emotion of sympathy. Thus they suggest expressivism as a meta-ethical theory instead of refuting it. That they express an emotion does not imply that they may not also state a moral fact. So I say that they only suggest an emotivist analysis without implying one.

But these core moral beliefs are not Huck's only moral judgments. He has other moral beliefs which fail to motivate him and which are inconsistent with his regard for Jim. They fail to motivate him at all once he renounces morality as he conceives it, but he continues to take these to be genuine moral requirements. They remain moral beliefs, but do not express any moral emotions or attitudes on his part. Thus expressivism cannot be the correct meta-ethical account of these judgments. And in addition to these two sets of moral beliefs, there are others that Huck ought to hold on grounds of consistency with his core beliefs that he fails to hold, for example that all slaves deserve the same moral regard and ought to be helped.

If the core judgments of more typically morally minded people also express such emotions as sympathy, guilt, pride, anger, and disgust, for them too these are not the only sources of moral judgments. They are also rationally required to accept a constraint of consistency or coherence on their moral beliefs: they must not judge cases differently without being able to specify a morally relevant difference between them.[18] And the judgments outside the core to which they are committed by this constraint may not express the same emotional commitments as those in the core, even if they accept these judgments, as Huck does not.

Whether this lack of commitment amounts to irrationality will be addressed below. The point here is that a distinction can be drawn between core moral judgments that express deeply felt attitudes and other judgments that agents take to be moral, or to which they are committed on grounds of consistency, that need not express such attitudes. Thus my interpretation of the Huck Finn case and his failure to be motivated by his explicit moral judgments does not imply a rejection of expressivism or acceptance of either conventionalism or realism on the meta-ethical level.

Expressivism may well provide the best account of our core moral judgments. But this core varies from individual to individual and may be vanishingly small for some. If an expressivist account will not capture all of a person's moral judgments, and may not capture any, the analysis so far leaves open the question whether a rational person must be motivated by moral demands at all. Huck Finn is morally motivated,

---

although not by his explicit moral judgments, and he is rational, but is his sort of motivation deriving from his emotion of sympathy for Jim rationally required?

V

In the first section I argued that Huck Finn's core moral judgments are implicitly contained in his emotion of sympathy for Jim. I pointed out that emotions in general, at least intentional ones, contain such implicit judgments or beliefs as well as dispositions to react to their objects. We may add to these aspects bodily changes or symptoms, and sensations, sometimes analyzed as perceptions of these bodily changes. When I fear a snake, I implicitly judge it to be dangerous, am disposed to flee, might tremble and feel increased heart beat or feel a chill run through me. Our focus, however, is on the judgments implicit in emotions, and especially on the moral judgments implicit in moral emotions such as sympathy. These emotions, I argued, may reflect genuine moral reasons, but they do not typically arise through the deliberate weighing of the reasons that would justify the judgments.

When I am sympathetic to the plight of another person, my sympathy may be fitting in relation to her plight, may involve implicit awareness of the moral reasons to help her. But I might also feel sympathy for Jim, whom I, unlike Huck, know to be only a fictional character. Such emotions arise immediately from cues often subconsciously processed, and they prompt immediate reactions, or at least dispositions to react. These dispositions can be suppressed when it is known that action is out of place or impossible, but the other aspects of the emotions do not necessarily alter in response to the recognition that the reasons that may be reflected in their judgments do not obtain in particular cases. I might continue to fear a snake after being informed by a reliable source that it is not dangerous, and I might continue to feel sympathy for Jim when I know he is not real. Such feelings can be condemned as irrational, but they may be better seen as indicating again the largely arational way that emotions arise and persist.

Might certain emotions and the judgments implicit in them neverthe-less be rationally required by the reasons that make them appropriate when they are? In general, this seems again not to be the case. When fear is appropriate in the face of danger, we nevertheless do not typically blame or hold the person to be irrational who faces the danger fearlessly. We are more likely to praise her unusual courage (although we also sometimes condemn fearless actions as rash or unnecessarily risky). Likewise, when anger at a slight would be fitting, we do not condemn as irrational the person who remains calm or forgiving; and when pride would be warranted, it is not irrational to remain modest or even self-effacing. Thus, in general, emotions seem not to be rationally required even when they would be fitting or appropriate, even when there appear to be reasons to feel fear, anger, or pride. Not only is the lack of such usual emotional reactions not irrational, it may well be admirable.

Huck Finn's sympathy is entirely appropriate and reflects the genuine reasons to help Jim escape his plight. Might there be something about moral emotions, and specifically about the concern for others expressed in this emotion of sympathy, that makes them rationally required when other emotions are not? Put another way, is it irrational to lack this emotion, when it might be not only rationally permitted, but praiseworthy, to lack others? Answering this question requires brief further analysis of rationality, irrationality, and the rational constraint on moral judgments mentioned earlier. Once more we may narrow the task by focusing on Huck Finn's case.

I have argued that Huck is not irrational in the way that previous interpreters have held him to be. Practical irrationality consists in self-defeat, just as does irrationality in belief. The aim of belief is truth. Thus an irrational belief is one that flies in the face of known or available evidence, since evidence indicates truth. An irrational belief is defeating of its own aim in the way that it is acquired or persists. The aim of action is the fulfillment of the prioritized motivations that prompt the actions. We act in order to fulfill our concerns or motives in acting. Irrational people defeat their own strongest concerns or deepest aims by failing to specify them when they are general or by failing to act on them when they are specific, usually by acting on a more superficial urge instead. They fail to act on those reasons that indicate ways to satisfy these deepest concerns. Rational people avoid such self-defeat. They are coherent in their motivations and actions, acting on the strongest reasons that exist in light of these motivations. Priorities among desires change with contexts and opportunities for satisfying them, but rational agents do not sacrifice satisfaction of deeper concerns, those that connect to many others, to more superficial urges.[19]

---

[19]   For expansion on these points, see A. Goldman, *Reasons from Within*, ch. 2, section 3.

Huck Finn does not appear to be irrational in the ways just described. He acts on his emotion of sympathy instead of on his explicit moral judgment, but I claimed that this emotion reflects a stronger moral reason for him, in that his concern for Jim and their friendship is deeper than his concern (or lack of it) for doing what his society deems right, for following the only moral requirements as he conceives them. In acting on his stronger reasons he is perfectly rational, coherent in his motivations and actions, and not self-defeating. But I also pointed earlier to a rational constraint on moral judgments that Huck does violate. We must ask whether in violating this constraint he is practically irrational in a way that shows moral concern to be rationally required.

The constraint in question requires not judging cases differently without being able to find a morally relevant difference between them. To judge one case right and another wrong when they are similar in every morally relevant respect is to promote and defeat the same moral value at stake in the same way, again a form of incoherence. Huck violates this constraint first by failing to grant the same moral regard to other slaves that he grants to Jim. His sympathy for Jim is personalized—it grows directly from his personal relationship with his friend—and it does not generalize to other slaves, who of course deserve equal moral status simply in virtue of being human. When asked whether anyone was hurt in a boat accident that Huck made up, he responds, "No'm. Killed a nigger." He certainly is guilty of moral inconsistency here.

Second, he is guilty of an even more obvious though less easily detectable form of inconsistency in implicitly sensing the strong moral reasons to hide Jim while explicitly judging that he ought to turn him in. (Again there is irony in this inconsistency, since the far more common form is to be explicitly fair or nonracist but implicitly or subconsciously racist.) He judges the same case in incompatible ways without reconciling these conflicting attitudes. He is morally incoherent in these two ways, the first being the more common form, but is he thereby practically irrational?

If he is, then first, his case may once more fail to show that rational agents need not be motivated by their moral judgments, and second, his case may instead show that some moral concerns are rationally required, given other concerns. It is indeed very tempting to assimilate moral incoherence of the sort suffered by Huck Finn to practical irrationality as characterized above. Both are forms of incoherence, which is why we can describe the constraint on moral reasoning as a rational constraint. And moral judgments, after all, are typically intended to guide actions, and are therefore practical. Don't all forms of practical incoherence amount to practical irrationality? My answer is no, when we take practical irrationality in its primary sense of self-defeat. While moral incoherence amounts to promoting and failing to promote the same moral value in relevantly similar contexts, it does not amount to self-defeat for the agent himself, as does genuine practical irrationality. To see this, we may first consider a more typical case and then return to the case of Huck Finn.

VI

Moral incoherence occurs when an agent fails to extend a concern to others who fall under the same relevant description as those who enjoy such status, as Huck Finn fails to extend moral concern to all slaves. A common form of such incoherence occurs these days in our attitudes toward animals. A meat eater who considers it seriously wrong to eat dogs might well be incapable of finding a morally relevant difference in this regard between dogs and pigs, although he enjoys his BLTs completely guilt free. While his carnivorous action lacks justification by his own lights, it does not defeat any aim or purpose that he accepts as his own. In fact, it satisfies his desire for gustatory pleasure, although it balances that desire in an arbitrary way against the reasons for not killing, accepting an arbitrary subclass of these reasons as his own.

If practical irrationality consists in self-defeat, then a failure to respond to such moral reasons does not appear to be practically irrational, unless it is itself a case of weakness of will, which many such cases are not. The meat eater in question is not giving in to an irresistible urge at the expense of a deeper concern when he orders his bacon. He has no concern for the pigs. He may even recognize that what he does is wrong in this instance by his own lights, but that recognition will not move him to abstention. He is morally inconsistent, as he may acknowledge, but his inconsistency amounts simply to a narrowing of the scope of his accepted moral values in an arbitrary way, in a way that cannot be defended by appeal to any moral reasons.

Moral values may have limited motivational force for agents who must balance them against nonmoral concerns. These limits may be expressed in ways that are morally arbitrary but that enable agents to better achieve their personal aims. If the latter is true, then the agents who limit their moral concerns in these ways are not defeating their strongest aims and are not practically irrational. Even if they care about only a very limited number of people and cannot justify limiting their concerns to those few, they do not defeat their own aims in doing so. They fail to extend the motivational force behind their core moral beliefs to other judgments implied or supported by those core judgments, but this does not defeat any motivations they have and may even serve to better fulfill them.

Huck Finn is not motivated by self-interest in failing to extend his moral regard to slaves other than Jim. He may in fact be serving his self-interest by his attitude in better fitting in to his corrupt society and limiting the risks he takes, but this is not his motive. But neither is he defeating his own aims and motivations by his inconsistency. If the meat eater who will not eat dogs is not practically irrational, then neither is Huck. He suffers from an extreme form of a moral malady a lesser form of which infects most of us non-saints: a failure to extend moral concern or sympathy and resultant altruistic action to all those who are not relevantly different from those whose distresses we do seek to alleviate.

When I convince my ethics class students that they morally ought to contribute substantially to the alleviation of hunger in distant areas of the world, the vast majority even of those who acknowledge this obligation remain unmoved to fulfill it. To hold us all practically irrational for such moral failings is to extend the notion of irrationality far beyond its standard use and meaning. There may be an element of moral hypocrisy of which the agents are unaware in all these cases, but moral hypocrisy or inconsistency does not amount to irrationality, the self-defeat of one's own aims.[20]

Failure to extend moral concerns in a fully coherent way does not amount to practical irrationality any more than would failure to extend aesthetic taste in a transparently coherent way. Appreciating Haydn but not Mozart, or Haydn's Symphony 101 but not 104, would be highly unusual, aesthetically arbitrary, and even incomprehensible and indefensible, if the aesthetic reasons to appreciate the 101st apply also to the 104th. But once more, unless the listener had the unusual aim of appreciating all Haydn symphonies or all composers in the classic tradition, her arbitrarily limited taste would not be practically irrational. If asked why she passed up a chance to hear the 104th in concert, an acceptable response would be "I do not care for that symphony." Her lack of appreciation cannot be defended

---

[20] For a full defense of this notion of irrationality, see *Reasons from Within*.

by appeal to aesthetic reasons, but it does not defeat her own aims and may serve them better if she has other things to do. Neither then is Huck's arbitrarily limited moral concern practically irrational.

VII

If extending such concern coherently is not required by practical rationality, then lack of a rational requirement seems even clearer for those who lack moral concerns altogether. They are not guilty of moral inconsistency, of narrowing the scope of moral values they accept in an arbitrary way. Such persons, complete amoralists, are classified as psychopaths, however. Arguments against the claim that moral concern is rationally required often appeal to such characters. But they are widely recognized to be abnormal and psychologically impaired. Debate then ensues whether their impairment is affective or cognitive, or both, and again, whether they use moral terms in the same way we do.[21] Given the inconclusiveness of this debate, the argument is better made by appeal to more psychologically normal individuals, such as Huckleberry Finn and us.

While Huck is not unusual in seeing all moral demands as imposed by society and God, he is atypical in having his core moral judgments expressed only implicitly in his sympathetic feeling for Jim and so failing to translate into explicit judgments of right and wrong. Most people's core judgments largely overlap with their society's ethical code, and most people's judgments of right and wrong derive from more concrete reactions to right- and wrong-making properties. These judgments might seem to derive at least in part from social programming or education, although the origin of their motivational force might lie elsewhere. It might be claimed in light of efforts at moral education that, independent of emotional development, there is another more purely cognitive route to moral maturity that rational people must take.

We saw in the previous chapter that cognitive development is required for the attainment of full moral maturity, in that moral agents must be capable of decentered attention, perception, and thought. But this is not the sort of capacity typically developed by taking ethics courses. And we

---

[21] For a recent version of this debate, see Shaun Nichols, *Sentimental Rules* (Oxford: Oxford University Press, 2004), ch. 3.

also saw that emotionally mature empathy is central for full moral agency. One of the central moral lessons of Twain's novel lies in his showing us precisely how moral concern develops more directly through emotional attachment in personal relationships.

We saw that also in the previous chapter's analysis of Austen's *Pride and Prejudice*. These are entirely realistic accounts of moral development, however much the contexts and styles of the two novels differ. Our concerns for others, like Huck's and Elizabeth Bennet's, also develop outward as our relationships expand, until, perhaps like her but unlike him, we come to an appreciation of common humanity. Developing affect is the key to such moral development, as it is in Huck's case, not coming to appreciate newly learned arguments. We may project that he would further develop into a fully mature moral agent along the same path, certainly not by formal moral education.

If there is a route to required moral motivation through an argument that all rational people can grasp, no one has given the argument. When my students fail to extend concern to distant people or future generations, demonstrating the most common form of partial amorality, their fault is not a failure to understand the argument that such people are not relevantly different from others. The students' fault is not a fault of reason, but of lack of real extended sympathy, predictable from lack of personal contact. If moral concern were a requirement of reason that all rational people could grasp, then, since my students are rational people, all I would need to do to get them to feed the starving in Africa would be to present them with the simple argument just indicated. Despite the desires or pretensions of classes in ethics, such is not the case.

For Huck Finn, by contrast, all the arguments he knows fall on the wrong side, but as Mark Twain himself noted in a journal, his heart is fortunately in the right place, at least when it comes to Jim on the river. Huck is not unlike Everyman: a bit more corrupted by his corrupt society than is Everyman these days, but a bit better in his ability to escape its rules and trust to his natural moral feelings when out on the river. Most important, his route to real moral motivation is that of Everyman. It is by way of developing moral emotions toward other people and their actions, emotions that arise from personal interactions and exchanges with them and that embody implicit awareness of moral reasons without being rationally required.

7

What we learn about rules from *The Cider House Rules*

I

As noted earlier, in a well-known collection of essays, Martha Nussbaum has argued that novels are indispensable in teaching and learning ethics in the right way. A large part of such learning consists in developing the capacity to perceive and respond to complex, nuanced situations having numerous morally relevant features deriving from particular relationships and past commitments that combine these context-sensitive features in unique and unpredictable ways. Careful attention to detailed, intricate stories with finely sketched characters develops such capacity far better than does reading analytical philosophy papers. Only such narratives capture the particularity and complexity of morally charged contexts with their myriad of morally relevant features in unique blends. Typical philosophers' examples in their applied ethics parables, by contrast, are truncated, highlighting only those properties that suggest applications of the authors' favored rules.

This claim regarding the invaluable contribution of fictional literature to moral education is clearly tied to her perceptual model and particularist theory of correct moral judgment. General rules play only a very minor role in this theory, correct judgment in morally difficult situations never being simply a matter of applying such rules to the cases in question. Each particular situation calls for weighing unique combinations of morally relevant factors that may not be relevant, or relevant in the same way, in other contexts. There is indeed a minor role for rules to play, but this is primarily the use of rules of thumb without independent moral weight as initial guides to what to look for in the way of morally relevant features. These initial rules of thumb must be adapted to and modified by application to the specifics of concrete situations and particular relationships, always ultimately to be supplanted by fully nuanced moral perception. Nussbaum writes:

> In these essays, and in the novels, much is made of an ethical ability that I call "perception," after both Aristotle and James. By this I mean the ability to discern, acutely and responsively, the salient features of one's particular situation… one point of the emphasis on perception is to show the ethical crudeness of moralities based exclusively on general rules, and to demand for ethics a much finer responsiveness to the concrete—including features that have not been seen before and could not therefore have been housed in any antecedently built system of rules.[1]

Novels teach us to perceive in this way when we attend to all the details of their extended narratives and character portrayals. Especially relevant are the complex and changing relationships into which the characters enter, and the different ways in which the characters and narrators view these relationships. No set of formulable rules could capture all the relevant moral features of these relationships and their context relativity. General rules can substitute for fully context sensitive perception only in the public sphere, when decisions must be made for the general public without knowledge of particulars, and where we do not trust the independent judgments of public officials to be unbiased. For competent judgment in the more typical private sphere, we must attend fully to the concrete and particular, and it is novels that train us to do so:

> novels, as a genre, direct us to attend to the concrete; they display before us a wealth of richly realized detail, presented as relevant for choice.[2]

Other advocates of the supreme relevance of fictional literature to ethics follow Nussbaum in this regard. Anthony Cunningham, for example, writes that novels enable us to see the "complexities of life and character":

> The errors of ethical theory can best be corrected by a moral philosophy that pays attention to particular people leading particular lives, complete with rich emotional attachments that are prey and sometimes prone to conflict…literature can play a role in such a moral philosophy. By providing detailed descriptions of the complex interior life of fictional characters embroiled in the messy business of living, fine

---

[1] Martha Nussbaum, *Love's Knowledge* (New York: Oxford University Press, 1990), p. 37.

[2] Nussbaum, *Love's Knowledge*, p. 95.

literature directs our attention to the subtleties and nuances of what should rightly command our attention...By drawing our attention to morally salient features of life and character, novels can sharpen our ability to perceive moral subtleties and nuances...To do justice to particular people and their circumstances, we must paint the kind of subtle, detailed pictures that can bring them to life in all their complexity, the kinds of pictures good literature can paint...The right kind of novel—one with detailed character portraits of particular people embroiled in complex, meaningful situations—can help us refine our moral vision.[3]

Once more it is moral perception of complex relations among morally relevant features in concrete situations that novels can train, guiding us away from reliance on simplifying general rules.

Nussbaum's paradigms of such literature are the novels of Henry James, certainly apt paradigms of subtle, complex, and highly nuanced prose. James' form of writing as much as his content conduces to the sort of moral perception she seeks. One might nevertheless note that, if it takes the ability to grasp Henry Jamesian prose to become a highly moral person, then most of us surely are going to hell. In this chapter I want to press again by example a different criticism of this view of the moral worth of novels. It is not that fiction is not valuable in teaching us to grasp complex moral truths, but that it is more valuable than this view indicates, or valuable in a different way. Novels not only train us to attend to the particular, but can equally importantly teach us important general moral truths. We have seen that we can learn the general features of moral development and the nature of moral motivation from *Pride and Prejudice* and *Huckleberry Finn*. In this chapter we will see what is generally necessary for sustaining a strong moral identity and the motivation to act on moral considerations, as well as the result of lacking these necessary conditions: disintegration of the moral agent or self.

In this chapter we will analyze a novel that itself thematizes the uses of moral rules. What better way to show the incompleteness of Nussbaum's view of the philosophical importance of novels and the particularist moral theory from which it follows than by reference to a novel that is itself largely about general moral rules and their place in proper moral reasoning? *The Cider House Rules* shows rules to be far more important to ethical behavior than the particularism of Nussbaum and others allows. We see in the attitudes of the novel's characters toward rules that they can

---

[3] Anthony Cunningham, *The Heart of What Matters* (Berkeley: California University Press, 2001), pp. 3, 5, 84–5.

and often should be far more than mere rules of thumb, disposable indications of the morally relevant features of unique situations. We will see that rules must sometimes be obeyed even when agents think they can do better by reasoning in the particularist manner from all the apparently relevant features of a situation.

It is worth emphasizing at the start that *The Cider House Rules* really is a book about rules, with much to teach us about their proper use and abuse. Given its title, it is somewhat remarkable that some reviewers and critics seem unaware of this theme. One sees the novel as being primarily about "belonging" or family; several see it as primarily about abortion (more plausible, although abortion laws are only one set of rules the book addresses); and one who does note the central theme of rules thinks that the lesson here can be summed up in the single misguided thought that everyone must develop their own set of rules (a thought that the novel itself shows to be misguided). I found only two commentators who focus on the theme of rules. But they see this theme as underdeveloped, only suggested in the novel:

> In *Cider House*, then, Irving explores many aspects of a paradox created by the conflict between rules and human realities, between social law and personal freedom, between abstract value and biological life... The rules of society and those we establish for ourselves are at best necessary compromises between contending absolutes... this vital and universal theme remains only partially developed in the novel, more potential than actual.[4]

On the contrary, I will show that the conclusions that can be drawn from the novel regarding the place of rules in practical reason are as rich as any that can be found in philosophical works on the topic, although, of course, these conclusions are only implicit in the attitudes of the characters and in what befalls them in the narrative as a result of these attitudes. Attention to this narrative reveals the narrowness of particularist meta-ethics.

Certainly this novel is not as widely read as Austen's or Twain's. But as a final preliminary, I can offer only the barest summary of the novel's plot, at best to recall its outline to those who have read it, or at least seen the movie (written by Irving and faithful to the book as far as it goes, despite omitting two main characters and several minor ones, as well as fifteen years of the central adulterous love affair). Dr. Wilbur Larch runs an orphanage in a deserted and dreary lumber town, St. Cloud's,

---

[4] Carol Harter and James Thompson, *John Irving* (Boston: Twayne, 1986), p. 139.

in Maine, where he also delivers babies and performs secret and illegal abortions. The two oldest orphans there, returned after unsuccessful placements, are Homer Wells and Melony. Homer becomes Dr. Larch's de facto intern, although he comes to disapprove of abortion after, as an impressionable teenager, finding a discarded fetus. Melony, a tough and unhappy adolescent, initiates Homer into sex and exacts a promise that he will never leave her. Homer breaks the promise when he gets an opportunity to leave St. Cloud's (names are significant here, as in Dickens) for the sunnier coast. He leaves with Wally and Candy, a very attractive unmarried young couple who come to the orphanage for an abortion. Homer becomes their friend and falls in love with Candy. He goes to work in Wally's family's apple orchard, joining a group of black migrant workers led by Mr. Rose.

Wally goes off to war; Homer and Candy have an affair and produce a son, Angel, who they say has been adopted from the orphanage by Homer. Wally returns from the war paralyzed; he and Candy marry; and Homer and Angel live with them, while Homer intermittently continues the romantic relationship with Candy. Melony tracks Homer down after fifteen years and confronts him with his duplicitous life. After this confrontation and the death of Dr. Larch, Homer realizes that he must break off the affair and tell the truth to his son and Wally. Angel has fallen in love with the daughter of Mr. Rose. But she is pregnant by her father and receives an abortion from Homer when he learns of the situation. She then stabs her father and escapes. Homer returns to St. Cloud's with a new identity and false medical credentials provided by Dr. Larch and takes over the orphanage and abortion clinic. Melony dies in an electrical accident, and Homer turns his romantic attention to Nurse Caroline. He will continue with Dr. Larch's work despite strong personal misgivings about performing abortions. He will follow a rule to perform them, which he can discard only if the legal rules prohibiting them change:

Sometimes, when he was especially tired, he dreamed that abortions were legal—that they were safe and available, and therefore he could stop performing them (because someone else would do them).[5] (585)

---

[5]   John Irving, *The Cider House Rules* (New York: Ballantine, 1985). Page references in the text are to this edition.

Thus, he will follow a rule to perform them as long as there is a legal rule prohibiting them, a policy that will tell us much about the proper attitude toward rules.

II

At first thought, directed at the novel's initial hero, one might see the book's message as rule-skeptical, as supporting Nussbaum's particularist moral view, though supporting it as a general meta-ethical truth thematically, and not just as a reflection of method or style. Dr. Larch, who certainly shares the role of hero with Homer, has no use for rules. He refuses to be influenced by laws or the ordinary moral rules of society, acting always from sympathetic feelings, as when performing abortions for desperate women, and sometimes acting from intentional defiance of authority. He delights in fabrication, making up fictitious histories, forging medical records, providing a fake heart problem and a new identity for Homer as Dr. Stone, and lying to the board of directors of the orphanage. Society's rules, such as the law against vandalism, mean nothing to him:

> The reported vandalism to the so-called sawyer's lodge had upset Larch less than it had disturbed certain townspeople who had witnessed the damage done by Homer and Melony—mostly by Melony, Dr. Larch was sure. What are abandoned buildings for? Dr. Larch wondered—if not for kids to vandalize, a little? (102–3)

Responding to the personal needs of women, he has nothing but a similar contempt for more serious laws prohibiting abortions. Having seen first-hand the result of refusing to provide an abortion, his attitude is a response to the fears and needs of individual women and to his experiences of abuses of unwanted children.

Even when he seems to have his own rules about performing abortions, refusing to do late term procedures, he is responding to needs, medical and otherwise, in individual cases. Before late term, his rule is that of individual choice, a rule not to have a rule. And even when he performs the same procedures always, it is not because of a rule to do so. We are told in the opening sentences of the book that he performs circumcisions on all newborns, not as a rite or law, but in response to the medical need for hygiene. He describes the reverence for law and religion of his fictional character, Fuzzy Stone, as "convincingly creepy":

> He even had young Dr. Stone propose that *he* replace Dr. Larch...and that by this replacement it might be demonstrated to Dr. Larch that the law should be observed, that abortions should *not* be performed, and that a safe and informative view of family planning (birth control, and so forth) could in time achieve the desired effect ("...without breaking the laws of God or man," wrote the convincingly creepy Fuzzy Stone). (268)

Nurse Caroline, a minor but perceptive and sympathetic character, describes Larch as "not a systems man, just a good one" (473). Elsewhere in the book he is described as a saint and a god at St. Cloud's. He lives in clouds, is celibate, writes his own histories, and rules over the orphanage. Homer describes him as playing God:

> Dr. Larch, Homer knew, played God in other ways; it was still Homer's cautious opinion that Dr. Larch played God pretty well. (97)

Homer cannot figure out what the rules at St. Cloud's are:

> What were the rules at St. Cloud's? What were Larch's rules? Which rules did Dr. Larch observe, which ones did he break, or replace—and with what confidence? (379)

Gods need no rules, and Larch, having none himself, refuses to impose them on others as well:

> Who am I to advocate honesty in all relationships? he wondered. Me with my fictional histories, me with my fictional heart defects—me with my Fuzzy Stone... "I have no quarrel with anyone at prayer," Wilbur Larch said. "Prayer is personal—prayer is anyone's choice. Pray to whom or what you want! It's when you start making rules..." (362, 372)

He teaches Homer medicine only with actual, hands-on cases. He calls the orphans "princes" and "kings," indicating his belief that they, like royalty, should be above rules too.

A more minor but equally admirable character in the novel, Candy's father Ray Kendall, seems to have a similar skeptical attitude toward rules. A lobster fisherman and master mechanic who takes care of all the equipment at the orchard, he picks his own hours for work and attempts to build a torpedo, undoubtedly illegal, in his house. And once more the other lobstermen learn their trade not by learning a set of rules, but by imitating

Kendall's individual decisions. Another minor character, meddling Mrs. Goodhall of the board of directors of the orphanage, also reinforces the rule-skeptical view, not by being rule-skeptical herself, but the comical opposite. She is a rule-fetishist, looking down, for example, on any public show of affection outside marriage. As the one ridiculous character in the novel, she makes strict adherence to rules look ridiculous.

But despite our attraction to the characters of Dr. Larch and Ray Kendall and their contempt for rules and laws, despite the rampant disregard for rules throughout the novel by the migrant workers and others, contempt for rules is not the novel's message. The feature of the story that brings this out most strongly is the fact that all the main characters who die in the course of the narrative are done in precisely by disregarding rules, overestimating their own expertise and capacity for personal judgment in their areas of expertise. The young Dr. Larch ignores rules against sex with prostitutes and contracts a debilitating venereal disease that leads him to be celibate from then on. The old Dr. Larch is killed by an accident with the ether that he knows as a doctor but addictively misuses, ignoring the rules for its proper use. Ray Kendall, the master mechanic, is blown up by his own illegal torpedo, again a victim of broken rules. Mr. Rose, who is an expert with a knife, dies by a knife in the hands of his daughter, or more precisely allows himself to die because of the guilt he feels for having broken the most serious rules in his behavior toward her:

Mr. Rose had managed to soak the blade of his own knife in his wound, and the last thing he told Homer was that it should be clear to the authorities that he had stabbed himself. If he hadn't meant to kill himself, why would he have let himself bleed to death from what wasn't necessarily a mortal wound? (576–7)

Melony, who becomes a skilled electrician, electrocutes herself when relaxing on the job, forgetting the rules for handling electrical equipment:

In the event of her death (which was caused by an electrical accident), Melony had instructed Lorna to send her body to Dr. Stone in St. Cloud's... in Lorna's opinion, something to do with how relaxed Melony had become was responsible for her electrocuting herself. (585–6)

Homer and Candy escape death but not pregnancy when they ignore rules for the use of condoms.

Surely this common thread in the narrative is nonaccidental. Once more Nurse Caroline has it right: "It is because even a good man can't always be right that we need a society, that we need certain rules" (473). Even those with expert personal judgment cannot ignore rules that limit their authority to act solely on such personal judgment. Even saints need rules, since, unlike gods, they and we cannot always trust their personal decisions. Rules exist first of all to supplant such judgment when it is more likely than not to go wrong, when individuals miscalculate their ability to judge correctly in the absence of the rules. Those who take themselves to be experts may be most prone to such errors. Philosophers have pointed to the use of rules in avoiding errors in personal judgments, but the novel makes the danger of ignoring rules in such contexts more vivid and motivating by having us vicariously experience the dire consequences that can result.

In order to appreciate more subtle distinctions among rules and the proper and improper contexts for their use, we must turn to other characters in the novel with more complex attitudes toward them. Like Dr. Larch, Mr. Rose is contemptuous of society's laws and rules, which he sees as imposed by whites on blacks, for whom they are at best irrelevant. Given their source in the context of grossly unequal power, even seemingly innocuous rules, such as the cider house rules themselves (rules for the safety of the workers tacked up on the wall of the cider house by the orchard owners), will be ignored or resisted. The workers cannot read, and so giving them written rules mocks the attempt of white men to impose rules on them. But Mr. Rose makes up his own rules:

Mr. Rose knew the rules: they were the *real* cider house rules, they were the pickers' rules... "Mr. Rose does what he wants," Wally said. "He's got his own rules," said Homer Wells. (540)

Unlike Dr. Larch, Mr. Rose imposes his rules on others, on the other migrant workers. His rules reflect raw power relations. They are aimed at survival in an oppressive white society, prescribing how to act toward both blacks and whites. In a knife fight, one can cut a black man, but not so badly as to get the police involved, and one can cut only the clothes of a white man:

We got our own rules too, Homer...' bout lots of things...' bout how much we can have to do with white people...we got our rules about that...And about fightin'...with each other...One rule is, we can't cut each other bad. Not bad enough for no hospital, not bad enough for no police. We can cut each other, but not bad. (455)

Mr. Rose is always calm, reserved, and polite toward his employers, but avoids excessive contact with them. When Homer confronts him with his incestuous relationship, he politely points out that Homer's relationship with Candy breaks the rules too, and he reminds Homer constantly that his people have their own rules (namely, his rules). In his society of migrant workers, for example, abused wives never seek the protection of the police and their white laws. In contexts of oppressive power relations, the rules of the oppressors will be ignored or resisted even when benign, and the rules of the oppressed will reflect only the power relations among the different strata. But, as noted, Mr. Rose's death results from his ignoring rules that all must obey and from his final acknowledgment of that fact:

"You breakin' them rules, too, Homer," Mr. Rose whispered to him. "Say you know how I feel." (576)

Strict rules prohibit incest and child abuse; they aim to curb emotions that might lead to such behavior. Some rules and their justifications apply universally, and we ignore them at our peril.

The other major characters in the novel must discover through years of life experience which rules of society are justified and when to obey them. These are the two orphan heroes, Homer and Melony, and to a lesser extent Candy and Wally, who are half-orphans (she having no mother and he no father), and Angel, who is said to be an orphan but lives with three parents. By setting his novel in rural Maine in the first half of the last century, and by choosing orphans as his central characters, Irving emphasizes the theme of searching for a moral compass in the form of acceptable social rules. While the America of that time may have been more rule-bound than our present society, Dr. Larch reflects the skepticism of government rules more typical of Yankees in Maine:

"Once the state starts providing, it feels free to hand out the rules too!" Dr. Larch blurted hastily. It was a Yankee thing to say—very Maine. (473)

And isolation from society and its rules is far more pronounced for orphans in rural Maine. They must find their moral compass from scratch. Even more so for Homer and Melony, whose only surrogate father is the rule-skeptical Dr. Larch. As was the case with Darcy and Elizabeth Bennet, a typical moral development from initial internalization of parental rules is not a possibility for them. They must develop throughout life a proper view of rules to live by, although the right rules apply to all.

Homer characterizes himself always as the ultimate outsider or "Bedouin," as he self-consciously tries to decipher the rules governing the various groups in which he finds himself, including the somewhat comical rules of adolescent lovemaking, which he must learn by trial and error:

He was beginning to see it was a yes–no set of rules he had encountered; he was permitted to rub her tummy, but not to touch her breasts. The hand on her hips was allowed to remain there; the hand on her thigh, in her lap, was moved on... Homer Wells was forced to accept that what they called "necking" was permitted; what they called "making out" was within the rules; but that what he had done with Melony... to all of that, the answer was "No!"

In his case, the theme of "waiting and seeing," repeated often to him by Candy, and the fifteen years of living in moral limbo with only his emotional attachments and misgivings to guide him, underline the theme of the quest for the proper set of social and personal rules. But outsider that he is, search he must, for we are told several times that orphans above all need routine. As lone individuals trying to make the best judgments and decisions they can, they need the aid of simplifying rules when situations become too complex. Sympathetic emotions alone, important as they may be (as emphasized in the previous chapter), do not suffice for correct judgments.

While Homer accurately sees himself as an outsider, the ultimate outcast in the novel is Melony. She wanders from town to town entirely on her own and must compete for a living in a tough, male-dominated, rural society. As a teenager she is lawless and destructive, responding with only hostility to a hostile world. But in the course of making her way through generally unfriendly environments as a lone woman, she comes gradually to accept a more general rule, Hobbes' "Copper Rule" to do unto others as they do unto you: an eye for an eye, but also a return with interest of the few gifts she receives. Thus she meticulously repays all her debts, positive and negative, as she sees them. She comes to an intuitive grasp of this rule through hard experience. But after years of searching for Homer, whom she initially takes to be a moral hero despite his broken promise to her, she learns that she has found her moral compass, a rule to live by, before he is able to achieve a similar clarity.

Indeed, his moral awakening is prompted only by the confrontation with her and her immediate grasp of his situation. She vividly brings home to him the rules he is breaking:

I figured you for that—you know, the missionary. The do-gooder with his nose in the air... You've got your nose in the air—I got that part right. But you ain't exactly no missionary. You're a creep. You knocked up somebody who you shouldn't 'a' been fuckin' in the first place, and you couldn't even come clean about it to your own kid. Some missionary! Ain't that *brave*? In my book, Sunshine, that's a creep. (498)

His long, slow process of "waiting and seeing" what the right rules are is abruptly ended by her sudden reappearance and blunt words. Only then does he see that long-term deception of his son and sleeping with his best friend's wife violate rules for truth-telling and trust that must be obeyed. The one person, the ultimate outsider, whose experience has ingrained moral rules on a clean slate, becomes his moral beacon:

He had always expected much from Melony, but she had provided him with more than he'd ever expected—she had truly educated him, she had shown him the light. She was more Sunshine than he ever was, he thought. (586)

Homer nevertheless is not only the central character, but the true hero of the novel, for it is he alone who comes to a complete understanding of which rules must be obeyed and when they must curb strong feelings that would prompt violations. Throughout most of this long coming-of-age novel his judgments and behavior are guided by his emotional reactions and resultant affective attitudes, not always as reliable as those of the more mature Dr. Larch. As a young teen he comes to oppose abortion after being repulsed by the sight of an aborted fetus. Only slightly older, he falls immediately in love with Candy and blindly enters a long-term romantic relationship with her. And his sympathy for Wally and aversion to causing him distress prevents his revealing the true nature of their relationship. While such emotional reactions may in some contexts be an initial guide to right behavior, they cannot be fully trusted as bases for moral decisions in complex situations.

Homer's need to rely on more firmly established rules is symbolized in the novel by the flash of the cider house roof when he is looking out of his window and thinking of Candy:

Out in the orchards, the roof of the cider house flashed to him... How could I not be in love with Candy? he wondered. And if I stay here, he asked himself, what can I do?... And if I go back to St. Cloud's, he asked himself, what can I do? (270)

He is lost without a set of rules to guide him at least initially. The cider house is the site of their lovemaking, but also houses the rules that stand for all rules in the novel. The flashing light turns out to be a reflection from a piece of glass that cuts his hand when he investigates its source, the symbolic price for ignoring the symbolized rules. At the time Homer views the cut as a possible message, but cannot yet grasp its significance. The message lies not in the particular cider house rules, reasonable in themselves but unreasonably imposed and invariably ignored, but in the genuine rules he must still discover through the maze of useless rules like those in the cider house.

After his epiphany occurs in the encounter with Melony, Homer finally comes to a sophisticated if implicit understanding of when and which rules are required. First, he learns to specify vague moral rules correctly. We think of a rule against lying, but as Dr. Larch illustrates, there is no acceptable rule against lying per se. Unlike Dr. Larch, who lies or fictionalizes whenever it makes him feel good to do so, Homer comes to see when a narrower rule applies. He continues to lie to the board of directors of the orphanage about his identity, his credentials, and his abortion practice in order to be able to serve there. But he recognizes that he can no longer base his serious personal relationships on long-term deceptions. One cannot lie to one's loved ones despite strong feelings in favor of doing so. Better to end whatever aspects of the relationships depend on such deception. The rule must correct for the emotion-based behavior when one cannot trust to one's strong feelings.

Second, Homer comes to accept what is perhaps the most philosophically interesting truth about rules: that one must obey genuine rules even in some contexts in which one believes one can do morally better by acting on personal judgment.[6] Homer not only continues to oppose abortions personally; he knows from Wally and Candy having sought one just because they wanted to wait a while to have a child that some are clearly unjustified from almost any perspective. And yet, having overcome his aversion to ever performing abortion procedures by seeing the necessity of doing so for Mr. Rose's daughter, he comes to realize that he lacks the knowledge and authority to make these decisions on a case-by-case basis. He cannot know the situations of individual women as they themselves know them, and so he must accept a rule to provide abortions on demand when it is medically safe to do so.

---

[6] A fact denied by some writers on the subject: see Larry Alexander and Emily Sherwin, *The Rule of Rules* (Durham: Duke University Press, 2001), p. 37.

Doctors as a group have a collective obligation to allow women control over their bodies, and precisely when laws convince most doctors not to do so, Homer must obey the rule expressing the moral imperative whatever his personal feelings and judgments might be in individual cases. While ignoring a too general rule against lying by telling the board he will not perform abortions, he accepts a rule to perform them that is required in the social context in which he finds himself, precisely because of a legal rule prohibiting them. His implicit grasp of the proper attitude toward moral and social rules is now indeed sophisticated, and we can learn from seeing it as the culmination through life experience of a long process of moral development.

III

To summarize, what we learn about rules from this novel, if we draw the proper inferences from the attitudes, behavior, and fates of its characters, is rich and complex, not to be captured in a simple phrase or two. Wally indicates as much to Angel when teaching him to drive before the legal age: "Some rules are good rules. But some rules are just rules" (467). Mr. Rose, by contrast, fails to recognize this complexity and variability when he equates his incest with Homer and Candy's affair as equally in violation of rules. He pays with his life, while they suffer from their duplicity but also produce a loving son. The theme of "waiting and seeing" also indicates the difficulty in achieving a proper regard for the place of rules in moral reasoning. In this story rules are not simply preliminary guides to personal judgments without independent weight. They are not simply rules of thumb, as particularists hold. Yet neither are they routinely to be applied as the norm for moral judgment. They must supplant personal judgment in certain contexts, and not only in the context of public decision-making.

As to their proper contexts and effectiveness, we noted first that rules must be imposed by authorities accepted by those subject to them, if they are to be effective. The cider house rules, while reasonable demands for the safety of the workers, do not meet this requirement. Even benign rules are useless if imposed by sheer power on alien and alienated groups. Rules so imposed that are also unjustified cause harm even when ignored, as we see in the case of abortion laws imposed by men on women, which should be ignored but result in some unsafe abortions when they are, and in Melony's ignoring rules against lesbian relationships, which is again warranted but leads to hardships. Only by great ingenuity does Dr. Larch avoid the harm that would be caused by rules imposed by the incompetent board of directors. Rules allocate authority for decision-making, and they must reflect where justified authority lies.

Second, even justified rules that are accepted must nevertheless be broken when there are clearly overriding reasons for doing so. There is a justified rule to keep one's promises, but the rule can be violated even sometimes for purely self-regarding reasons. Homer must break his promise to Melony never to leave her in order to have a chance at a life beyond the orphanage. And sometimes rules that are almost universally binding must be broken to serve vital interests of others. Homer must accept fake medical credentials, even though the rule for licensing doctors is legitimate, since that is the only way he can serve the women and children at the orphanage. Mr. Rose's daughter breaks a most serious rule by stabbing her father, but that is the only way to escape from him. All these are justified violations of justified rules, some vitally important. In each case there are the strongest of reasons for breaking the rule, without which the violation would not be justified.

Third, lacking such clearly overriding reasons, we must sometimes obey rules even when we feel that we could do better in the individual case by acting on personal judgment. One context in which we must do so is when we cannot rely on personal judgments that may be partial or clouded by untrustworthy emotions. In the novel, Homer cannot trust his feelings when it comes to his relationship with Candy and Wally, and Mr. Rose certainly cannot trust his feelings toward his daughter. Another such context is when we lack the authority to act on our own judgments because of obligations of and to groups to which we belong. Rules allocate authority within groups and by doing so solve collective action problems. They prevent unacceptable aggregate outcomes that would result from unimpeded individual decisions, however individually rational those decisions might be.

As a member of the medical community capable of performing safe abortions, Homer must do so despite personal misgivings. As Dr. Larch points out, he might have a personal choice if enough other doctors were willing to serve women in need; but, given that the medical profession at the time was not fulfilling its collective obligation in this regard, Homer was morally required to bring it closer to doing so. In these contexts in which individual judgments are likely to produce collectively unacceptable results, we must accept rules and stick to them unless there are overwhelming reasons for making exceptions.

These general truths about the proper uses of rules can be gleaned from the novel if, as pointed out, we make the right inferences from the events in the story. In the first section of this chapter I expanded on Nussbaum's claim that novels have certain advantages over philosophical arguments in teaching ethics by claiming that they not only can show us how to attend more finely to particular complex moral contexts, but can also demonstrate general moral truths that take us beyond particularist insights. *The Cider House Rules*, which develops the theme of adherence to rules, is particularly apt in this regard. The novel is partly about the abortion issue, partly about race relations, partly about the need for family, but its main theme is the use and abuse of rules.

One might question this claim by noting that only philosophers already familiar with various positions regarding rules could draw the inferences that we have made explicit. Novels do not present arguments, and only analytical arguments can establish the sorts of distinctions I have drawn in regard to the proper uses of rules. We might be able to reconstruct these arguments and ensuing distinctions by reference to examples provided by fictional narratives such as *The Cider House Rules*, but, it might be objected, it is the arguments themselves that are crucial, and better to have them explicitly stated, as philosophers do, than only obscurely implicit in the fictional narratives.

I grant that it requires some philosophical acumen to draw the correct moral inferences from the events in the novel (otherwise, why write this chapter?). But having these lessons about rules taught to us by means of such detailed narratives still has its pedagogical advantages. It brings home to us, makes concrete, what are otherwise abstract arguments, in this case by having us vicariously experience the consequences of ignoring rules that must be obeyed and of following rules, such as abortion laws, that should not be followed. The chief advantage is motivational, which is key in ethics, since moral truths are meant to guide our conduct and not simply add to our beliefs. On the one hand, we all tend to overestimate our power of correct judgment, but witnessing the lives and deaths of these characters will make us more cautious about ignoring rules that are to guide judgments in certain contexts.

On the other hand, being the imitative and conformist creatures that we are, we often follow rules unthinkingly, but confronted by these stories, we cannot help but reflect consciously on when we should be following them and when we should not. We hone our moral judgments not only of particular cases, but in regard to the proper use of general guidelines, underestimated by particularists. I argued in earlier chapters that bringing moral judgments to action is a distinct moral capacity and end of moral development. Novels such as this not only provide contexts for the exercise of such judgments, but motivate us to act on them by making us see, indeed experience, if only imaginatively, the consequences of acting and not acting on them.

Philosophers may supplement their arguments and analyses with examples, but their examples will never be as nuanced or complete as the extended narratives in novels. This may be one reason why counterarguments and counterexamples to their analyses are so often easy to come by. We have seen that we need extensive sets of detailed examples to capture the subtle distinctions among contexts in which rules are proposed and imposed, and this need will exist in analyzing other complex moral issues as well. As Nussbaum argues, such narratives help us to see subtle differences in morally relevant contexts, but seeing these differences can lead us to draw generally relevant distinctions, and not simply help us to perceive particular situations more attentively.

Equally important, these distinctions can lead us to act differently in light of them. Irving himself might have had only an implicit grasp of a completely proper attitude toward rules, as revealed in his characters and their fates, but in comparison to an explicit but abstract philosophical argument, he can better motivate that attitude in us. In living the lives of his characters, we come to actively approve or condemn the ways the judgments that guide their lives are made. The fact that we ourselves must reflect on and draw inferences from their behavior makes us more likely to be motivated by our conclusions.

I shall end by briefly expanding on another point made by Nussbaum, as applied to *The Cider House Rules*. She argues that novels serve their moral purpose as much through their form as their content, and they serve it best when form and content are mutually reinforcing. We saw that in an earlier chapter in the way that Hemingway's prose style reinforces the thematic content of *The Sun Also Rises*. Henry James' depiction of delicate, many faceted, and highly nuanced moral relationships by means of equally delicately crafted (if not convoluted) prose is Nussbaum's excellent example. But how *The Cider House Rules* says what it has to say about rules is another equally apt example.

In broad outline, this is a classic coming-of-age-through-journey-and-return novel very much in the tradition of Dickens, who is often mentioned and quoted in it. Homer, like an orphaned Dickens hero, leaves home on his own, has a series of challenging adventures, and returns a different person to his proper role or place in life. Several reviewers remark that the narrative is clear and almost totally linear, in contrast to some of Irving's earlier novels. Thus, he seems here to follow the rules for standard, traditional narratives. But once more a closer look reveals his attitude toward these rules to be more complex and subtle, mirroring the proper complex attitude toward moral and social rules.

First, the narrative pace is uneven: despite the length of the novel, it covers a crucial fifteen years in the lives of all the characters in one chapter. Second, what we expect to be the climactic scenes are missing altogether, scenes in which Homer and Candy finally reveal the truth to Angel and Wally. Third, and perhaps most obvious, key events in the narrative, including deaths of major characters, are revealed in the most offhand ways. The reader is unexpectedly informed of Ray Kendall's death, for example, in a parenthetical phrase midway through a long paragraph describing clandestine meetings between Homer and Candy:

> The way they sat by the pool reminded them both of how they used to sit on Ray Kendall's dock, before they'd sat closer together. If ever they were too conscious of this memory—and of missing the dock, or of missing Ray (who'd died before Angel was old enough to have any memory of him)—this would spoil their evening by the swimming pool and they would be forced back to their separate bedrooms, where they would lie awake a little longer. (470)

These violations of the rules of narrative writing are surely not literary lapses on Irving's part. Occurring in what is otherwise a standard if well-written narration, they must be seen as a mirror in form of the central thematic content of the novel: the very complex ways in which rules must function in our decision-making.

Rules must reflect proper distributions of authority, and when they do, they can solve collective action problems. They can coordinate collective outcomes not achievable by individual choice, however rationally guided and morally perceptive. But even legitimate rules must be disobeyed when there are overwhelming reasons for doing so. In other contexts, such rules must supplant personal judgments about the best courses of action, when individual agents are likely to overestimate their ability to judge. We learn these general moral truths from the novel, which is better suited than philosophical argument alone to motivate us to reflect on and respect them.[7]

In the previous chapter on *Huckleberry Finn*, we saw how important the development of proper empathy and sympathy is in the attainment of full moral agency. Sometimes, as in Huck Finn's case, we should trust to such feelings to override our reflective judgments based on internalizations of society's rules. But in *The Cider House Rules*, we see that the opposite is also sometimes the case. In some contexts we must defer to rules and even allow them to curb our strongest feelings, even feelings of love, as guides to proper conduct. Morality is indeed a difficult and messy business. And Martha Nussbaum, whose particularist view of morality has been shown to be as narrow as the opposed rule-bound view, is nevertheless right that novels, with their detailed narratives, are the optimum vehicles for revealing this complexity. *The Cider House Rules* is as good as any for imparting this supremely general philosophical lesson.

[7] Or, if we prefer to make up our own rules like Dr. Larch or Angel, whose love for Mr. Rose's daughter is thwarted by the corrupt racist rules of his society, we become like them writers of fiction or novelists.

8

Nostromo and the fragility of the self

In the previous chapters of this section we have seen how novels, by tracing the lives of their characters through many years and through life-changing relationships and events, can teach us what is generally involved in full moral agency and in the development of a moral identity. We saw that Jane Austen, in contrast to more one-sided contemporary theorists of moral development, was aware of the several different cognitive, emotional, and volitional capacities acquired by fully mature moral agents—empathy for the long-term needs of those at some psychological distance, decentered perception of opposed morally relevant factors or interests, a properly deferential yet critical attitude toward social rules, and the will to act on one's reflective moral judgments. We saw in *Huckleberry Finn* what is more specifically involved in moral motivation, and again, how it typically develops. And we saw in *The Cider House Rules* how complex the proper attitude toward conventional moral rules needs to be.

It is noteworthy, if predictable in hindsight, that one of the first modern novels, written at the turn of the last century and prophetic in style, content, and political vision, would thematize not moral development, but its opposite, the disintegration of moral agency, a significant part of a healthy human self. Here we see in reverse what is required not simply for developing, but for sustaining, full moral agency. And we see the effects of lacking these necessary conditions: the fragmentation of the moral agent, indeed the disintegration of the self.

I

Once again, however, most literary criticism of *Nostromo* has focused not on this philosophical theme, but on Conrad's nonlinear view of history.

This view is half Marxist, in that "material interests" are seen to shape the course of historical movement, but nonprogressive, in that, while his fictional new republic of Sulaco has made some progress in achieving prosperity and social order, the latter remains repressive, and new revolution and chaos seem imminent at the end of the novel.

The story begins with a riot in the town of Sulaco in the midst of yet another revolution in the country of Costaguana. The plot only returns to the riot over a hundred pages later and then again near the end of the novel in Captain Mitchell's distorted historical narrative. The central events of the novel take place during a few days toward the end of the 19th century, but the focus early on shifts from the 16th century to ten years or so before and after the main events, chronicling the history of the San Tomé mine, the early relationship of the young Goulds in Europe, and the subsequent history of Sulaco after becoming the new Occidental Republic. These shifting and sometimes confusing and chaotic scenes present a vivid picture of the colorful but violent setting of the Latin American state.

There is at first no linear development in the story, but constantly shifting tableaux, disorienting the reader in a temporal sequence that is "irrecoverable," according to one prominent critic.[1] In fact, in the second and third parts of the novel we do get a good idea of the sequence of events immediately preceding, during, and after the crucial several days of the separatist revolt. But the multiple strands of the first part that come together only later surely do reflect Conrad's pessimistic view of the course of history. That view is reinforced by the intimation that fresh violence will follow the end of the narrative, both in the form of an attempt to annex the rest of Costaguana, from which Sulaco had separated, and in the form of a Marxist uprising against the European ruling elite. And the historical narrative of the successful revolution that precedes the novel's conclusion is put in the mouth of the half senile and always comical Captain Mitchell.

Conrad's dark view of historical movement is matched by his cynical attitude toward political factions on both the right and the left in his prophetic vision of the 20th century. The regime of the benevolent dictator Ribiera is supported by the main characters in the novel, and we are clearly

---

[1] Albert Guerard, *Conrad the Novelist* (Cambridge, MA: Harvard University Press, 1958), p. 211.

to sympathize with the defeat of the greedy and evil Monterists who overthrow Ribiera. But the Monterists oppose foreign imperialism, and Ribiera is a tool of both Gould, a protagonist, and Holroyd, the American capitalist who hypocritically seeks to bring a "purer form of Christianity" to the natives. Conrad seems leery of the American imperialist colonialism that he sees coming, but no more sympathetic to the lower classes or their Marxist instigators. The Marxist who seeks Nostromo's aid at the end of the novel is described as anything but a future hero:

There was no one with the wounded man but the pale photographer, small, frail, bloodthirsty, the hater of capitalists, perched on a high stool near the head of the bed with his knees up and his chin in his hands…remaining huddled up on the stool, shock-headed, wildly hairy, like a hunchbacked monkey.[2] (445)

As opposed to historical fiction in which progress is the culmination and confirmation of individual endeavors in concert, we find social change here determined by impersonal material forces, but in a dismally repetitive process that subverts all individual efforts at progressive reform.

As noted, critics have mainly addressed such historical themes in the novel, seeing them as being of greater interest than its characters. One major critic sees the two hundred pages in the last parts of the novel that focus on the characters and their fates as superfluous, unnecessary excess.[3] Another writes that "historic process could be seen as the real subject of the story, more important than any of the people in it,"[4] while a third holds that the characters exist for what they represent rather than for what they are.[5] I profoundly disagree. My focus here will be exclusively on the characters as individual selves who tell us much about the nature of character and the self. I believe Conrad's focus is the same. The incredibly rich fictional history that he creates in this novel is still only contextual backdrop for the deeply revealing, however unsuccessful, interactions among the characters.

There are several major clues in support of this claim of literary priority. The first is that disorienting shifts occur not only in the temporal

---

[2] Joseph Conrad, *Nostromo* (New York: Doubleday, 1960). Page references in the text are to this edition.

[3] Albert Guerard, *Conrad the Novelist*, p. 203.

[4] Eloise Knapp Hay, *The Political Novels of Joseph Conrad* (Chicago: Chicago University Press, 1963), p. 162.

[5] Jocelyn Baines, *Joseph Conrad* (London: Weidenfeld & Nicolson, 1959), p. 299.

sequence, but in spatial perspectives and narrative viewpoints as well. Descriptive passages veer from majestic, sweeping landscapes of mountain and sea to visual details of mundane, intimate interiors and actions.[6] Many characters early on appear and then vanish, and multiple narrators tell the story. The permanent backdrop of mountain and sea contrasts with the fragility and futility of the characters and their actions, for whom and for which there is no internal probing or explicit psychological interpretation. The main characters, especially Nostromo himself, are portrayed initially by others, seen only from their shifting and often contradictory viewpoints.

That we have changing narrators, points of view, and spatial as well as temporal perspectives indicates a stylistic symbolism not limited to the theory of historical change over time. The spatial shifts direct our attention to the smallness and vulnerability of human projects in a vast and indifferent nature. The changing narrators force us to see the characters always through the eyes of others, stylistically indicating the importance of the social aspect of psychological identity, the fact that individual identity is possible only in community, and the evanescence of the self from the purely first-person point of view.

A second clue to the centrality of character study in the novel, the lack of dominant focus on the philosophy of history, is the fact that the key historical events are largely omitted from direct narration. Nostromo's daring ride to bring back the army of Barrios, the defeat of Montero by that army, the saving of Gould by his miners—all these events that would be climactic in a historical adventure story are only indirectly mentioned after the fact, and mostly in Captain Mitchell's offhand and rambling account to an inattentive visitor to the town. If the theory of history were the main focus of the novel, central points in the historical narrative would be highlighted.

The challenges to readers in the first part of *Nostromo*, the fact that they cannot locate themselves in the sort of imaginative games that current literary theorists like to ascribe,[7] make it fitting to characterize the book, as many critics have, as one of the first modern novels, despite its lack

[6] Compare Ian Watt, *Joseph Conrad, Nostromo* (Cambridge: Cambridge University Press, 1988), p. 42.

[7] Kendall Walton, *Mimesis as Make-Believe* (Cambridge, MA: Harvard University Press, 1990).

of explicit inner psychological exploration of its characters, as in later stream-of-consciousness narrative. The interior mental lives of these characters, as opposed to their actions, interactions, and descriptions of each other, are not in focus in this novel. This lack has been seen as a shortcoming by some critics, or once more as a sign that the book is really about social history, but again I disagree. The style of narrational externality and distance is better characterized as reflecting the major theme of the novel—the psychic disintegration or fragmentation that leaves these characters mere shells without coherent inner selves to explore.

The lack of intelligible purpose to history and its social and political movements with which individuals could identify parallels and only partly causes this pathological process in the individual characters, which is the book's main theme. The continuous destruction of the social order is a contributing backdrop to the destructions of the individual selves of the main characters, more sharply focused in the later parts of the novel, leading up to the literal deaths of both Nostromo and Decoud. Character and self are superficial and fragile in this novel, highly vulnerable to the terrible circumstantial luck to which the political chaos subjects them. It is the nature of the self that its vulnerability reveals that will be my focus here, as it was Conrad's.

II

Conrad's skepticism about the substance and stability of character predates by a century the same topic now prevalent in contemporary social psychology and philosophy. A brief survey of the conflicting claims in that contemporary literature will help to clarify the concept of the self that Conrad shares with those who later attack and defend it, and will enable us to better locate his position.

Traditionally, it has been assumed (and perhaps even more so by novel writers) that individual persons have characters or selves consisting of stable and robust dispositions to react in ways that can be classified as virtues or vices. This assumption guides our practice in evaluating persons by their actions and holding them responsible. Character traits are robust when exercised across virtually all relevant circumstances. We assume that a kind person will act kindly whenever called for, that an honest person will tell the truth even when a lie might benefit her, and so on. Good character, we assume, stands up to adverse circumstances, and is indeed tested and identified by actions in those situations that tempt transgressions. People ascribe these traits to themselves as well as to others; they identify with certain of their assumed traits and identify themselves in these terms. They believe they can be identified by their deepest and most robust dispositions or motives that motivate a great many specific actions in various and varied circumstances.

While individuals identify with certain of their deep motivations or values, other desires may feel alien. A person can be mistaken about some of these deep motivations, and then her self-image comes apart from her real self, which consists in those stable dispositions that actually determine how she acts. But ideally the self exhibits coherence across several dimensions. First, in a healthy psyche, second-order desires match first-order motivations: we endorse or desire to have the desires that we do have. Second, these motivations match our evaluative judgments about what is good or bad for us, what we have reason to pursue or avoid. Our deepest motivations with which we identify ultimately determine what reasons we take ourselves to have, if we are coherent selves. They set limits to what we rationally will or will not do. Our central values fix our priorities and rule out certain demands as constituting reasons for us. The self is defined by what is most important to us, what we try to live up to and hope not to betray.[8]

Our deepest motives may lack deeper reasons for having them, but they should cohere with each other and in that sense provide a mutually supporting set of reasons for acting in a variety of ways as the circumstances call for. These self-constitutive motivations make up a set of prioritized values that give the self complexity and depth. They are the source of long-term plans that give coherence to our lives over time as we act to fulfill them. If we are to endorse and take them to determine our reasons for acting, we must be capable of rationally and critically reflecting on them. Responsiveness to reasons implies the capacity to criticize our own motives in light of others and of opportunities to successfully act on them.

While our central motivations fix our priorities at given times, these priorities and the motives behind them must still be subject to revision with changing situations.[9] Reasoning in light of them serves to resolve

---

[8] See, for example, Harry Frankfurt, *The Importance of What We Care About* (Cambridge: Cambridge University Press, 1988).

[9] Compare Bernard Berofsky, "Autonomy without Free Will," in *Personal Autonomy*, James Taylor, ed. (Cambridge: Cambridge University Press, 2005).

inconsistencies, determines how to translate them into action, and adjusts them to new information. Such rational reflection on our motivations, which is the mark of a rational, functioning self, requires a plurality of concerns whose priorities can be adjusted as situations allow for their fulfillment in action. We revise some goals in light of others, and so the ability to reflect and revise requires a set of ongoing concerns.

Third, then, one's actions must be coherent with one's values. If one is to endure as a self-directed agent, opportunities must present themselves for translating one's values into actions that realize them in the world. To be self-directed is to act on self-endorsed motivations most important to one at the time, motives that one takes to provide one's strongest reasons. One must be capable of carrying out one's plans,[10] but not with a fanatic obstinacy that signals that one is a slave to one's desires that then may be felt as alien and oppressive. A unified self is an autonomous agent capable of self-directed action aiming at his conception of the good. Such an agent has integrity or character, the strength of will necessary to act on his relatively fixed values in situations in which it may be difficult to do so.

Difficult, but not impossible. The first way in which the natural, and especially the social, world must cooperate in sustaining functioning selves is in affording opportunities for such self-directed action. If one's motivational set leads only to constant frustration in action, the self that is identified with that set is at risk. Outer life must express inner life. A second related way in which the social world must cooperate in the creation and sustenance of individual selves is by providing suitable social roles that individuals can fulfill in ways coherent with their values. In fact, such roles are a major source of individuals' values, but they must cohere with each other in a social system so as again not to lead to constant conflict and frustration.

A third requirement of the social context is that it reinforces the self-images that individuals develop over time. Persons' self-images may be largely idealizations, but such ideals may be necessary to their psyches and must be socially reinforced to survive. One's self-identity is at least in part relative to the ways others see one. When a person's self-image diverges sharply from the ways others see her, there is again danger of psychic disintegration, as there is when self-image diverges from motives

---

[10] Michael Bratman, "Planning Agency, Autonomous Agency," in *Personal Autonomy*, James Taylor, ed. (Cambridge: Cambridge University Press, 2005).

that actually guide actions. The self is partly a personal construction from identification with certain central motives and values, and partly a social construction, and once more the two must cohere for the individual agent to remain unthreateningly self-directed.

People construct their own selves in part by constructing narratives in which they are the central characters,[11] and they present themselves to others through these narratives that others may or may not accept. They have difficulty opposing others' views, especially others' views of them. Their self-esteem, which sustains their sense of self, is tied to their reputations with others. When others ascribe a trait to a person, that person is more likely to act in line with that trait. Then too, one's deepest motives need reaffirmation or confirmation in one's intimate relations. Nowhere are these points more evident than in the characters in *Nostromo*.

In all these ways the requirement of coherence for functioning selves capable of self-directed action and long-term plans extends outward from one's internal motivational set to the social environment in which one acts. This means that the health and very survival of the self is subject to factors beyond one's control. While a person of integrity or strong character is supposed to stand up to adverse circumstances, character can be overwhelmed by sufficiently hostile environments. And, as Thomas Nagel points out, we judge people's characters by what they do in the situations in which they find themselves, even if they would have behaved completely differently had those situations never obtained for them.[12]

Since others' assessments of a person depend on circumstances that elicit actual behavior, and since future behavior depends in part on others' expectations, it seems that not just success or failure, but character itself is subject to what Nagel calls circumstantial moral luck. We are praised or blamed for actions that would not have occurred had circumstances beyond our control been different. Such vulnerability to blame can, however, generate alternative explanations for weakness in the face of adversity or temptation. Since character is unpacked dispositionally, it can be debated whether action seemingly out of character reveals a mistake about the dispositions an agent had all along, or a change in

[11] Daniel Dennett, "The Origins of Selves," in *Self and Identity*, Daniel Kolak and Raymond Martin, eds (New York: Macmillan, 1991).
[12] Thomas Nagel, *Mortal Questions* (Cambridge: Cambridge University Press, 1979), ch. 3.

those dispositions. As we shall see in the next section, the character of Nostromo dramatically raises this very question.

Character, we noted, consists of stable and robust dispositions classified as virtues or vices. A person identifies himself by identifying with these central dispositions, and others identify him by ascribing them. Fictional characters in novels typically exemplify such traits, and if we are to learn anything about real people from reading fiction, real people seemingly must exemplify them too. But contemporary psychologists and philosophers following them have questioned the reality of such character, claiming that character traits or behavioral dispositions are far less stable and robust than common sense assumes.

They claim that experiments have shown that behavior is determined by situation far more than by character traits. Even seemingly minor variations in circumstances alter behavior, which cannot therefore be lined up with professed or commonly ascribed values. Such factors as mood as altered by trivial events, time pressure, and the presence and pressure of others turn out to be far more predictive of helping, ignoring, or harming others than are assumed character traits. Subjects who had just found a dime were far more likely to help a woman pick up papers dropped on the street; seminarians in a hurry to keep an appointment to give a talk were far less likely to help a stranger seemingly in need; and normal subjects ordered to play roles involving harm and cruelty were very likely to comply.[13]

Critics, however, have recently questioned the sweeping conclusions drawn from these experiments. In the dime and dropped papers case, the need for help seems as trivial as the mood change, so it is not so surprising that the one would vary with the other. In the seminarians' case, the obligation to be on time to give a talk, which might be thought to affect future career opportunities, seems as important as the need of a person, possibly a derelict, on the side of the road, so it is not so surprising that help would vary with pressure to be on time. In general, multiple dispositions or character traits might oppose one another in different situations that determine their priorities in those contexts without calling into question their existence. Thus, people have strong institutional norm obeying dispositions as well as benevolent and harm-avoiding ones. The former are

---

[13] These experiments are well summarized in John Doris, *Lack of Character* (Cambridge: Cambridge University Press, 2002).

biologically predictable since necessary for much basic learning, including language learning. Such robust and stable dispositions might well explain willingness to harm when pressured by perceived institutional obligations or authorities.[14]

In regard to fictional literature and its capacity to teach us about real human nature, two questions can be posed in light of this recent debate. The first is the question at the center of the debate: "Are people as dispositionally unstable as currently claimed?" The second is the question whether fictional characters display such robust character traits as to be way out of line with true human nature. Assuming a positive answer to the first question, which I would not assume except for the sake of arguing its irrelevance in the case of Conrad, the second question might be answered generally affirmatively.

But Conrad is perhaps the greatest exception. He does not take a stand on whether minor variations in circumstances alter behavior, since his characters are subject to extreme adversity and temptation. But what we find are repeated dramatic variations on the theme of what happens when circumstances overwhelm character, effecting a complete breakdown of the self. And, by contrast, we can infer what a healthy self or firm character ought to be, whether most people are so or not.

Breakdowns, as we learn from the novel and will see in more detail in the next section, occur in either of two ways. The result is either fanaticism, obsessive clinging to a single purpose or cause that maintains psychic unity at the cost of alienation and loss of control, or fragmentation and disintegration, loss of any sense of purpose or self. The fanatic is guided by a single motivation that obscures all others and remains beyond the capacity for criticism, consideration of opposing reasons, and therefore critical endorsement. The healthy self is multi-dimensional; the fanatic's single overriding motivation is not only compulsive, but more vulnerable to irremediable failure. Often it is a motive formerly rejected or subordinated to others, and the agent may remain self-deceptive about its current domination of him. The opposite pathology, the extreme identity crisis, involves the disappearance of any idea of a good to pursue, irresolvable conflicts within any remaining motivations, complete

---

[14] John Sabini and Maury Silver, "Lack of Character? Situationism Critiqued," *Ethics*, 115 (2005): 535–62; Rackana Kamtekar, "Situationism and Virtue Ethics on the Content of Our Character," *Ethics*, 114 (2004): 458–91.

loss of self-esteem, and finally, loss of a sense of who one is and of any significance to events.[15] When a person loses her sense of self, her personal narrative no longer makes sense to her: past events in her life seem unconnected to present and future.

By contrast, self-construction from identification with and critical endorsement of central motives taken to provide reasons for pursuing values, and the resultant self-image that coheres with one's social role and reputation, give a sense of direction to one's life and a sense of freedom or mastery over events. Such self-identification serves a unifying function that makes sense of one's personal narrative. Action seems self-directed, expressive of one's character, and under one's control, achieving the values pursued, and leading to fresh intentions and plans. Such an integrated self is necessary for a sense of meaning in life, meaning deriving from the coherence over time of events under one's control. In *Nostromo*, as we shall now see, this concept of the self and its function can be inferred from the failures of its characters to live up to it.

III

With background provided, we can now examine the characters in the novel directly. Nostromo himself obviously stands at the center of the novel (despite the denial by some critics of the obvious), and he is most emblematic of the themes regarding character and self described in the previous section. One claim emphasized there was the dependence of the self and self-image on social reinforcement, the need for one's dispositions to be socially sustained, and Nostromo is an extreme example. At the beginning of the story, his private self is simply his public self, and that is why we see him initially only through the eyes of other characters.

The match is not entirely healthy since Nostromo can be seen as obsessively concerned with his reputation and is accused of being so by Teresa Viola, his adopted mother. On the other hand, his primary motive can be seen as a throwback to an earlier ideal of honor in a novel already described as transitional and concerned with transitional historical themes. His sole concern with being admired by others does already render him vulnerable, but to the extent that he is capable of reflection, it is self-endorsed

---

[15] Compare Charles Taylor, *Sources of the Self* (Cambridge, MA: Harvard University Press, 1989), p. 68.

without illusion early on. We all need social reinforcement, Nostromo
only more than others.

As intimated, Nostromo is not reflective; nor does he have a developed
sense of self, relying entirely on others to provide his self-image. He acts
mainly on instinct, but when it comes to dangerous situations, his natural
instincts appear perfect, which makes him the perfect hero for the peril-
ous missions in the revolutions and counter-revolutions in Costaguana.
He saves the defeated benevolent dictator Ribiera, enlists the bandit
Hernandez as a leader of the anti-Monterist forces, brings back the army
of Barrios to Sulaco, quells a riot of peasants in the town, and takes a shipment of silver out to sea to prevent the Monterists from seizing it.

But despite his heroic deeds and dashing image, there are from the
beginning the seeds not only of fanaticism, but of both conflict and contradiction in his character. Contradictions are already apparent in the
early descriptions of him by others. While Captain Mitchell, his boss,
praises him as entirely trustworthy and capable, in fact "incorruptible"
(the image widely shared by the community), Teresa Viola, who perhaps
knows him best, sees him as both subservient and selfish:

"Ah! the traitor! The traitor!" she mumbled, almost inaudibly. "Now we are
going to be burnt; and I bent my knee to him. No! he must run at the heels of the
English... He think of the casa! He!" gasped Signora Viola crazily. She struck her
breast with her open hands. "I know him. He thinks of nobody but himself." (31)

And the contradictions are apparent in his roles and actions as well, even
in the multiple ironic names he is given. Despite being most instrumental
in the successful secession of Sulaco, he is entirely a-political. He unwittingly ushers in the age of capitalism and colonialism in the Latin republic, yet his actions are completely divorced from any motives that might
politically justify them.

He is a man of natural instinct, yet everything he does is for show,
egoistic yet entirely other-directed. He is a man of the people, yet at the
service of the elite rulers. He can overcome mountains and the sea, control men and women, yet he is easily controlled by the European capitalists, used by Mitchell, Dr. Monygham, and the mine owners, Gould and
Holroyd, for their own purposes. Until his one failed mission, he remains
unaware that he is being used, even when Teresa Viola mockingly points
it out to him. His multiple names reference these contradictory roles:
"Nostromo," Italian for mate or boatswain (he was a sailor and is captain of the longshoremen), but also an abbreviation for "our man" (man

of both the people and the aristocracy); "Gian Batista," his Christian
names (John the Baptist, heralding a new economic religion); and finally,
"Captain Fidanza," when he becomes least loyal and trustworthy.

These seeds of contradiction in his personality and public persona
do not bear self-destructive fruit until the climactic failed silver mission. Seeking to transfer the silver to a friendly cargo ship, the boat of
Nostromo and Decoud is instead struck by Sotillo's enemy vessel, barely
making it to the island where Nostromo leaves Decoud with the now
hidden silver to seek help. When Nostromo finally returns to the island
after being diverted to a desperate ride to bring General Barrios back to
Sulaco, Decoud is missing, having committed suicide by using four silver
bars as weights to drown himself.

Nostromo is now the victim of extreme circumstantial moral luck.
The silver is thought to be sunk. With Decoud gone, no one knows its
location, and Nostromo believes he would be accused of stealing if he
returned the remainder with four bars missing. He feels betrayed by
Decoud and those who sent him on a dangerous mission with a shipment
of silver that was insignificant in relation to the mine's lode. His moral
identity now appears to be beyond his choice and control since he can
no longer make his public image match his self-knowledge. His fear of
being thought corrupt corrupts him. Slowly stealing the hidden silver is
then seen by him as an act of revenge against those who betrayed him:

Yes, four gone. Taken away. Four ingots. But who? Decoud? Nobody else. And
Why? For what purpose? Did he take them in revenge... and yet had laid upon
him the task of saving the children? Well he had saved the children... Who
cared? He had done it, betrayed as he was, and saving by the same stroke the San
Tomé mine, which appeared to him hateful and immense... "I must grow rich
very slowly," he meditated aloud. (394, 400)

That no one is incorruptible given extreme enough adversity and
temptation may not be an interesting inference in today's context of more
radical situationist claims. But the situation leading to Nostromo's transgression is more morally ambiguous than so far described and explicit
in the novel. While it is undoubtedly true that he could have remained
morally pure in different and more ordinary circumstances, that he is
therefore a victim of circumstantial moral luck in deserving condemna-
tion for theft, he is already partially compromised before the decision to
steal the silver. He has betrayed Teresa Viola on her deathbed by refusing
to find her a priest, deciding instead to bolster his public image by leaving

to seek General Barrios (the necessity of choosing being another piece of moral luck):

> She was dead. But would God consent to receive her soul? She had died without confession or absolution, because he had not been willing to spare her another moment of his time. (336)

And he has betrayed Decoud by leaving him for so long on the island without adequate supplies.

Thus, his treachery against Gould and Holroyd, to whom the silver belongs, is not his first, although he sees these last three as having betrayed him. Indeed, he blames his transgression on their having wronged him, but it is clear that whatever moral sense he had is largely gone before the decision to steal the silver, which is therefore made easier. Then too, he could have simply left the silver hidden and lost without slowly enriching himself with it, so that circumstances did not force his decision to the extent he thought.

Nostromo's moral standing being already partially compromised, the interesting question arises whether his climactic decision to steal the silver represents a radical change in character, a revelation of true, already existing character, or an indication that character itself is the myth that situationists claim. And there may be no answer, certainly no clear answer, either in the case of this fictional character or in real life.

The first answer, a change in character, is suggested by the fact that Nostromo might well have remained "incorruptible" to the extent that his actions would have continued to have been entirely in line with his public image had he not been subject to such extreme circumstances, in which his reputation would have suffered more by the return of the remaining silver. Circumstances, it seems, can affect not only praise or blame received, but that deserved. While it takes time to acquire a stable disposition, it seems that one can dissolve in an instant of contrary choice. Misfortune, failure, or temptation can alter the entire pattern of one's future actions. Character is determined by choices, as well as determining them. Nostromo becomes secretive and untrustworthy after his choice to steal the silver, as he would not have been otherwise and was not before.

The second answer, that Nostromo's act merely reveals his previously existing but unknown character, is supported by the claim that true character is tested only in adverse circumstances involving difficult choices or temptations. And even after stealing the silver, Nostromo's concern for his reputation remains at least for a time his main motive. Thus, returning to Sulaco, he is immediately convinced by Dr. Monygham's flattery to undertake the dangerous ride to find Barrios. He accepts yet another desperate mission in order to maintain a public image now known by him to be false. He does so at the expense of both Teresa Viola and Decoud, but that only shows again how obsessive his concern for his public image has been all along.

If there are no grounds for choosing among the first two answers, this might well suggest the third—that character itself is an illusory social construction. Conrad himself suggests as much in the voices of his more cynical characters, Decoud and Monygham. When another character is described as sure of himself, Monygham answers: "If that is all he is sure of, then he is sure of nothing. It is the last thing a man ought to be sure of" (251). Whether or not such statements indicate skepticism about the existence of the self or character on Conrad's part, it is clear that its fragility is a main theme of the novel. What is most clear and interesting is the self-fragmentation, disintegration, and then fanaticism into which Nostromo descends after his fateful decision to steal the silver.

As indicated, his public and private self, formerly indistinguishable, now come completely apart. As he grows into the rich Captain Fidanza, his public image is for a time even enhanced, but it is an entirely false identity. Conrad describes his state:

Nostromo had lost his peace; the genuineness of all his qualities was destroyed. He felt it himself, and often cursed the silver of San Tomé. His courage, his magnificence, his leisure, his work, everything was as before, only everything was a sham. (416)

He becomes Fidanza when he can no longer be trusted; in becoming his own man, he loses his former self. A life totally on display for others becomes entirely secretive and alienated from those with whom he might be intimate.

He had never been on intimate terms with those with whom he shared the adventure of saving Sulaco. On the boat with Decoud, they each remained locked within their own worlds:

This common danger brought their differences in aim, in view, in character, and in position, into absolute prominence in the private vision of each. There was no bond of conviction, of common idea; they were merely two adventurers pursuing each his own adventure, involved in the same imminence of deadly peril. Therefore they had nothing to say to each other. (241)

While Decoud acts from love of Antonia and Monygham from love of Emilia Gould, both are entirely opaque to Nostromo, who takes no interest in their motives. They act together in isolation, often talking past one another. With Monygham he acts in vain, even though their mission to save Sulaco is successful. Monygham can never reveal his love for Emilia, and Nostromo can no longer make his image match reality. After the theft of the silver, all moral limits are gone, and he becomes even more isolated. He betrays both Viola daughters, the sole characters with whom he could have been intimate and whose affirmation could have supported the identity he was striving to adopt.

After a lighthouse is built on the island where the treasure is hidden, Nostromo installs the Violas there as its keepers. The lighthouse, a symbol of the public eye in which he had thrived, is now a mortal danger to him, a threat to expose his secret. He becomes engaged to Linda Viola as a way to keep returning to the island, has an affair with the more morally lax Giselle, but lies to her about his motives and cannot bring himself to reveal the secret location of the treasure. His former self, which might have been saved by her collusion, has by now ceased to exist, as Conrad makes clear in allusions to death:

the confused and intimate impressions of universal dissolution which beset a subjective nature at any strong shock to its ruling passion had a bitterness approaching that of death itself... his excitement had departed, as when the soul takes flight leaving the body inert upon an earth it knows no more. (333, 393)

The disintegrated self is replaced by a new fanaticism: he is now a slave to the silver he has stolen. The periodic visits to the treasure to appropriate more of it become his sole guiding motive, but he is completely alienated from it. Indeed, it is entirely alien to his former dispositions. He had cared nothing for money, as was clear from his having given the silver buttons on his coat to a street girl; and his complete lack of material concern was another object of Teresa Viola's scorn. But now the desire for the silver, for "becoming slowly rich," is felt to control him like an addiction. Although neither man is initially motivated by it, Nostromo, like Charles Gould (to whom we turn next), is thoroughly corrupted and ultimately ruled by the silver and the material greed it stands for.

In the end Nostromo is killed by the old man Viola in a case of mistaken identity. The case is ironic since Viola mistakes him for the man he takes to be Giselle's lover, when Nostromo is the real lover of his daughter. Doubly ironic, since by then Nostromo has no true identity capable of self-directed action. His image for others, his former obsession, is preserved in death by Linda's enduring love and by Emilia's refusal to reveal the stolen silver (revealed to her by Nostromo on his deathbed) to Monygham, who wants to see Nostromo as having been as corruptible as he was. But the lasting image of magnificence is an illusion of a self that long ago ceased to exist, if it ever did.

IV

The other major characters in the book, already mentioned as variations on the same theme, are Charles and Emilia Gould, Decoud, and Dr. Monygham. Charles Gould, the proprietor of the silver mine, is a variation on the descent into fanaticism. His is more gradual and less dramatic than Nostromo's, and mostly offstage, but equally or more obvious. Like Nostromo, he has a reputation for being incorruptible. Both belie that public image, Nostromo by a catastrophic act and Gould on a slippery slope of slow moral decay. Again like Nostromo (and like Elizabeth Bennet, Darcy, Huckleberry Finn, Homer Wells, and Melony), he lacks parental guidance toward self-development in his youth.

Nostromo, we saw, betrays his surrogate parents. Gould, having been sent away to Europe as a child, later rejects his father's emphatic advice in seeking to avenge his memory by restoring the mine. Finally, like Nostromo, he is rendered vulnerable by his primary motivation, in his case by linking the central project of his life to a hoped-for progressive course of history unlikely in the turbulent context of Latin America. As noted earlier, the fictional but reality-based history in this novel is both a symbol for and partial cause of the fragile and fragmented psyches of several of the main characters.

Gould's initial motives are moral: to avenge his badly treated father by redeeming the silver mine for which he was victimized, and in so doing to bring prosperity and peace to Sulaco and Costaguana. But the actions he must take to keep the mine running in the totally corrupt political environment undermine the motives initially behind them, including most obviously the motive of creating a moral social order:

> In his determined purpose he held the mine, and the indomitable bandit (Hernandez) held the campo by the same precarious tenure. They were equals before the lawlessness of the land. It was impossible to disentangle one's activity from its debasing contacts. A close-meshed net of crime and corruption lay upon the whole country. (291)

Totally corrupt means cannot sustain a moral end.

The slippery slope that begins with briberies, political deals, and the installation of a new friendly dictatorship, necessary to save the mine, compromises the values that the silver was to express and serve. The mine itself, initially seen as a means to admirable social goals, becomes the only end for Gould, when he must constantly sacrifice his moral sense to its survival. Political circumstances will not allow the joint realization of the means and the end, and so the means become the end. Like Nostromo, Gould, an innately good man, is the victim of bad circumstantial moral luck, and the result is a gradual descent into fanatic pursuit of the single goal of maintaining the profits of the mine.

This choice of an ultimate amoral motive comes about not through rational assessment, but by small incremental steps, much as Millgram's subjects would not initially choose an extremely painful shock, but arrive there at the bottom of a slippery slope. Gould is probably unaware of his loss of moral purpose, but his obsession increasingly dehumanizes him, turning him completely uncommunicative and isolating him even from his wife, the only character who retains a moral compass throughout:

> His taciturnity, assumed with a purpose, had prevented him from tampering openly with his thoughts; but the Gould Concession had insidiously corrupted his judgment. (293)

His marriage a failure, he becomes sterile in every way. His silence at first could be interpreted as a refusal to engage in empty political rhetoric, so prevalent around him, but later it is more plausibly seen as an inability to express a self that is no longer there.

If he could critically analyze his actions and express his motives, he probably could not live with himself, and so his lack of dialogue with others undoubtedly matches the same lack in himself. He is living a lie that he cannot tell. He is no longer self-directed and in control of his motivations and actions, but a fanatic driven by the silver that controls him to save it for himself and his financier, Holroyd, at any human cost. This fanaticism is most clearly evidenced by his willingness at the end to blow up the mine rather than let it fall into others' hands:

He was prepared, if need be, to blow up the whole San Tomé mountain sky-high out of the territory of the republic. This resolution expressed the tenacity of his character, the remorse of that subtle conjugal infidelity through which his wife was no longer the sole mistress of his thoughts, something of his father's weakness... (294)

Loss of the mine would destroy even the shell that remains of his self. If he retains any motive other than profit, it is the near equivalent one of avenging the father he never knew, filling the hole in his self-development with this monomaniacal pursuit of material profit.

The next major character is Decoud, a Frenchified wholly cynical dandy, whose attitudes perhaps best match Conrad's own, but who echoes Nostromo's disintegration, as Gould mirrored his fanaticism. Although as a cynic he is less prone to self-deceptive illusion than is Gould, his motives are equally divided and fail to be adequately reflected in his actions. His detached and ever-critical rationality does not allow identification with his own emotions or actions. Initially he is a journalist spokesman for a cause in which he does not believe, presenting a false front by advocating liberal views he does not share. He then initiates and leads the separatist movement, all the while seeing politics as a "farce." He is the pathological opposite of a fanatic, totally uncommitted to any cause in which he participates. He thinks that he is politically engaged in order to keep his love, Antonia, in Sulaco. His love for her is the one thing he is not cynical about, but even that may be deceptive and not fully genuine. Years before she had snubbed him in Paris and attacked his flippancy, so that now it appears to be her approval for which he really yearns.

His isolation on the island with the treasure after the failed mission with Nostromo might seem fitting for a man who is already so detached from others in his society. It seems a fitting conclusion to his aloof cynicism. But in fact the physical isolation completely undoes him. As opposed to the glorification of nature in earlier Romantic literature, here nature only clarifies by contrast the impermanence and ultimate futility of all human endeavor. Especially at night, Decoud feels surrounded by a vast, silent nothingness, and he loses his sense of location in the world. As the physical integrity of his body is felt to dissolve from lack of perspective, his psyche cannot survive the complete lack of social input or connection. Society is necessary even for an outsider, for being an outsider is still a social role. Decoud needs other people, if only as a brunt for his sarcasm. His detached, ironic attitude fails him when he is literally detached:

> Solitude from mere outward condition of existence becomes very swiftly a state of soul in which the affectations of irony and skepticism have no place... After three days of waiting for the sight of some human face, Decoud caught himself entertaining a doubt of his own individuality. (396)

His scorn can now be turned only on himself, and it is so directed with devastating effect.

His mission with Nostromo having failed, he feels there is no reason left to act, nothing left to live for. There is no activity that could any longer distract him with an illusion of importance:

> In our activity alone do we find the sustaining illusion of an independent existence as against the whole scheme of things of which we form a helpless part. Decoud lost all belief in the reality of his action past and to come. (396)

Nor can his love for Antonia, such as it was, sustain him in isolation. He pictures only disapproval from her whose approval alone he sought. In his mind he sees her "looking on with scornful eyes at his weakness" (396). He recognizes that his moral standing with the community, and especially with Antonia, depends on the success of the political adventure that he takes to have failed.

He knows that we are rightly praised or blamed for what we actually accomplish or bring about, even if our success or failure is beyond our control. A relative of circumstantial moral luck, this is now called resultant moral luck,[16] and Decoud is a victim of the latter, as Nostromo and Gould are victims of the former. Conrad recognizes both types more recently discovered by philosophers, as Nostromo and Decoud both clearly see the sources of their downfalls, even if Decoud is mistaken about the fate of the separatist movement.

He, of course, is also in dire circumstances on the island without adequate supplies, but it is the failed mission that in his eyes merits only disapproval from Antonia and others in Sulaco. Left entirely to himself,

---

[16] Bernard Williams, *Moral Luck* (Cambridge: Cambridge University Press, 1981), ch. 2.

the man who founds the new republic finds nothing to support his continued existence. Once more the defeat of any motive with which he could possibly identify spells the disintegration of the self, and in his case leads to literal self-destruction or suicide.

The only two major figures in the novel who almost sustain or redeem their characters or selves are Emilia Gould and Dr. Monygham. Almost, but not quite. Like Decoud, Monygham is a cynic and pessimist, but he also has a strong moral sense. His psychological progression in the story is the opposite of the other characters, since at the start we find him already shattered by his past. Like Lord Jim, he had failed to live up to the high standard of loyalty and courage he had set for himself, having revealed under torture by a former regime the names of friends being sought. He has failed to live up to his self-image, however ideal it was, and, although now better than his public image, he has lost all self-respect. He is a wreck both physically and psychologically. Despite being once more a victim of circumstantial moral luck, he suffers from extremely debilitating guilt and self-loathing, and makes himself an outcast from society.

His redemption comes later in the novel, when, spurred on by a secret love for Emilia, he atones for his earlier lack of courage by deceiving at the risk of his life the enemy, Sotillo, decoying his army out of Sulaco and saving the new republic. His public image is also restored, when he once more becomes a respectable doctor. But the self-redemption is at best partial. It is fitting that it is accomplished through an act of deception, since, while not self-deceptive as are the other characters, he continues to live a lie. Although he generally says what he thinks and feels, he cannot reveal his overriding motive, his deep love for Emilia; and he sees her suffering without being able to do anything about it. His love is both unrevealed and unrequited.

In the end, she does not even return his trust, refusing to reveal Nostromo's secret to him, and he takes her silence as an ultimate defeat. His self-redemption is not confirmed by the person who prompted it, the one person he cares about, and his public persona remains sharply divided from his private. In addition, while his profession is saving lives, he is partially responsible for the torture and death of the pathetic merchant, Hirsch. Given his still-fractured state, the fact that he has more self-integrity than the other characters at the end of the novel only highlights more clearly the theme of the fragility of the self.

Emilia Gould is the one character who maintains a moral mission throughout the story, but in the end it is a failed moral mission. Her main motive lies in serving others, at first especially her husband. Her self is once more defined by her relation to others, by her charity toward them. She comes to realize, however, that whatever charity she can perform is offset by the exploitative actions of her husband. She becomes increasingly isolated from him, torn between her loyalty to him and her recognition of the fanatic capitalist he has become. She likens her betrayal by Charles to Linda Viola's betrayal by Nostromo.

In the end she is still at the center of society in Sulaco, but the loneliest of all the characters:

Small and dainty, as if radiating a light of her own in the deep shade of the interlaced boughs, she resembled a good fairy, weary with a long career of well-doing, touched by the withering suspicion of the uselessness of her labors, the powerlessness of her magic...Mrs. Gould's face became set and rigid for a second, as if to receive, without flinching, a great wave of loneliness that swept over her head...an immense desolation, the dread of her continued life, descended upon the first lady of Sulaco. (413–15)

In her, the most self-integrated and moral character throughout the novel, we nevertheless see once more futile actions, isolation from others, a public persona different from the private, and desired, if not actual, self-destruction.

I will not comment on the minor characters at any length, simply note that they follow the same pattern. The old man Viola, mentioned earlier, has fought for the poor and oppressed in Italy, yet he has nothing but scorn for the poor natives of Costaguana and depends on the rich capitalists in Sulaco. His actions are unwittingly motivated, as he kills Nostromo, his surrogate son, by a mistake that is not really a mistake, refusing to acknowledge the identity of his victim. The American financier Holroyd bankrolls the silver mine at the center of the story as a kind of hobby. He hypocritically speaks of bringing a pure form of Christianity to the benighted natives, when we suspect that his only real motive is further profits for himself.

Don Jose Avellanos, Antonia's father, lives for a free and peaceful republic of Costaguana, but dies after his history of the country is destroyed by rioters, and he has agreed to the secession of Sulaco, betraying his patriotism and respect for the law of the country. Antonia shares her father's mixed political motives, loves Decoud, but is at least partially responsible for his suicide. The fur merchant Hirsch's only motivating emotion is fear for his life, but his cowardly vulnerability costs him his life. Even the rioting mob, a final minor character, seeks loot, not political freedom or stability. In all these characters we find yet again actions seemingly out of line with character, motives that are self-defeating or completely frustrated by circumstances, and public professions seemingly out of line with private motives, all calling into question yet again the coherence or unity of the self.

V

I will summarize. The characters in this novel first of all fail to live up to their public images or professed social roles. They are all, with the possible exception of Emilia, moral frauds. The heroes of the revolution are shams, their reputations empty shells. They all act publicly for purely private and hidden motives, their actions divorced from motives that would justify them in the public eye. Nostromo, the incorruptible, becomes a thief; Gould, a moral reformer, becomes an exploiter and underhanded dealer; Monygham, extremely loyal, has betrayed his friends; Decoud, skeptic and leader of the secessionist revolution, becomes an illusionary romantic and thinks politics a farce.[17] All victims of circumstantial moral luck, they betray society as society betrays them.

A relatively stable social order, reinforcement of social roles and self-images, all being necessary to sound and stable individual selves, here the social chaos following the destruction of social order mirrors and contributes to the destruction of the individual psyches of the characters. Images of immobility recur throughout the novel—the old man Viola, Nostromo on his deathbed, Charles Gould when he first meets Emilia, and the natives of Costaguana. It is as if these characters are falsely posing, and this dominant image suggests the futility of actions in contexts in which they cannot succeed. Character and self are realized through the fulfillment of long-term plans, but in the violent context of Costaguana, plans are continuously frustrated or, if they succeed, as does the secession, it is posthumously, not through the actions of those who intend them, and their success appears short-lived.

Second, each character is isolated from the others, especially from those intimate relations that might fulfill and confirm their identities.

---

[17] Compare Suresh Raval, *The Art of Failure* (Boston: Allen & Unwin, 1986), p. 74.

This includes relations with parents, comrades in arms, and lovers. As noted, each acts privately in shared missions, keeps motives hidden, and misjudges the motives of the others. Each fails in love, and therefore fails to be saved by those who might have redeemed them. Nostromo chooses the sexy Giselle over the more stable and substantial Linda, who truly loves him, and he chooses the silver over both. Gould likewise chooses the mine over his wife, while Monygham cannot reveal his love for her. Decoud feels his love evaporate when physically isolated from Antonia. And both Gould and Nostromo betray parental figures, Gould in the very act of trying to avenge his father, who had sternly warned him against reactivating the mine. Thus, all personal relations among these characters fail: none is open, intimate, and successful. None has his or her identity confirmed in another.

Finally, each character fails to live up to his own ideal self-image. Faced with near impossible situations or irresistible temptations, none can be the character he aspires to be. The silver, meant to be an agent of reform, is the agent of corruption in the cases of Nostromo and Gould, and it is the literal weight that drowns Decoud. Conrad suggests through several characters that some degree of illusion or idealization is necessary to one's self-image as a unifying motive. But when the standard is set high, as it is by Gould, Monygham, and Nostromo, failure becomes more probable. On the other hand, the cynicism of Decoud fares him no better, and he must pose for himself the illusory ideal of a love ultimately defeated by his own cynicism. Whether failing a dramatic test, as do Nostromo, Monygham, and Decoud, or having their long-term projects gradually eroded, as do Charles and Emilia Gould and Don Jose Avellanos, the disconnect between ideal self-image and fulfillment of plans that might realize it is devastating.

None of the characters in this novel controls their own destiny, or ultimately their own motivations. Each is overwhelmed by blind chance, material forces, greed, and corruption. In the wake of such failure, idealism gives way to disintegration and then to obsession or fanaticism. Loss of illusion turns to cynicism or the urge for self-destruction. All the characters are variations on this theme of the fragile and ultimately fragmented self. The reader cannot identify with any of them (a cause for misplaced criticism by some critics), simply because there is not a coherent inner self with which to identify. All are vulnerable to the situations they face, vulnerable to being undone by circumstantial and resultant moral luck.

By seeing these characters as contrasting types, we can easily infer what is necessary for a stable character or self. An individual needs a realistic but motivating self-image, a plurality of concerns and plans, reinforced or confirmed by others and by actions in an accepted social role. Motives can then be rationally assessed and actions self-directed. Conrad, implicitly aware of these requirements, is an exception to the many novel writers who think of their characters as exemplifying fully stable traits, inferable from the smallest samples of behavior and always explanatory of those behaviors. Confidence of such stability in the self may be misplaced in both novels and real life. Given the extremity of the dramatic situations in *Nostromo*, Conrad does not tell us just how fragile character is. But then neither do contemporary psychologists, given the triviality of the situations they typically describe.

Philosophers have recently paid much attention to this literature in social psychology. They would profit from more attention to the extended narratives of fictional lives in novels with themes of moral progression, positive and negative.

Index

causal inference 93
Chandler, Raymond 86
character
  development
    narrative patterns in 19
  disintegration 109, 184, 188, 192–3
  motivation 29, 180
  traits 179–80, 183
  see also moral development
Christianity 23, 177, 187, 196
Christie, Agatha 85, 86, 88, 93n,
    94, 104
Cider House Rules, The
  characters in moral quandaries 19
  interpersonal relations in 18
  rules, attitudes towards 21–2, 36,
    156–74
circumstantial moral luck 182, 187, 195,
    197, 199
Clark, Michael 142
Clockwork Orange, A 73
cognition 6–9, 12, 21, 24, 82–3,
    94, 103
cognitive engagement 7–8, 12, 14–15,
    91–2, 96, 100, 105
cognitivists 114
  see also imagination; inductive
    inference;
    inferential ability; memory;
    scientific reasoning
Cohen, Michael 84n, 90n
coherence 17
Colby, A. and Kohlberg, L. 111n,
    114n, 116n
comedy 51
  see also humor
communication
  interpretation and 53
Conan Doyle, Arthur 56, 59, 93n
conflict 12
  see also dramatic conflict
Conrad, Joseph 30, 57–8, 175–7, 179,
    184, 189–90, 198–9
  see also *Nostromo*
Constable, John 30
conventionalism 148
Cooke, Thomas 86
Copland, Aaron 34
Copper Rule, the 166
Cornwell, Patricia 88
corruption 192, 198

crime 85–6, 88, 95–6, 106, 192
  see also detective fiction; mystery genre
criticism
  objective of 50
  see also art criticism; interpretation,
    theory of; literary criticism;
    music criticism
Crocker, Thomas 141n
Cunningham, Anthony 157, 158n
Currie, Gregory 58–9, 80
cynicism 68, 130, 193, 198

Da Vinci, Leonardo 58
  Last Supper 58
Dadlez, E. M. 117n
Damon, William 112n
Danto, Arthur 26
Davidson, A. E. and Davidson,
    C. N. 76n
Death of a Salesman
  self-deception in 25
Deaver, Jeffrey 95
deliberation 140–3
Dennett, Daniel 182n
denouement 56, 100
Derrida, Jacques 80
detective fiction 15, 84
  American detective stories 90
  criticism of 86–7
detectives:
  anti-heroes 89
  archetypical 86, 91–2, 98–9
  continental 89
  heroes 87–8, 93, 97, 102
  heroines 99n
  identification with 100–2
  moral ambiguity of 103
  outsider 103
  reasoning of 92–6
  see also hard-boiled American
    tradition; mystery genre
Dewey, John 4
Dexter, Colin 87, 89, 94
Dibdin, Michael 87
Dickens, Charles 85–7, 173
Dickson Carr, John 90, 94
distributive justice 113
Doris, John 183n
Dove, George 95n
dramatic conflict 7
  see also conflict